TED HUGHES

ALSO BY ELAINE FEINSTEIN

Poems
City Music
Selected Poems
Daylight

Translations
Selected Poems of Marina Tsvetayeva
Poems of Margarita Aliger,
Yunna Morits and Bella Akhmadulina

Biography
Pushkin
A Captive Lion: the life of
Marina Tsvetayeva
Lawrence's Women: a life of
D. H. Lawrence

Novels
The Border
Loving Brecht
Dark Inheritance

TED HUGHES

The Life of a Poet

ELAINE FEINSTEIN

W. W. Norton & Company
NEW YORK LONDON

For Arnold

Contents

Illustrations

Acknowledgements

The author (EF) gratefully acknowledges the following sources from which she has drawn and quoted: Ted Hughes *New Selected Poems* 1957–1994 (Fabers, 1995); from 'The Rock', in Geoffrey Summerfield's *Worlds* (Penguin, 1974); from MSS 644 in Special Collections Department, Emory University, Atlanta, Georgia; from EF interview with Donald Crossley; from Anne Stevenson's papers held in Cambridge University Library ADD MSS 4451; from *Poetry in the Making* (*1967*), reissued in (ed) William Scammell, *Winter Pollen* (Faber and Faber, 1994); from a telephone conversation with Alice and John Wholey March 2001; from Drue Heinz interview with Ted Hughes 'The Art of Poetry', in *Paris Review* © (1995, no 134) (reprinted by permission of Russell and Volkening, New York, as agents for the *Paris Review*); from Keith Sagar, *Laughter of Foxes* (Liverpool University Press, 2001); from Margaret Drabble, *The Peppered Moth* (2001); from Ted Hughes letters to Gerald Hughes MSS 854 Special Collections Department, Robert W Woodruff Library, University of Emory; from Lucas Myers *Crow Steered, Bergs Appeared* (Proctor Press, Tennesee, 2001); from a letter to EF written by Dr Gwen Black; from Tom Pero's article, 'An Interview with Ted Hughes'. *Wild Steelhead and Salmon Magazine*, Winter, 1999, partially reprinted in the *Guardian*, 9 January 1999; from Mrs Kathy Severn's letter to Ted Hughes (1984), Special Collections Department, Emory; from a letter from Mrs Mary Morris to Ted Hughes 1984 in Special Collections Department, Emory; from EF interview with Professor Michael Podro; from a letter to EF from Dr Gwen Black 1999; e-mails from Michael Boddy February–April 2001, and a photograph of Michael Boddy and Joe Lyde; from EF interview with Karl and Jane Miller 1999; from Karl Miller, *Rebecca's Vest* (Hamish Hamilton, 1993); from *Hawk in the Rain*

(Faber and Faber 1957); from Glen Fallows, 'Ted Hughes: Reminiscences', in *The Martlet* (1999), an occasional Pembroke College magazine; from EF interview with Professor Brian Cox, and from Brian Cox, 'Ted Hughes (1930–1998). A Personal Retrospect', *Hudson Review* Vol: Lll, no 1, Spring 1999; from EF interview with David Ross; from a letter to EF from Professor John Honey, Professor of History, Botswana University, posted December 8 1999; from a letter to EF from John Coggrave 16 October 1999; from D. D. Bradley, *Pembroke Annual Gazette*, no 73 (September, 1999); from EF interview with Brian Cox, 1999; from Thom Gunn, *The Occasions of Poetry* (Faber and Faber, 1982); from emails received from Daniel Weissbort; from Phillip Hobsbaum, 'Ted Hughes at Cambridge', *Dark Horse*, no 8, Autumn (1999); from Anne Stevenson, *Bitter Fame* (Viking, 1989); from letters to Lucas Myers, MSS 865, Special Collections Department, Robert Woodruff Library, Emory; from Robert Graves, *The White Goddess* (1948); from A. Alvarez, *The Savage God* (1971) and *Where did it all go right?* (2001); from *Howls and Whispers*, Gehenna Press (Northampton, 1998); from Karen V. Kukil, ed: *Complete Journals of Sylvia Plath* (2000); from *Birthday Letters*; from Aurelia Plath (ed) *Sylvia Plath's Letters Home: Correspondence 1950–63* (Harper and Row 1975); from Karen V. Kukil, *Sylvia Plath's Journals 1950–62* (Faber and Faber, 2000); from Erika Wagner, *Ariel's Gift* (2000); from Sylvia Plath *Collected Poems* (1981); from Ted Hughes, *Gaudete* (Faber and Faber 1977); from Ted Hughes, *Capriccio* (Gehenna Press, 1990); from Ted Hughes *Rain Charm for the Duchy* (1992); from Ekbert Fass, *Ted Hughes: The Unaccommodated Universe* (Black Sparrow Press, 1980); from EF interview with Karl Miller (1999); from Professor John Beer, 'Ted Hughes and the Daughters of Incomplete Being' (kindly shown to EF in MS); from Letters to W. S. Merwin, MSS 856, Special Collections Department, Robert W Woodruff Library, Emory; from Tim Kendall, *Sylvia Plath*, seen in MS; from Diane Wood Middlebrook, *Anne Sexton: a biography* (Virago, 1992); from EF interview with Peter Redgrove (1999); MSS 866, Special Collections Department, Robert W Woodruff Library, Emory University; from EF interview with Ruth Fainlight (2000), and Sylvia Plath's letters to Ruth Fainlight, held by Ruth Fainlight; from EF interview with Suzette Macedo, 1999; from Anne Stevenson's archive held at Cambridge University Library ADD MS 94451; from Paul Alexander, *Rough Magic* (Da Capo Press edn. 1999); from William Scammell, ed *Winter Pollen*; from Ted Hughes, *Birthday Letters* (Faber and Faber, 1988); from EF interview with Elizabeth Compton Sigmund (1999); from Janet Malcolm, *The Silent Woman* (Alfred A Knopf Inc, 1993); from EF interview with Mira Hamermesh (2000); from EF interview with Clarissa Roche 1999; from Clarissa Roche memoir in Edward Butscher (ed) *Sylvia Plath: The woman and the Work*; from EF interview with Al Alvarez and his wife, Anne (2000); from David Wevill's letter to Anne Stevenson (1989) among her papers at Cambridge University Library; from letters in Brenda Hedden's possession from Ted Hughes, and conversations with Brenda Hedden, letters and faxes May–July 2001; from EF interview with Fay Weldon 1999; from Eda Zoritte-Megged's memoir 'Intersections', first published in Hebrew, *Mosnayim*, 9, September/October 1984; from Yehuda Amichai (ed Ted Hughes and Daniel Weissbort) *Selected Poems* (2001); excerpt from 'The Arraignment' by Robin Morgan (1970, 1990). (The poem first appeared in *Monster* (Random House, 1970) and was subsequently reprinted in *Upstairs in the Garden: Poems Selected and New*, 1968–1988 (W. W. Norton, 1990), reprinted by permission of the author, care of Edite Kroll Literary Agency Inc, 12 Grayhurst Park, Portland, Maine 04102, U.S.A.); from Emma Tennant, *Burnt Diaries* (Canongate, 1999); from e-mails from Jill Barber, and a conversation with Jill Barber in Wen Wah Restaurant, Hampstead 1999; from Ted Hughes letter to Keith Sagar, quoted in Nicholas Gammage (ed), *The Epic Poise: A Celebration of Ted Hughes* (Faber and Faber 1999); from letters to Keith Sagar quoted in *The Laughter of Foxes*; from Ted Hughes introduction to Pilincsky's *Selected Poems* (Carcanet, 1976); from Ted Hughes, *Tales from Ovid* (Faber and Faber, 1997); from Carolyn Wright, 'What Happens in the Heart,' *Poetry Review*, vol 89, no 3, 1999; from Newman (ed) *The Art of Sylvia Plath*; from Alvarez review of *Birthday Letters, New Yorker*, 2 February 1998; from Ted Hughes, *Alcestis* (*1999*); from Ted Hughes *Howls and Whispers* (Gehenna Press, 1998); from Ann Skea's paper delivered to Ted Hughes conference in Lyons 2000, downloaded from www.ann.skea.com.

I should like to thank Lucas Myers, Peter Redgrove, Daniel Weissbort and Mike Boddy, who found photographs of their younger selves for me; Jane Donaldson for supplying me with a photograph of Assia Wevill and information about its provenance; and Eda Zoritte-Megged who let me use extracts from 'Intersections', her memoir of Assia, and also sent me copies of a photograph of Assia and her child Shura. I should also like to thank Mark Gerson, Susan Plath Winston, and other agencies listed on p ix for the use of illustrations. I am also grateful to the many people who have helped me in numerous ways, but do not wish to be named.

Finally, I should particularly like to acknowledge the help of Steve Ennis, Curator of Special Collections Department of the Robert W. Woodruff Library, University of Emory, Atlanta, Georgia, not only for his invaluable assistance while I was exploring Ted Hughes' archive on the two extended visits I made to Atlanta, but also for his patience in dealing with a stream of later inquiries by e-mail.

ELAINE FEINSTEIN

Introduction

Early in November 1998, a few days after my husband and I returned home from Ted Hughes' funeral, an Irish American writer whom I had met at the Galway Literary Festival telephoned. W. W. Norton wanted to commission a biography of Hughes and he wondered if I might be interested.

I knew there was an important story to tell, and one that was still unexplored, even after biographies of Hughes' dead wife, the American poet Sylvia Plath. Her suicide in 1963 had etched into the consciousness of a whole generation the image of Ted Hughes as a callous husband whose infidelity drove her to kill herself one frozen February morning in London. Those of us who knew him recognized this as a caricature of a man whose life, if far from conventionally blameless, was always lived with warmth and generosity. My hesitations lasted no more than a few weeks, although I did not begin work until February 1999.

Hughes' bestselling *Birthday Letters* – a sequence of lyrics cast as a continued conversation with Plath – has already gone some way towards a new understanding of how strongly Plath and Hughes were shaped by their passionate love, and the damage they did to one another nevertheless. The story of Ted Hughes, one of the towering figures of twentieth-century poetry, starts long before their meeting; even earlier than his arrival in 1950s Cambridge as a precociously gifted, stubborn young genius who had to confront that class-ridden social world. His story begins in the Calder Valley.

This is the first biography of Ted Hughes. It is not only a book of literary criticism, but an attempt to understand the man behind the poems and to tell the history of his life as he experienced it. He knew that such a book was inevitable, as he wrote in a letter to Aurelia Plath in 1975 when he was reading the galleys of *Letters Home*: 'Sooner or later all this will be quite clear to anybody who's interested ... An impartial scholar will no doubt put all these notes in quite pitilessly.'[1]

My intention is to give the portrait of a complex man who defiantly rejected the sexual puritanism of his upbringing; a man intrigued by the occult neoplatonism that preoccupied Shakespeare and Yeats but who nevertheless had a down-to-earth Yorkshire shrewdness; a man whose sharp eye for the English countryside went alongside a fascination with poets from Eastern Europe, who understood the human brutality of the twentieth century.

Hughes was never to be free from Plath, but his tragic history did not stop with her death. It was the discovery of his affair with Assia Wevill that led Plath to order Hughes out of their Devon home, and Assia, née Gutman, was in some ways as fragmented and vulnerable a human being as Sylvia. Very little has been written about Assia, partly because Ted discouraged it. All that most people saw was her beauty, her natural poise and her sophistication. Yet Assia, too, killed herself, along with their young daughter, Shura. To survive those deaths, and continue writing, took a granite endurance. He was helped in this by his love for his two children from his marriage to Plath, the loyalty of his sister Olwyn, and his second wife – the beautiful and much younger Carol Orchard.

Hughes' main archive is in the Robert Woodruff Library in Emory University, Atlanta, Georgia, once the heart of the Deep South, now a prosperous cosmopolitan city which could hardly be less like the feral landscape of Hughes' poetry. I should particularly like to thank Steve Ennis, the Curator of Special Collections there, who not only helped me to find my way around the 108 feet of library shelving, but was both hospitable and friendly during my two visits. His assistant, Kathy Shoemaker, was also a great help. I am also grateful to Anne Stevenson for generously opening her archive at Cambridge University, which she had hitherto sealed until after her death; and to Daniel Weissbort for introducing me to the archive of *Modern Poetry in Translation* in King's College, London.

I should also like to thank Ted's childhood friends, fellow students, poets, critics, those who knew both his first wife, Sylvia Plath, and his later partner, Assia Wevill, as well as the many others who were willing to talk to me or who wrote me helpful letters or emails: notably Donald Crossley and his wife, John and Alice Wholey, David Ross, Lucas Myers, Professor Brian Cox, Daniel Weissbort, Michael Boddy, Professor John

Honey, D.D. Bradley, Dr Gwen Black, Glen Fallows, Fred Grubb, Dr John Press, Professor Michael Podro, John Coggrave, Philip Hobsbaum, Peter Redgrove and Penelope Shuttle, Karl and Jane Miller, Al and Anne Alvarez, Keith Sagar, Suzette Macedo, Ruth Fainlight, Mira Hamermesh, Clarissa Roche, Elizabeth Compton Sigmund, Brenda Hedden, Eda Zoritte-Megged, Jill Barber, Anne Stevenson, Tim Kendall, Professor J. Beer, Fay Weldon, Dannie Abse, Jeremy Robson, Harold Pinter, David Pease, Emma Tennant, Carolyne Wright, Andrew Motion, and to Rebecca Wilson, Francine Brody, Victoria Webb, Celia Levett (copy-editor) and Margaret Body (index). Jill Bialosky and Ion Trewin were generous and supportive editors.

I should particularly like to thank my secretary, Jane Wynborne, for her care and for her indefatigable good humour; and my husband, who accompanied me to Atlanta for my first month's stint at Emory and who read the last draft of the manuscript punctiliously.

Elaine Feinstein
May 2001

ONE

Childhood

Edward James Hughes, the third child of William and Edith Hughes, was born on 17 August 1930 in Mytholmroyd, a village set in a narrow cleft of the Yorkshire Pennines. The valley owed its livelihood to wool weaving, first as a cottage industry, then in factories powered by the water mills of the industrial revolution. Even today, chimneys for mills, known as 'lumbs', mark the whole landscape. Mytholmroyd, too, had its 'lumbs' and there was a Moderna blanket factory over the canal bridge near Hughes' family house, although by the 1930s the Depression had begun to close down the village textile industry.

The Hughes family lived at 1 Aspinall Street in Mytholmroyd for the first seven years of Ted's life. This was a respectable row of grey and yellow Yorkshire brick houses, far less cramped than those of the industrial Midlands. Several of the other families in the street were related to the Hughes family. Ted's Aunt Hilda lived at number 13, and his Uncle Albert at number 19, both siblings of Edith and also part of the Farrar family, who could trace their descent back to the Norman Ferriers and could number Nicholas Ferrar[1] among their forebears.

The Hughes family went to the Methodist Zion Chapel every Sunday while the children were growing up, although Edith had been brought up as a Wesleyan and William's family were High Church. The people in Aspinall Street valued thrift, hard work and cleanliness, strengths that enabled Ted, like D.H. Lawrence, to manage on little money with some grace in later life. He was less attracted to the Puritan ethic that underpinned these habits. In the last quarter of the eighteenth century, Parson Grimshaw, a hell-fire Methodist, had preached in the nearby pulpit of Haworth, where the Brontë family were to live, and the people of the valley still remained some of Wesley's most fanatical enthusiasts. Like

5

many other energetic small boys, Ted found Sunday attendance so boring that he sometimes liked to imagine himself as a wolf running wild in the woods. In later life he wrote of the Zion Chapel holding women 'bleak as Sunday rose-gardens' and men with 'cowed, shaven souls'.[2] He even wrote: 'But everything in West Yorkshire is slightly unpleasant. Nothing ever quite escapes into happiness.'[3]

In those days Aspinall Street was not yet covered with tarmac, and housewives were proud of their white doorsteps. Donald Crossley, a childhood friend who lived at number 9, remembers how

> Mrs Baldwin in the top house would come out – in those days they wore these aprons and a fancy cap on their heads – and she would come to the door and play Old Joe with us. Because they were very prim and proper and used to swill out – they came and swilled the flags with a brush and water. And then they put a white stone on the step – you had what was called a scouring stone and they put this white mark on the step. And woe betide you if they'd just done it one morning and going to school you trod on it, you were in for it.[4]

William Henry Hughes, Ted's father, was a carpenter by trade, a strongly built man, although not as tall as his two sons grew to be. His mother, Polly, had been widowed young, and had had to bring up three children with very few of her own family around to help. In William's youth he had been a keen footballer; he played for Hebden Bridge and had been invited to become a professional. In those days, however, footballers were offered less money than he could earn as a carpenter, so he decided against it.

William was one of only seventeen survivors of a whole regiment of the Lancashire Fusiliers who had been slaughtered at Gallipoli and, in Ted's memory, he was so shattered by his experience that he remained reluctant to speak of it even when other soldiers were exchanging stories. In his son's poems, William is usually sitting in a chair, wordless; but on Sunday mornings Ted and his sister Olwyn, who was two years older, sometimes lay one on each side of their father listening to stories of the First World War.

Photographs show William looking jolly enough, and Ted recalls that his laugh had indeed survived 'nearly intact',[5] despite all those memories of soldiers slithering about in the mud. But nightmares had him calling out in his sleep. William had been a brave soldier, carrying back injured men from the front line many times until he collapsed with exhaustion, and winning the Distinguished Conduct Medal for his heroism. He was wounded several times, once in the ankle by machine-gun fire, and was only saved from being hit in the heart by his paybook, which stopped a piece of shrapnel. He was fortunate to survive another occasion, when a shell failed to go off as it buried itself between his feet.

Men from every part of the valley had died in those battlefields, and sometimes an entire street of families lost their sons through a mistaken order to advance. Ted could never escape the sense of a whole region in mourning for the First World War. In later life he refused to wear a poppy on Remembrance Day. The image of his father in his poem 'Dust As We Are' is almost that of a corpse, or a piece of funereal statuary with 'marble white' muscles. Ted's vision of trench warfare – the ugliness of the landscape and the helplessness of those trapped within it – came from the stories of other veterans, including his Uncle Walter, who felt himself cursed by a German prisoner before going up the line, only to be hit by a bullet in the groin.

William had golden hair which, as a child, Ted liked to comb, learning as he did so the fragility of the human skull beneath. In his poems his father is often perceived as walking like one of those war-wounded in tranced shell-shock who haunt the post-war German cinema as somnambulists. Yet even when economic depression took hold of the cotton towns of South Lancashire and the wool towns of the West Riding, William Hughes continued to provide adequately for his family.

Ted's mother, Edith, was a Farrar and proud of it, but there was no sense in the Hughes family, as there had been in that of D.H. Lawrence, of a mother who was a class above her husband. Edith was handsome and immensely capable. She had olive skin, the hair of a Red Indian and strong features. Her three children, to judge from photographs, took their good looks from her, although Olwyn had fair hair as a child and Ted's was brown rather than black. Edith is remembered by Ted's friend Donald Crossley as 'a really lovely woman. I can't ever remember her raising her voice to me – I used to go playing in there with Teddy. When it was raining, we went playing in one another's houses ... There was a long kitchen ... Women in those days were more or less supposed to stay at home and look after the family, which they did. I don't think Ted's mum ever went out to work.' Crossley's own mother worked as an odd weaver; that is, part-time on the factory looms while her children were at school.[6] Feminism was not an issue in these parts, though Hughes recalls: 'Actually my father regularly washed up – he liked it.'[7] Edith was thrifty, and prided herself on being a good manager. She could make jam and gooseberry pies and traditionally Northern dishes, though later on Sylvia Plath would complain about her cooking. She also had the dressmaking skills of the period, and could cut out patterns, stitch and machine seams. She was a good, hard-working mother and housewife, and she wanted the best for her children.

For all her practical common sense, Edith had a strong sense of the supernatural. In Hughes' story 'The Deadfall',[8] which was at least partly based on memories of his childhood, he speaks of a woman dreaming of the cries of dying men on the night of the Normany landings. He relished her belief in ghosts. Miriam, Edith's sister closest to her in age, had died in her teens and Edith frequently spoke of feeling her sister's presence sitting on her bed. In one of Hughes' late poems, written on the anniversary of his mother's death on 13 May, he describes her vision of Miriam changing over the years into the figure of an angel. In that poem, too, he describes his mother telling Miriam real or imagined events of the life she had shared with Ted: galloping out, for instance, over the heather to bring him a new pen, or reflecting that what she had enjoyed most was thinking of her children simply being alive somewhere.

Hughes once described the whole village as dark, with the sun hardly rising about Scout Rock in winter, yet in many ways it was an idyllic childhood. Banksfield Road, which ran across Aspinall Street, led directly into fields after only a few houses. The boys growing up there had easy access to farmland and trees. They could swim in the Calder river in summer and play cowboys and Indians and hide-and-seek in Redacre Wood. Even Zion Chapel was a social centre for dances and amateur dramatics as well as functioning as a place of worship.

The group of friends who centred around Ted – Brian Seymour, Derek Robertson and Donald Crossley, who was rather younger – would play together after school or during the school holidays. Perhaps none of the boys in that group of friends had Ted's native talent, but none was given the same opportunities either. One became a lorry driver. Crossley, who later in life was a skilled painter of local landscapes, left school at fourteen to take a job as a presser in a clothing factory, learning little more than how to use a bucket of water, a cloth and a wooden block. They played together happily enough as young children, sometimes pretending to be trappers looking for birds and foxes, or fishing in a canal a few yards behind the terrace house where he lived. With a long-handled, wire-rimmed, curtain-mesh net, the boys fished for loaches. These were slug-gish cigar-shaped fish fringed with beards and moustaches, which lived in crevices between the stones on the old sides of the canal, and poked their heads out when the boys stamped their feet. Loaches could be tickled gently until they swam into a net. Ted liked to keep those he caught in a two-pound jam jar, which his mother allowed him to stand on the kitchen windowsill, or outside the kitchen door in bowls and buckets. The canal itself, which seemed so magical to Crossley as he recalled his boyish memory of it, is scarcely four feet wide, its water still and brackish in appearance. At the other end of the towpath, where there is more of a current, stands a pub called Stubbings Wharf. Ted's father went there by bus on a Sunday and sometimes took his youngest child with him.

The boys shared the usual love of mischief, and sometimes liked to dam with stones a stream of water that ran down Banksfield Road, which produced a great flood when it was let out. Crossley remembers Ted as having a tremendous laugh. There is still some sign of an early painting on the wall of 1 Aspinall Street under the arch where Ted, who had found a tin of Colman-mustard-coloured paint, had followed a bump in the brickwork to outline a skull and crossbones. Crossley was eleven months younger than the other three boys and smaller, and so was 'often put on'. He spoke without rancour of a time when Ted and a group of friends tied him to a tree in Redacre Wood. On Guy Fawkes night – called 'Plot Night' – the boys used to collect wood there for a fire that they then built on a piece of spare land opposite Ted's house.

Ted's passion for animals was known to the family from his earliest childhood and for his fourth birthday he was given a thick, green-backed book of photographs of them, along with descriptions of their natural history that were rather too adult for so young a child.[9] He liked to try and copy these pictures, and was excited by his childish attempts to draw them. He was more successful in making plasticine models of them. On Saturdays, when the family went shopping in Halifax, Ted was allowed to choose lead animals from Woolworths, until he had so many species that they stretched round the fender.

He enjoyed collecting living creatures even more, catching mice by snatching them from under the sheaves at threshing time, and finding frogs in ditches. He liked to keep the creatures in his pockets. Crossley recalled how a girl called Betty Lumb, a bit older than himself, told him just before Ted died that he had once put a frog down her back at primary school. 'So I wrote to Ted and said, "Do you remember putting a frog down Betty Lumb's back?" and back came the letter, "Yes, I do remember putting a frog down her back. Does she remember stoning me? I remember getting a stick and trying to fend them off like a whirling dervish." '[10] It is entirely typical of Ted that, ill as he then was, he had written back to a boy he remembered from sixty years earlier, and that he should at the same time offer him the hospitality of his house at Moortown and Court Green.

Ted was clearly the hero of friends his own age, but it was his brother, Gerald, ten years older, who was the most important figure in his own early childhood, making it a paradise by teaching him to fish, trap animals and shoot. According to Crossley, Gerald was even more handsome than Ted, with a magnificent build. He was a highly talented boy, with a gift for painting, particularly in watercolours.[11] He had a passion for hunting and shooting, which were not common pursuits among other people in the village. William had no interest in them, although Ted's Uncle Walt seems to have been involved on some excursions. But the fourteen-year-old Gerald got up at four every morning to climb the hillside and shoot whatever he could find. He took his younger brother with him from the age of three or four. They camped in the neighbouring valleys of Hardcastle Crags and Crimsworth Dene, where Gerald taught Ted how to set up a tent and to light fires. Edith had great faith in the common sense of her children and never worried about them. At first, Ted acted as retriever, picking up the animals that his brother shot; later on Gerald taught the boy to use a gun. There were rabbits, magpies, owls, weasels and curlews to be shot. What Ted enjoyed about shooting was the way it made him alert to the whole landscape, so that he was aware of every bird and animal alive in it. Gerald was a very imaginative boy himself, and liked to pretend he was a North American Indian from the palaeolithic age; Ted in later life spoke of 'living in his dream'.[12]

It was Gerald who took him climbing to the top of Scout Rock. Ted remembered the alarming exhilaration of being up there at the age of six, in another world that he had been trying to imagine for so long. Beyond the Rock lay the moors, the landscape in which the Brontës had been at home. Ted was too young then to do more than relish the vast skies, violent winds, the scent of peat and heather, and to register the horizon that made a visible magical circle surrounding him. The moors were far too wide for a young child to think of crossing them, but his childhood was given space and life by these explorations.

Ted remembered one particular expedition to camp with his brother and their Uncle Walt in Hollins Valley as the most important single experience of his life up to the age of twenty-five. It remained so vividly in his memory that thirty years later he could remind Gerald that he only shot one rabbit on that occasion and that a small bird shot in a young tree had been pointed out to him by his uncle.

Some part of that childhood delight still lived on in Hughes when he wrote of the valley as part of Elmet, the last Celtic kingdom in England, whose main stronghold was Heptonstall. In the seventeenth century this inhospitable terrain made an excellent hideout for those in flight from the law; Defoe, for instance, hid there from his creditors.

Even as a boy, Ted could see that the wildlife of the moors had a harsh struggle for survival,[13] yet in later life Hughes speaks of climbing back down into the comfortable valley as a return to the pit, and of passionately wanting to escape the constricted life there. 'At the same time, all that I imagined happening elsewhere, out in the world, the rock sealed from me, since in England the world seems to lie to the South.'[14]

In 1937, however, the boy's whole landscape changed. Edith came into a small legacy after the death of her mother, and William was able to buy a newsagent's and tobacconist's shop. The family moved to Mexborough, an industrial town in South Yorkshire, and the shape of Ted's childhood was changed at a stroke. His brother Gerald, now seventeen, did not move to Mexborough with the family but chose instead to take a job as a gamekeeper in Devon. However, he must have returned often to see his family and Keith Sagar in *Laughter of Foxes* quotes an Indian war-song that Gerald chanted to his brother when Ted was about nine:

> I am the woodpecker
> My head is red
> To those that I kill
> With my little bill,
> Come wolf, come bear and eat your fill
> Mine's not the only head that's red.[15]

Mexborough is a bleak mining town, which at that period was blighted by the effects of the industrial slump and was so deeply pervaded by pollution that those who lived there 'lived in it, coughed in it, spat it out, scrubbed at it and frequently died of it'.[16] Even after the industrial revolution had begun to grind to a halt, pitheads and cooling stations continued to mark the landscape. The terraced houses of the workers who sustained the mine-owners' prosperity still stand, barely touched either by the Second World War or by much in the way of gentrification.

The Hughes family had no history of involvement with the terrible colliery accidents, recorded in sepia photographs in the town's museum. Yet Ted, returning to the town in the aftermath of the death of John Fisher, his favourite teacher, from lung cancer in the 1980s, remembered the pervasive, sulphurous odours in which he had spent the early part of his life, almost without noticing them.

Equally pervasive was the ethos of self-denial. 'Pleasure deferred', Margaret Drabble calls it in *The Peppered Moth*. Hughes, in letters to his brother,[17] saw it as the refusal to acknowledge that one's own desires had any legitimacy. He was in rebellion against such joyless virtues. He was entranced by Lawrence and Blake, and could have echoed the aphorisms from 'The Marriage of Heaven and Hell'.

Ted, by his own account, was uninterested in working hard at primary school but at eleven he won a place at Mexborough Grammar School easily enough, following in the steps of his sister Olwyn. The school had a tradition of good teaching; indeed Drabble's mother won a place to Newnnham College, Cambridge, when a pupil at the school some twenty years earlier.

Freud once said that a mother's favourite son is strengthened by that approval for the rest of his life. Over the years Olwyn has always said that her mother loved all her children equally. However, there is a scrap of a note written to Gerald[18] which suggests that Ted always believed her eldest son was his mother's favourite. Lucas Myers, a close friend of Ted's from Cambridge days, remembers a letter from him in 1958 in which he wrote that 'a younger brother could never grow up with the completeness of the elder'.[19] His awareness of his position in the family may have derived from his study of anthropology. In the *Paris Review* interview he spoke of those who came from a close-knit family: 'The moment you do anything new, the whole family jumps on it, comments, teases . . . There's a unanimous reaction to keep you how you were.'[20]

Ted missed his brother Gerald, who had made his childhood so happy for him, although he soon learned to explore on his own, often getting up early on purpose before school as his brother had taught him. He discovered two rivers – the Don and the Dearne – in walking distance of his house. Close by those rivers were hollows where the wildlife was prolific. He found that if he silently climbed up the side of one of these hollows and peered over the hedge, he could frequently surprise some creature there, busy with its own vivid life.

His friends at primary school were the sons of colliers and railwaymen; Ted would play with a gang of boys 'kicking about the neighbourhood' after school, but he kept his weekends for himself. At Mexborough Grammar he made friends with John Wholey, a boy in Olwyn's class. Wholey was the son of the head keeper on Crookhill, a local estate, which was later sold to Doncaster local authorities as a sanatorium for TB patients. John's father had once worked as a gamekeeper for Lord Halifax, the first Earl, who had served as Foreign Secretary under Sir Anthony Eden. Wholey was fascinatingly knowledgeable about country life and Ted learned a great deal from him. His friendship with John gave him access to acres of parkland, woods and a huge lake, where he had his first experience of fishing for pike. It was with John Wholey, too, that Ted put three baby pike into a fish-tank at school, feeding them regularly at first. The boys forgot about them over a school holiday, and returned to find the three fish reduced to one:[21] an act of cannibalism recorded in Ted's poem 'Pike'.

Ted's interest in pike fishing in his teens approached an obsession. He spoke of dreaming regularly about pike and about one particular lake where he did most of his fishing. 'Pike had become fixed at some very active, deep level in my imaginative life.'[22] It was as if pike had become symbolic of his inner, vital being, though he would hardly have been able to articulate that thought in his teenage years. He remained more interested in the world outside school than anything he learned there, and he returned to Mytholmroyd in the long school holidays to visit his Aunt Hilda and to see his old friends. But the move to Mexborough was in other ways crucial to his development as a poet.

His father's newspaper shop was big and busy, with excitements of its own. Ted was able to read the comics and boys' magazines freely there, and these were to be the basis of his first attempts at storytelling. He also formed the habit of buying the *Shooting Times* and the *Gamekeeper*, which he read avidly, since he continued to be obsessed with shooting, fishing and trapping. These magazines made a link between the world of outside-school freedom and the world of book-knowledge, which he might not have acquired while Gerald was there to teach him all he needed to know. In the early days the Hughes home held few books, although Edith read poetry and particularly loved Wordsworth. The only stories that Ted heard as a young child were ones told by his mother and usually made up by her.[23] It was Edith who brought a children's encyclopaedia into the house; it included a section on folk tales, which Ted read with great delight.

Gerald's absence was felt by the whole family. Ted must have observed how much his mother missed her older son. Among the fragments of undated letters from Ted to Gerald, one scrap, typed from a letter written just before Ted and Sylvia Plath left Great Britain for the United States, makes the point sharply: 'I will write a journal to Ma. She was very pleased at hearing from you frequently. You must remember that you're her best in a way I never could be and that your writing regularly could make up for my not writing, whereas my writing every day could not make up for your silence.'[24] Edith missed her elder son all the more when, two years after the move to Mexborough, the Second World War broke out and Gerald enlisted in the RAF.

Mrs Hughes received her first ration books in January 1940. These allowed her four ounces a head per week of bacon and ham, twelve ounces of sugar and four ounces of butter. Meat rationing began in March of the same year, with one shilling and ten pence per head allowed for everyone over the age of six.[25] By July, tea was also rationed, which most families found a particular hardship. Similar restrictions on sugar were felt as a serious deprivation, and by March 1941, jam, marmalade and syrup could only be bought with coupons.[26] Tinned salmon, although not rationed, had virtually disappeared from the shops and by the end of 1940 even the most provident housewife had bare cupboards.

In the cities it was a time of great austerity. It was rare to get more than one egg a fortnight, although pregnant mothers received special rations. Dried eggs, with their odd taste of cardboard, were imported from America, which seemed a land of plenty far away on the other side of the Atlantic. Dried milk was also brought in after November 1941, when the ration of fresh milk was reduced to two and a half pints a head per week. Women used cheese rind for flavour and begged scraps of bacon rind from their butcher.

These restrictions were felt less harshly by the Hughes household, however, because a system of barter prevailed among local shopkeepers. Nettleton, the butcher, for instance, was happy to exchange meat for a supply of Craven A cigarettes from the Hughes tobacconist shop; Eric Barker, a grocer in Mytholmroyd who owned a catering firm, often arrived at the Hughes home with jam, cheese and bacon. Small corner shops were allowed to give regular customers who had registered with them unrationed items such as coffee and pepper, an advantage available to Mrs Hughes.

Nevertheless, the evil of wasting food was one of Lord Woolton's most persuasive wartime campaigns. As school children, Ted and Olwyn would have been able to supplement home rations with school dinners, but it has to be said that in the context of wartime Britain, fishing, trapping rabbits or shooting birds for the pot was the most natural human activity. The parkland at Crookhill provided a rabbit or even a partridge from time to time. John Wholey said of his own mother: 'Her house rule was that she would cook anything, provided it was given to her oven-ready.'[27] The young boys, accordingly, learned how to pluck and draw the creatures they shot.

Arguably, learning to cope with material scarcity fitted Ted admirably later on for the life of a writer and poet. Clothes rationing made making do and mending a virtue; however, it is unlikely that Ted took a great interest in his clothes. Nor did he greatly mind the restrictions on the use of hot water, although any American of his generation would have taken a daily shower for granted. This was as well, since to use only five inches of bath water was regarded as patriotic.

Not everything in Mexborough during the war was bleak. There was a music hall – despite the town's reputation of being the comedian's grave – cinemas and dance halls. Mary Hutchinson (née Morris) a friend of Olwyn's, who knew Ted only as her kid brother in Mexborough Grammar School days, wrote to Ted to congratulate him when he was made Poet Laureate. She reminisces: 'I stayed sometimes at the shop in Main Street, Mexborough, when school dances or the like went on too late for me to get back to my home in Radmarsh. Your mother was such a dear kind soul; you were such a horror of a little brother.'[28] Ted did not yet share Olwyn's friends, or her social world. At this stage, Olwyn seemed to know far more about books and people than he did, and to be altogether more grown-up, though she was only two years older.

At about the same time that Ted entered Mexborough Grammar School, he discovered the town library. He read *Tarka the Otter* by Henry Williamson many times, and began to find new links between his own private world of woods and rivers and the world between book covers. He remained resistant to 'anything that needed ink',[29] until he discovered that the stories he liked to tell amused his classmates. These stories were usually set in jungles, Africa or the Wild West, and were filled with fantastic happenings derived from comics.

When he was thirteen, excited by hearing his teacher reading *The Jungle Book* in class and perhaps identifying with Mowgli, a boy living on his own among animals, he borrowed Kipling's *Selected Poems* from the town library. He soon found that he was enjoying poetry more than prose, particularly Kipling's powerful rhythms and long lines. Ted's father, who knew stretches of *Hiawatha* by heart, had perhaps played a part in this too; Ted wrote several comic poems in Longfellow's rhythm with which he amused his classmates. He also began to read the Bible, particularly Job, The Songs of Songs, Isaiah and Ecclesiastes.[30]

Gerald's absence, Hughes wrote to Keith Sagar

> left me to my sister – who took his place as my mentor. She was the prodigy at school – and I see now she had a marvellously precocious taste in poetry ... When my teacher began to make remarks about my writing, my mother went out and bought a whole library – second hand – of classic poets ... So, I was in that cooker from the age of about eleven – totally confident that I belonged in it, so by sixteen I had no thought of becoming anything but a writer of some kind, certainly writing verse.[31]

Perhaps the pressure 'cooker' Ted spoke of was no more than the school push towards university. The teachers recognized quite soon that they had a remarkable talent on their hands. And after the 1944 Education Act they were aware that a clever child from any background could hope to go to university; for the most brilliant, even Oxbridge was open. Whatever attitude Ted later took to Cambridge, he was fortunate that his innate talents were developed in ways that could easily have been misdirected or even overlooked. Dedication to writing and a belief in the power of poetry to heal the human spirit marks Hughes' whole being as almost no other poet since Lawrence. In a black moment of depression, much later in life, he may even have had that dedication in mind as being the moment he threw up the chance of an ordinary, happy life.[32]

Ted's earliest poems were about fishing and shooting. He was encouraged by Miss McLeod, the headmistress at Mexborough Grammar School, and by Pauline Mayne, a young English teacher who held John Fisher's post while he was in the armed forces. She picked out a line in a poem that Ted had shown her about a expedition for wildfowl, which described the hammer of a punt gun breaking in the cold 'with a frost chilled snap', and told him, 'That's poetry.'[33] Ted was delighted to discover how easily he could find the right words to convey the sharpness of his impressions, and that early praise helped him to decide that writing was something he really wanted to do. Partly to equip himself for the job, he began to learn poems that he liked by heart and to imitate the style of poets he admired.

When he was fifteen his passion for animals, too, became more complicated. He had always most valued in them the fact that they had their own life, quite separate from his own. Now he began to consider that he was disturbing that life; it was a part of his beginning to imagine the inner being of the creatures themselves, an act of empathy that lies behind some of his most celebrated poems.

Male Yorkshire society is a powerful one, and a boy who grew up in it would be expected to demonstrate some prowess in games. William Hughes loved to watch football long after he was able to play himself; Ted, however, took no interest, although he did excel at throwing the discus, in which he competed in the inter-school sports, barefooted like the Greeks. His size and craggy good looks, alongside a mischievous lack of shyness with girls ruled out any danger of his being thought effeminate when he began to take pleasure in books.

John Fisher, quite apart from being a brilliant English teacher and a perceptive editor of the school magazine, offered a model for Ted's awakening interest in literature, which balanced the authority of strong women in his own home. Dr Gwen Black, who taught at the school at the time, suggests that Fisher exerted such an influence over Ted by being 'himself a charismatic character, with many of those personal qualities which became evident in Ted; a tall, athletic figure, a handsome face and a curiously potent attraction for the opposite sex'.[34]

It was certainly crucial to Ted's development that Fisher's bearing was at once so assured and so masculine. Mrs Kath Severn, a colleague of Fisher, who wrote to Hughes on 21 December 1984 to congratulate him on his appointment to the post of Poet Laureate, spoke of Fisher, who had died some years earlier, as having had great affection for his most distinguished pupil: 'You were mentioned frequently in our conversation, with myself mostly listening, and it was clear that you were a pride and joy in his life. This recent honour would have delighted him ... He was a good and generous friend to me, so I felt I must write. I could say so much more, but will not embarrass you ...'[35]

Ted was fortunate in his teachers, but his own ability to ferret out what he needed should not be underestimated. He went in search of folk tales himself, and books of them were far less common in those days than they are now. He came to Yeats, through *The Wanderings of Oisin*, for instance, and afterwards pursued all the Celtic folk tales he could find. But a

knowledgeable teacher was essential, and it was John Fisher who introduced him, once he was ready, to both Eliot and Hopkins. In these poets,
Ted recognized something he 'very much wanted, and set about taking
possession of both'.[36] His sensitivity gave him an insight into poets who
were then unusual favourites for schoolboys. He was fortunate in the texts
set him for English A Level study, which included *King Lear*, Hardy's
The Woodlanders and Shelley's *Adonais*; the last he learned by heart.
Perhaps *Lear* was the most important of these for Ted's developing inner
world.

When the war ended in 1945 the cinemas at Mexborough, like those
of the rest of the country, showed the liberation of Belsen. The impressionable fifteen-year-old boy watched the bones of men, women and
children being pushed by bulldozers into trenches for mass burial. (He
could also have seen the same images in *Picture Post*, on sale in his parents'
shop.) The imagination of a whole generation was marked by those
newsreels, perhaps especially in the rural parts of Britain where the war
had impinged less on civilians. Before these discoveries, the Second World
War had made decidedly less impact than the First. There were shelters,
from which German bombers could be heard, but the bombs that fell
were from stray planes unloading their cargo. It was Liverpool and Leeds
that took the real pasting. In the later years of the war, Lancaster bombers
could be seen moving in formation across the sky on their way east
towards Germany. As an adult Hughes wrote far more about the First
World War than the Second, but the impact of those films of the camps
came at a formative time. He had another direct experience of human
despair. When he was about twelve or thirteen, his Uncle Albert, a joiner
by trade whom he had known from his childhood in Aspinall Street,
committed suicide by hanging himself in the attic. Donald Crossley
speculated that Albert, whom Olwyn remembers as a gentle and courteous
man, might have started his own business and 'it weren't doing well'.[37]
Although the experience did not reach Hughes' poetry until decades later,
it must have played a part in forming his precocious awareness of grown-
up misery.

Some time in his adolescent years, Ted read Lawrence's work in its
entirety, except for a few of the poems and probably *Lady Chatterley's
Lover*, which would have been hard to obtain in Mexborough at that
time. *The Rainbow*, with all its rich awareness of the physical world,
confirmed Ted's respect for primitive instinct as a means of preserving his
own inner being. Perhaps he also absorbed Lawrence's vision of marriage

18

as the only heaven that human beings can enjoy. Dr Gwen Black remarked that the imagery in Ted's first published poems was 'almost incomprehensible to most of his peer group, the moon and the eye figuring large'. Those poems were published in the school magazine, *The Don and Dearne*, and show remarkable felicity. As a sixth former, Gwen Black noted, 'Ted displayed a style at once self-effacing and charismatic . . . One could not fail to notice the tall, shambling, handsome figure. Sixth formers were often held in some awe by junior and middle school pupils but even then Ted was something apart, he was a poet.'[38]

Among the Emory University collection of manuscripts there is a copy of 'Summer She Goes' with an accompanying sketch. This poem was written in 1946 to Jean Findley, a school beauty with whom Ted, then sixteen, had a brief flirtation. It was Olwyn who remembered its existence when he was putting together *The Hawk in the Rain*, in which it is included. Their friendship lapsed and Ted's first real romance was with Alice Wilson. A year younger than Ted, she found him both attractive and gentle. He introduced her to the countryside, of which she knew little before their relationship, and he took her on trips with a group of friends to go walking in Derbyshire[39] or on cycle rides for which they had packed lunches. He also introduced her to his friend John Wholey. Two years older than Ted, he was soon called up into the armed forces. Alice went on to correspond with Wholey all through the war, and afterwards married him. She found both the Hughes children impressive, and was in no doubt about Ted's talents.

The school, too, recognized an unusually gifted pupil and made the decision to put him in for Cambridge, which was then far from common for a northern grammar school. In 1948 Ted won an Open Exhibition to Pembroke College, Cambridge, although his entry was postponed by two years of National Service in the RAF as a radio mechanic.

He was stationed at an isolated radar station at Fylingdales in East Yorkshire, where he had nothing much to do, although he managed to fit in well enough in the barrack-room. Perhaps because of his size and quiet manner, he did not suffer from the teasing and bullying often meted out by other RAF conscripts to young men who loved reading. According to Michael Boddy, a friend from Ted's Cambridge days, Ted himself took part in several youthful pranks.[40] He grew a moustache for a while, although Gerald, who was in the RAF in Algeria and Egypt throughout the war soon laughed him out of it on his return.

Throughout his National Service, Ted was using his time to read and reread Shakespeare. No doubt he also read Robert Graves' *The White Goddess*, which had been given to him as a prize at Mexborough Grammar School. He liked to find a quiet field where it was possible to read poetry aloud to himself, and in this way enjoyed the whole of Spenser's *The Faerie Queene* and Milton. His dominant passion, up to and through university, was Yeats, who had first attracted him because of Irish folklore and who continued to enthral him because of his interest in the occult. By the time he got to Cambridge, Yeats was part of a personal canon that also included Blake, Wordsworth, Coleridge, Keats and Hopkins. One foreign poet excited him during his National Service – the German, Rainer Maria Rilke.

He amused himself at Fylingdales by listening to music on the radio, and once heard an inexplicable noise – from a station found by twiddling the dial to improve reception – which he took to be a great battle but later discovered was the sound of a sheep-shearing, something uncommon in Yorkshire at the time. The landscape of his Service years is evoked in early poems such as 'Mayday in Holderness' and 'Hull's Sunset Smudge', which describes how the river Humber flows into the North Sea. All through this period he looked forward to Cambridge and the thought of receiving an even more fruitful education than he had received from John Fisher. He went on writing. The earliest poem that he kept was 'Song', written when nineteen while he was on night duty just after beginning his National Service. Between that and 'The Thought-Fox', he later claimed,[41] lay six years of confusion.

TWO

Pembroke College

In October 1951 Ted Hughes went up to Pembroke College, Cambridge, to read English. He was twenty-one and after two years in the ranks of the RAF, with its usual drudgery of boots and kit and poor food, the change in his situation was startling. He was given a fine set of rooms in the First Court, the oldest part of the college, to the left of the main gate. As in all men's colleges, a bedder came in every day to bring him shaving water, deal with the washing up and make his bed.

In autumn 1951, while most of England was still drab and dingy in the aftermath of the war, Cambridge was much as it had always been. The stone of the Wren Library was a Florentine yellow in the sunshine; the lanes across the Backs smelled of leaf dust and wood smoke; the willows were gently reflected in the Cam. The gabled shops along Petty Cury bent forward like those in a children's fairy tale. Heffer's bookshop, with old-fashioned knobbed glass in its bay windows, offered free maroon leather pocket diaries, lecture lists and wall calendars to undergraduates. The usual means of getting about was on a bicycle, and these were often piled high outside Mill Lane lecture rooms, the main centre for Arts lectures, just across Trumpington Street from Pembroke College[1] and the famous cake-shop, Fitzbillies.

Some of the university rules were more suited to schoolboys than to ex-servicemen. Undergraduates were required to wear short gowns to attend lectures, see their tutors, eat in Hall, or go about the streets after dark. Any young man suspected of being a student and not correctly dressed could be challenged and fined. There was a Proctor – a senior member of the university – accompanied by two 'bulldogs' (often porters with a turn of speed), who could halt and question any undergraduate who thought to make an escape. All the college gates were locked at 10

21

p.m., and any undergraduate returning after that time had a fine of two pence; after 11 p.m. it rose to four pence. If he came back after midnight, he could either try climbing over the spikes on the back gates of the college, or face an interview with his tutor in the morning. However, undergraduates were left free to arrange their own hours of work. No one checked attendance at lectures; those reading English were taught to feel that reading in the library could be an equally useful mode of study. A large number of activities – dramatic societies, university magazines and amateur choirs – were encouraged.

At the end of a cobbled lane, past the Arts lecture rooms, stood The Mill public house, where in sunny weather undergraduates could stand outside to watch the waters race through the lock between the upper and lower reaches of the Cam. Close by, cows and horses strayed across the footpath of Coe Fen. Along Silver Street stood Newnham College, built in the nineteenth century for women undergraduates; the only other foundation that admitted women was Girton College, two miles out from the city centre. It was 1949 before female undergraduates were allowed to be full members of the University of Cambridge. Even then male undergraduates outnumbered female undergraduates by more than ten to one.

Cambridge made little concession to creature comforts. Food was not luxurious. To reach the few baths you had to cross a cold, draughty court. Yet the sense of a world of privilege was everywhere. In spite of the enfranchisement offered by the 1944 Education Act, the undergraduate population remained predominantly public school and upper middle class. Sports jackets with leather patches on the elbows were commonplace and men who had just been demobilized often dressed in pipe-stem tweed trousers. Some undergraduates, who fancied themselves as Sebastian Flyte from Evelyn Waugh's *Brideshead Revisited*, wore bow ties and brocade waistcoats.

The undergraduate literary magazine with most prestige was *Granta*. In the year before Hughes arrived in Cambridge it had been edited from Trinity, first by Peter Shaffer and then by his brother Anthony, reading History and Law respectively. Whoever took over the magazine had to be willing – and able – to take on its overdraft, which under Anthony Shaffer was about £500. In Hughes' first year *Granta* was edited by Mark Boxer, a handsome young man given to wearing green and 'notable for an olive Sephardic beauty – mossy eyes, wavy hair, graceful limbs',[2] who was to find fame as a cartoonist. Michael Podro, now a Professor of Art History at the University of Essex, was at Berkhamsted with Boxer, and reported

Boxer saying with shameless aplomb: 'The way the world works is that there is an apex – and that's where it's interesting to be.'[3] Undergraduates who aspired to journalism could write for the weekly newspaper *Varsity*. Among many other magazines that ran for no more than a few issues was *Chequer*, which was for a time edited by the poet Harry Guest and subsequently by Ronald Hayman of Trinity Hall.

Young men at Cambridge who thought of themselves as aspirant poets could feel their ambitions encouraged by writers of a previous generation, including George Barker and Dylan Thomas, who came to talk to the English Club. Robert Graves, then at the very height of his reputation as a poet, delivered the Clark Lectures. Stephen Spender launched his new cultural magazine *Encounter* at the Socialist Club. A chosen few would be invited to eat with these luminaries after their lectures. Ted Hughes made no move to be among them.

A particularly smart set of undergraduates, reading English, were centred on King's College and had connections to literary life in London. Several of the dons, including George ('Dadie') Rylands and Noel Annan, had been friends with members of the Bloomsbury Group, and continued to relish whatever was witty and frivolous. At a polar extreme was F.R. Leavis, at Downing College, who with his wife Queenie, had nothing but contempt for the King's College vision of literature as a delightful game, with social entry into amusing society as the natural reward. They had dedicated their lives to expounding the standards by which they felt serious writing should be judged, and had no time for those who saw literature as a means of self-promotion. Leavis had a wide influence, through lectures that were always packed, a network of former students and the critical journal *Scrutiny*, which had a worldwide reputation. He might have seemed a likely focus for Hughes' disaffection; yet although he enjoyed Leavis' lectures, Hughes did not, as he explained to Keith Sagar, enjoy his detailed practice of dissecting poetry.

Hughes' first year was a difficult one. In spite of the kindness of his college mentors and his own personal confidence and easy composure, to which many visitors to his rooms pay tribute,[4] Hughes was well aware of the class divisions that permeated the university, and he held on all the more obstinately to the Yorkshire accent that would have been used to place him instantly. As he wrote later, in his 'Soliloquy', he had a liking for

> every attitude showing its bone,
> And every mouth confessing its crude shire.[5]

23

Olwyn Hughes' copy of *The Oxford Book of Seventeenth Century Verse* is now in the college library, signed by her.[6] Ted would have been introduced to those poets in his first term for Prelims (as the first-year exams were called). He enjoyed Donne's vigour, and Herbert's clarity too, but declared the others were 'writing clues for crossword puzzles'.[7] His supervisor[8] for a time was Doris Wheatley and, when she wrote many years later to congratulate him on becoming Poet Laureate, she confessed that she had learned more from him about Dylan Thomas than he had absorbed from her about John Donne.

Hughes was well aware of the world of *jeunesse dorée* that centred on King's College, and the cultivation of an exclusive world of 'them' and 'us' embodied in the Pitt Club. As David Ross, a Cambridge friend of later years, put it: 'We hated everything about them.'[9] Hughes knew personally no undergraduates likely to emulate Boxer's effrontery in his first year. He may well have heard the stories of his unconventional behaviour, however. Towards the end of Boxer's third and final year, a poem by an aristocratic young man – Anthony Houghton, published in *Granta*, got Boxer into trouble. The offending lines, which admonished God to 'Get out of bed, you rotten old sod', seem mild enough these days, but they were seen as blasphemous by the university Proctors, particularly a Mr Prest, and Boxer was sent down. The lively wit that marked his presence marked his leaving also, and there are many who will remember his departure in a hired hearse: 'A funeral procession halted in King's Parade, a coffin was shown to the multitude and Mr Hugh Thomas, a president of the Union, climbed up beside the coffin to deliver a valedictory oration.'[10] In a letter written to Keith Sagar on 16 July 1979, Hughes refers to 'social rancour' as being one of the reasons he thought the university had proved such a destructive experience for him. His reaction was not dissimilar to that of D.H. Lawrence. When invited by Bertrand Russell to visit Maynard Keynes in 1915, he expressed his hatred of the chic Cambridge coterie who dominated the English literary centre.

Hughes' supervisor at Pembroke was Matthew Hodgart, Director of Studies in English. Hodgart recognized Hughes' exceptional talent, even though he did not always complete the obligatory weekly essays on time. His tutor, whose job was to oversee his moral welfare, was Antony Camps, a bachelor then in his thirties with a slight stammer. Camps regularly invited his students to tea and was 'immensely supportive to young men from working class backgrounds trying to find their feet in Cambridge'.[11]

The Dean of Pembroke, Reverend Meredith Dewey, lived in college and also took seriously the business of entertaining groups of under-graduates in his room for tea. He was formidable in conversation, however, 'since he would often disconcert undergraduates by apparent extreme rudeness; it took time to realise he expected them to answer back in bantering style'.[12] Other Fellows of Pembroke at the time included Professor Basil Willey, and the Master of the College was Sir Sidney Roberts.

Hughes loved to quote poetry by heart, particularly Hopkins and Blake. John Coggrave,[13] who went up to Cambridge in 1949, after his National Service to read English, remembers that the Hopkins poems that Hughes quoted most frequently were not tormented explorations of the poet's psyche but the exact renderings of the natural world in works like 'Inversnaid' and 'Woodlark'.[14] Coggrave also remembered an afternoon in his own rooms in Selwyn College where he gave a tea party for 'the Pembroke Crowd, and Ted took down my Blake from the shelves and began to read from "The Island of the Moon" ... I can see him now, reading with enormous energy this section in Chapter IV:

> If I had not a place of profit that forces me to go to church said Inflammable Gass Id see the parsons all hang'd a parcel of lying – O said Mrs Sigtagatist if it were not for churches and chapels I should not have livd so long – there was I up in a Morning at four oclock when I was a Girl. I would run like the dickens til I was all in a heat. I would stand still till I was ready to sink into the earth ah Mr Huffcap would kick the bottom of the pulpit out, with passion ... hed cry and stamp and kick and sweat and all for the good of their souls ...; I'm sure he must be a wicked villain said Mrs Nanicantipot, a passionate wretch. If I was a man Id wait at the bottom of the pulpit stairs and knock him down and run away. You would you ignorant Jade I wish I could see you hit any of the ministers. You deserve to have your ears boxed you do. – I'm sure this is not religion answers the other. Then Mr Inflammable Gass ran and shovd his head into the fire & set his hair all in a flame & ran about the room – No, No, No he did not I was only making a fool of you.

'He read this, as I say, with such intensity that we were riveted and when he finished he looked up with a ferocious glee that had us all in fits of laughter.'[15]

Even in his first year Hughes created a considerable impression on fellow members of Pembroke. There was gossip about his exploits in the

town, his drinking at The Mill, his climbing into college after an evening's
fun and snagging his gown on the spikes, 'but his everyday manner had
no display, no anecdotes, no imitation, no horseplay'.[16] Glen Fallows
remembers sitting opposite Ted Hughes in Hall waiting for Grace to be
said and noting with surprise that Hughes had not bothered to wear a
gown over his battered blue-grey herringbone jacket.

Brian Cox, who was reading English two years ahead of him at Pembroke, saw a great deal of Hughes at meal times, since undergraduates
were required to eat dinner in Hall and meals were already paid for. Cox
had taken a First Class degree in the English Tripos, and went on to
postgraduate work, so other undergraduates often brought poems for his
comment; yet Hughes not only did not show him poems but never even
mentioned that he was writing poetry. It was his presence that impressed
Cox: 'Craggily handsome, he radiated an extraordinary dynamism, a
power and integrity which later made his public readings so impressive
... He has often been compared to Heathcliff in *Wuthering Heights*. He
was already fascinated by the Ouija Board and there were Pembroke stories
about the frightening intensity with which he engaged in these activities.'[17]

Cox's introduction of the Heathcliff image here needs some comment.
D.D. Bradley, another contemporary, writes that Hughes 'delighted to
play Heathcliff. He had wandered as a boy naturalising and hunting over
Haworth Moor and in a sense *was* Heathcliff'.[18] It was an image that was
to follow Hughes damagingly in later life. Yet, for all his granite features
and love of the wild moors, it is a misleading comparison. None of his close
Cambridge friends saw him as dangerous, despite his size, or discerned any
malice in him; even casual acquaintances spoke of him as 'a gentle giant'.[19]
He soon attracted a 'Court of his own'.[20]

That Ted was deeply interested in the Ouija board, spiritualism and the
occult, however, is widely attested. Indeed, he delivered a paper called
'The Scope of Horror', which made use of his knowledge of astrology
and which seemingly enchanted those who heard him deliver it. Brian
Cox was both dismayed and alarmed to learn of this. A Methodist by
conviction as well as upbringing, Cox distrusted any such games with the
forces of darkness. He tells what may well be an apocryphal story about
an American who went to one of the sessions Ted held in his rooms:

> The other memory I have of Ted is that he was very interested in
> spiritualism and the Ouija Board. I never went to any of the sessions
> that he had, but one Pembroke story, for what it's worth, is that he

26

would hold sessions of this kind with such intensity – he was an extraordinary young man; you can imagine what he was like when he was 20 – enormous potency one felt, and there's a story that an American went to one of these sessions and Ted foretold his future in the most nightmarish terms and the man had a mental breakdown.[21]

We do not know the man, and Cox was certainly not present on the occasion, but this is one of the stories that undoubtedly circulated in Pembroke. Hughes, even at this early stage, evoked strange legends. Cox himself was deeply impressed by Hughes as a young man, later describing him as a 'strange mixture, a man of great benevolence and natural kindness, which at times seemed to conflict with the mythology of his poems'.[22] This was the Cambridge of Thom Henn and the Society of Psychic Research, into which many young men were drawn and lost. Although Hughes certainly knew of Lethbridge's research into psychic phenomena and the disputed discovery of the great Celtic moon goddess in the Gog Magog Hills, his own interests were reinforced as much by his passion for the poetry of the Elizabethan age as his love of Yeats.

Several members of the college spoke of Hughes' natural good manners. D.D. Bradley, in a memoir written after Hughes' death, remembered both his compelling voice and his expansive gestures, but he also comments on Hughes' natural reserve: 'Ted was not a great joiner in College activities, such as sports for example.'[23] Hughes had a gramophone in his room, where he liked to play music very loud, with a preference for Beethoven whom he admired for his titanic strength. He was no recluse. Indeed, his room often held six or eight friends 'slumped in chairs with the 9th Symphony echoing round them'. Bradley records: 'A great bow stood in a corner of his room and he spent several hours in archery practice.'[24] He also paid tribute to Hughes' skill at rapid drawing.

Ted had chosen to read English, believing that it would help his own writing to which he was already dedicated. This did not prove to be the case. Nor was he ever, during his undergraduate years, part of any literary set. There was one undergraduate, however, who might have changed Hughes' attitude to the uselessness of English Literature as an academic study. Thom Gunn was reading English a year ahead of Hughes at Trinity. Several of his contemporaries had already accepted him as the best poet of his time at Cambridge, but he and Hughes never met while under-graduates and, indeed, although they became good friends later, might not have hit it off if they had. In Gunn's first term he was an enthusiastic member of the Cambridge University Socialist Society, well aware none-theless of the stylish parties to which he was not invited. His first published poem opened every door. Gunn, the son of the editor of the *Daily Sketch*, had spent his adolescence in Hampstead and adjusted to Cambridge with remarkable ease, enjoying the sense of privilege, the libraries, the companionship of fellow enthusiasts and the Forsterian echoes there that could still be detected. Forster himself was resident in King's, and liked to invite selected undergraduates to tea.

By Gunn's second year a group was gathering together to discuss each other's poems, including John Coleman, later film critic of the *New Statesman*, and John Mander.[25] Meanwhile, Gunn attended all of Leavis' lectures. Where Hughes found English at Cambridge an almost unbear-able constraint, Gunn found it liberating to share his passion for literature. Unlike Hughes – and, indeed, most poets writing at that time – Gunn found Leavis' lectures 'helped me to deal with my own [emotions], by reducing their diffusion, by connecting them'.[26] Gunn was soon a friend of Karl Miller, then an undergraduate at Downing, to whom he made a habit of giving his new poems to read as he wrote them, and there were excited hours of conversation with other friends about Stendhal. All this suggests a social ease in an academic world, which perhaps explains how in later life Gunn found it possible to teach at a university while also developing as a poet. He liked 'the enclosed greenery of parks'.[27] Hughes did not. At the end of his first year in the Preliminary Examinations for the English Tripos, Hughes gained only a Pass degree. This must have been something of a shock for the boy who had been so effortlessly top of his school class, and who had won a College Exhibition, which Gunn had not.

Hughes went back to his parents, who by this time had moved to The Beacon, a house near Heptonstall in West Yorkshire. It was his first long vacation. Both his siblings were now overseas. Gerald, now married, had been as lost on his return to Mexborough after the war as the soldiers Ted described in 'A Motorbike', and he had no intention of staying. He and his wife Joan were already on the long sea-voyage to Australia. Olwyn was working as an au pair in Paris and writing very merrily of her life there.[28] Nothing much was happening in Heptonstall, as he wrote to Gerald; and after his near-failure in taking Cambridge examinations, Ted pondered, only half jokingly, that he was likely to be living on his sister in the future.[29]

Working in the way that Cambridge demanded proved perfectly manageable, however much Hughes disliked it. He might not have enjoyed being asked to produce weekly essays, but he obstinately refused to accept defeat. As the following year progressed, he began to enjoy college life, although never conventionally. Writing to his brother in 1953, he reports buying meat and roasting it in front of the fire in his room, 'which brings people slavering from the other side of College'.[30] John Honey, who went up to Pembroke on a History Scholarship a year later than Hughes, had many friends among the undergraduates of the college who read English. He recollects[31] a party in Hughes' rooms at which both Matthew Hodgart and David Daiches were present. He also remembered that Ted had a piano in his room (presumably hired) and that on this particular occasion, 'the party, including Matthew Hodgart and David Daiches,[32] [went on] playing and singing very bawdy songs late into the night, indeed report-edly continuing after I left to go to bed'.[33] Towards the end of his second year, although he had recovered from the initial culture shock of university and was well on the way to developing his own route through it, Hughes developed a resistance to writing the weekly essay that became so serious as to amount to a block. He had already determined that reading English under Cambridge constraints was not for him. Nevertheless, at the end of his second year he gained a creditable upper-second-class Honours degree.

Although in letters to Gerald he described many outlandish schemes for making money – for instance, mink-farming – which he hoped might bring his brother back to England, Ted remained stubbornly determined to make his way as a poet, and had no wish to be financially dependent in the process. He considered living cheaply at home and writing morning and night, while earning his keep by poaching the occasional deer; but emigrating to Australia seemed a far more attractive alternative.

Hughes had so far published no poems in Cambridge, but the most serious sign of his distress was the difficulty he experienced in writing them. Convinced that there was absolutely no value to him in the study of English as far as helping him to read or write poetry, he changed, as Cambridge rules allowed, to reading Archaeology and Anthropology for his third year.

In later readings of his poem 'The Thought-Fox', he often gave an account of the strange dream that prompted his abandoning the study of English Literature as an academic subject. He had spent all evening struggling to complete an essay of literary criticism. In his dream that night, a fox appeared that was the size of a wolf, and placed its paw, which seemed to be a bleeding human hand, flat palm-down on the blank space of Hughes' page, saying, 'Stop this – you are destroying us.' As it lifted the hand away from the page, Hughes saw the blood-print glistening wet. Hughes understood that mark as an image of his own pain at forcing himself to go against his nature. The poem was written two years after the dream, but the meaning was clear to him as he woke.

As he wrote to Keith Sagar, it was not that he lacked the ability to engage with the practical criticism of texts in a Leavisite fashion, or took no pleasure in exercising that skill; it was simply that he had stopped seeing the point of doing so:

> I connected the fox's commands to my own ideas about Eng. Lit. and the effect of the Cambridge blend of pseudo-critical terminology and social rancour on creative spirits and from that moment abandoned my efforts to adapt myself … it seemed to me not only a foolish game, but deeply destructive of myself.[34]

Most of Hughes' closest friends were made in his second and third years, among them undergraduates who had come up to college later than he did, as was the case with Daniel Weissbort, five years his junior. A curly-haired Londoner of Belgian Jewish descent, Weissbort came up in 1953 to read History, although he changed to Economics for Part One. He remained Ted's lifelong friend. Other close friends included Terence McCaughey, who was doing postgraduate research into Scottish ballads and went on to become a clergyman and a Professor of Trinity College, Dublin; Nathaniel Minton, who read Medicine; the lively and outrageous Joe Lyde, a Protestant from Belfast and a brilliant jazz trumpeter; and Michael Boddy, who played the trombone in Lyde's band. Boddy was a mainstay of the BATS (an amateur dramatic society at Queens' College) and played both the Ghost and the Gravedigger in *Hamlet* to some acclaim. Another member of the group was Colin White, a Scottish left-winger and a nephew of Keir Hardie. Lyde, now dead, was one of the people Hughes sought out with most enthusiasm when he returned to Cambridge as Boddy reports: 'Joe was very much involved in the ADC and so on until his final year (when I knew him) which he spent on jazz and his band, in which I played the trombone and tuba.'[35] Ted and his friends gathered at The Anchor to talk about politics, people they disliked – then designated as 'crumbs'[36] – but not much, in Weissbort's recollection, about poetry, although several of them were aspiring poets.

What they most liked was to sing songs, often Irish rebel songs such as 'The Wearing of the Green'. There are many tributes to Hughes' splendid rendering of 'Sir Patrick Spens'. Terence McCaughey, who was writing a thesis on Celtic folk songs, also had a fine voice and knew many unusual ballads.

David Ross, a young public schoolboy who came up in 1953, described the group as 'a sort of socialist group – only some of us voted Labour, but it had that feel about it. And I remember Ted talking to me on one occasion about "Class" – he was very well aware of class; it wasn't something he didn't notice ... it was virtually impossible not to notice it, and I certainly noticed it.'[37] According to David Ross, Ted's Yorkshire accent was never very strong.

Peter Redgrove, the distinguished contemporary poet, then an undergraduate at Queens' College reading Natural Sciences, gives a dramatic account of approaching Hughes, who was two years ahead of him. It is fascinating to find that Hughes had already acquired a large reputation as a poet even though he had still published nothing under his own name as an undergraduate. Redgrove was led to show Hughes the poems he had begun to write, largely through the encouragement of L.C. Potts, the librarian at Queens'. 'Someone said there was this marvellous poet and personality, Ted Hughes. So I dropped him a note – it was the custom then – and went to see him in Pembroke. He showed me a Beethoven death mask on the wall; he was playing late Beethoven, and he said, "This is what he looked like," and took the death mask off the wall and lurched it across at me. And the music was a cacophony to me then, because I had never heard anything like it. And that was how I met him.'[38]

Redgrove also remembers The Mill and The Anchor, both of which could be described as 'the pub just down from Queens', where they drank cider together. Hughes 'was never very much of a drinker, he didn't get drunk – not that I remember – and we used to have long conversations. He was very good at that – responding – and I was anxious to learn all the time from senior poets. I regarded him very much as a senior poet, because as a scientist I was searching out for what was real ... I was very upset and nervous, so I was looking for orientation and this man seemed to be utterly confident in everything he said ... it was as if he knew something we hadn't caught up with yet.'[39]

Peter Redgrove knew none of Hughes' other close friends at the time, and suggests that he kept his friendships separate. About the same time as Redgrove made contact with Hughes, Hughes also met Philip

Hobsbaum. In spring 1954 – that is, in Hughes' last year as an under-graduate – Philip Hobsbaum recalls meeting Hughes at The Mill. In summer it was possible to hire punts there, which undergraduates would take towards Grantchester. Except in warm weather, when people gath-ered on the bridge to watch the punting, the main attractions of the pub were that it was close to Mill Lane and that it sold Merrydown Cider, which was highly intoxicating.

Although Redgrove speaks, accurately enough, I imagine, about Hughes as a moderate drinker, David Ross attests to the wild drinking that was common among most undergraduates at the time, and D.D. Bradley vouches for one incident towards the end of Hughes' second year in which Merrydown cider was drunk to excess:

> I was returning one night, without a late pass and in some agitation – for even in the civilised reign of Tony Camps such matters were not insignificant. There appeared, staggering towards the gate along Trumpington Street, a respectable Cambridge couple, with Ted's limp figure draped across their shoulders. They knew where they were going and promptly transferred him to mine. Here was a predicament. I could not possibly heave Ted over the spikes of the back gate and I didn't know the reputed way through the Master's garage. The only possibility was to brazen it out. Fortunately the Porter who came to the wicket was Harry. A friend. 'Harry,' I said, 'Mr Hughes is very sick.' 'Yes, sir,' said Harry thoughtfully, and retired to the Lodge. All went well until, in Pitt Court, there was a voice in my ear, 'May I help you?' It was Tony Camps himself. As Tony shared the weight, Ted seemed to realise that a situation of some delicacy had arisen. Before passing out in our arms, he drew himself to his full height and said, in a voice of utter conviction, 'I'm very, very drunk. But if only you knew how pure and clean I feel inside.'[40]

Although this story is structured as a telling anecdote, Hughes' own words have a remarkable ring of truth. His memorable turn of speech – which Bradley refers to on other occasions as 'gnomic' – is instanced again in Coggrave's account of an incident outside the Mill with a 'soap-box evangelist holding forth on the need for religion. This triggered from Hughes a cry of, "We don't want religion, we want God." '[41]

For all the genuine humility of Redgrove's account of meeting Hughes, Redgrove rapidly found his way to the centre of a poetry scene of his own making. With Roger Bannister, who took a First in English, he set up the magazine *Delta* as a serious rival to *Granta*, to which it seems Redgrove did not aspire: 'It was that class thing – people were very snooty and very exclusive.'[42] In fact *Granta* was run less on any principle of exclusion than through a network of connections. Daniel Weissbort had a poem published in *Granta* when it was edited for a time by Jonathan Miller, with whom he had been at school. Karl Miller, then an undergraduate at Downing and a follower of Leavis, was a close enough friend of Mark Boxer to become the literary editor of *Granta*.

Philip Hobsbaum soon joined the editorial staff of *Delta*, editing issues 2 and 4 and including an Oxford poet, Edward Lucie-Smith, and two Downing College contemporaries, David Ward and Christopher Levenson. Philip Hobsbaum, himself from Bradford Grammar School, was a pupil of F.R. Leavis, and was outspoken in his dislike for poetry that he saw as too plainly derived from Yeats and Hopkins. He was described by Peter Redgrove[43] as unusually forthright in expression. Hobsbaum's recent memoir,[44] written after Hughes' death, confirms that he can still be abrasive. This is how he describes his first impressions of Ted:

> He was very tall, about 6'2", gaunt in body and face, but big-boned. Few undergraduates were classy dressers, but Ted was appalling. He had smelly old corduroys and big flakes of dandruff in his greasy hair. Also he talked out of the side of his mouth as if in a state of unbearable tension.
>
> Whatever we talked about at first, it certainly wasn't poetry. However, one evening he said – out of the corner of his mouth as usual – 'I hear you and Redgrove are starting a poetry magazine. Here are some poems I'd like you to look at.' And, with that, he shuffled off to the gents.
>
> The wad of manuscript he thrust at us was greasy and typed in grey characters, as though the ribbon in the typewriter had been used a great many times over a period of years and had never been changed.[45]

Hobsbaum asked Redgrove to look at Hughes' poems and Redgrove chose one for inclusion in issue 5 of *Delta*. This was 'The Woman with Such High Heels She Looked Dangerous', which plays with the image of a wolf that has become a woman.

It is interesting that, for all Hobsbaum's disparaging comments, he responded genially enough when Hughes appeared as the magazine was at proof stage and asked to be allowed to make a few changes to this poem. Hobsbaum agreed. He records: 'There was a kind of impressiveness about Ted even then, so I let him have his way, and he made a number of changes – every one, so far as I could see, for the better.'[46] Grudging as this praise may be, it is indicative of some inner confidence that was crucially important to Hughes' development, although it is likely he could make out easily enough the fastidious distaste in Hobsbaum's manner.

Exactly where then lay the 'devastation' of these university years of which Hughes speaks on several occasions? Perhaps it lay in his first disgusted understanding of the structure of the English literary world – that 'apex' of which Boxer chortled so breezily – along with the realization of his own situation on the peripheries. At any rate, although he found it hard to write poetry in his years as an undergraduate, his determination to dedicate himself to verse did not weaken. Karl Miller remarked: 'Ted seems to have made up his mind at an early stage that he was going to devote his life to poetry.'[47] It was an extraordinary conviction for a young man with no private income and no intention of battening on his family.

A couple of poems appeared in *Granta* by one 'Daniel Hearing' in June of Hughes' final year, which had been accepted by Karl Miller. It is intriguing that Hughes decided to submit work to *Granta* under a pseudonym. The poems were among those already shown to Philip Hobsbaum, who had grumbled at the greyness of the type and who had hesitated for several months while considering them for *Delta*. The use of a pseudonym suggests a decision not to put himself again in the position of supplicant. There is another possibility, however; another reason for the desire for anonymity: that he was not so much hiding as protecting possible changes of direction and development.

In later life he spoke to Drue Heinz, a wealthy patron of the arts and the publisher of the *Paris Review*, about his desire to keep several possible literary personalities alive, rather as Fernando Pessoa, the Portuguese poet, had done. Hughes spoke in that interview[48] of the way, that once you publish, your freedom is limited. He describes the exposure of a particular poem with a name attached as an assertion that would be bound to attract teasing, much as he had described in a close-knit family who unconsciously try to keep their perception of one another unchanged. However, he only used the device of the pseudonym in university magazines, though he went on to use the alias of Peter Crew for the poem he published in *Chequer*.

When Hughes went down from university, he was prepared to take any kind of work that would enable him to live, yet leave him with time to write. He did not attempt to find a job with literary or journalistic prestige. As a night security guard in a steel factory he earned £8 a week, which was only a little less than a 'supply' teacher, but he also took odd jobs for a time in a zoo and a rose garden. In a rare television reading of 'The Jaguar',[49] he mentioned with amusement that his job in the zoo involved hours of washing dishes in the cafeteria and not, as he must have hoped, caring for the animals.

Unsurprisingly, his parents were not best pleased with his occupations.[50] Ted was far from indifferent to money, for all his ability to live on little. Nor was he, in the ordinary sense, unworldly. His plan of saving enough to buy a Cambridge house, for instance, so that he could let it out to students, was a shrewd one.[51] Yet, as he reported to Gerald in the first year after his graduation: 'I shall have to get a proper respectable job, because if I don't Ma will just worry herself away.'[52] Without that pressure he might have taken a job on a North Sea trawler for the winter.[53]

THREE

St Botolph's

It was not uncommon for graduates, after taking their degrees, to hang around Cambridge for many months, as if their undergraduate years had been the most intensely enjoyable of their lives. This had not been Hughes' experience but he was drawn back nevertheless at most weekends for 'as long as his money would last to study in the library, write, and talk about poetry with friends'.[1] He was living in London, in a bedsitter at 18 Rugby Street lent to him by his friend Daniel Huws, who had published four poems in the same issue of *Chequer* as Ted. Huws was the son of a Welsh artist and a gifted woman from an English Roman Catholic family. Despite his Roman Catholicism, Huws was drawn to Graves' *The White Goddess* and the language of poetic myth there articulated. Ted, who had known *The White Goddess* since he had received it as a school prize, was particularly fascinated by Graves' attempt to establish the matrilineal structure of ancient societies.

The friends that Ted returned to meet shared his fascination with Graves' theories. They included David Ross, Daniel Weissbort, Peter Redgrove and Michael Boddy, who knew Hughes best in 1954–5. Michael Boddy, who had gone up to Queens' from Marlborough College, was reading for the Natural Science Tripos. He knew Ted through Joe Lyde, a wild, mercurial figure who delighted – as Boddy did himself – in 'gross impersonations, acts, ribaldry, physical humour'.[2] However, when Ted appeared, he at once became a centre of attention of another kind, 'because of his presence and his self-containment ... Ted was mostly a watcher, but joined in with an effective wit when he saw an opportunity. He was quiet, large, finely cut, still, friendly but enigmatic and reserved, and, above all, kindly.'[3] Boddy, who had his own literary aspirations, was – at twenty – much impressed by Ted's far greater sexual experience and his willingness to offer advice on how to treat women. Boddy described him as being at a bit of a loose end in those years but nevertheless someone who had 'the patience and good will to be something of an uncle to me for a while, or an elder brother. (I was a very young twenty-year-old when we met and badly in need of such a person ...) I have always retained fond memories of Ted and how we all relished his switches from "bloke" to "bard" if the occasion demanded, which seems to have stuck with him throughout his life.'[4]

In the final term of 1954–5 – that is, a year after he had gone down from university – Ted spent a fortnight sleeping on a couch in Michael Boddy's rooms in Queens' College. Unlike most of Hughes' other friends, Boddy was used to living in the country and knew about animals, birds and fish. He and Ted discovered that they had both won Henry Williamson's books as prizes at school:

> I mentioned I was having family trouble. 'You must be cruel,' he said, his voice rising. 'One must cultivate the practice of deceit.' He asked if I was the eldest of the family and I said I was. 'The eldest in the family must be the executioner ... You must emulate the actions of the weasel,' he said, leaving me stumped for a reply and wondering what my mother would do if I tried it.[5]

At Hughes' recommendation, Boddy bought *The New Waite's Compendium of Natal Astrology*, and was taken round the stacks of the university library to take note of other books on the occult. At the time he found it all 'pretty heady'. However, he now says: 'Sitting here in the clear light of an Australian summer it seems a fusty old nonsense ... The question is, did he believe any of this? Did I? Sometimes such stuff helps you to get into something more solid, more useful. A way of getting started, like sharpening pencils.'[6]

In retrospect, he has similar doubts about Hughes' fascinating instructions about the best way to seduce girls and then subjugate them, which he also took quite seriously at the time: 'The idea was to build up the relationship gently stage by stage ... until the poor woman was under the thumb without noticing it ... First say, "Bring me that cup." Then say, "Bring me that cup full of tea," until, I suppose, the woman was cooking a five-course meal, feeding the goldfish, walking the dog, and doing the laundry without argument.'[7]

Quite soon, Lucas Myers, an American and a relative of the poet

Allen Tate, joined the group of friends. Myers arrived in Cambridge the Michaelmas term after Hughes went down, having applied for admission to Cambridge on an impulse while still a merchant seaman. He was accepted by Downing College to read English, although, like Hughes, he went on to read Archaeology and Anthropology.

At Cambridge in the autumn of 1954, Myers submitted a poem called 'Dolphin Catch', along with another poem based on his shipboard experience, to *Chequer* magazine. His poems appeared alongside those of Hughes and Daniel Huws. A few days later Huws came up to Myers in the university library queue for the tearoom and introduced himself. It was not until January 1955, however, that Myers met Ted Hughes himself. They took to one another instantly. Hughes describes Lucas Myers as 'an especially close friend of mine. Luke was very dark and skinny. He could be incredibly wild. Just what you hoped for from Tennessee. His poems were startling to us – Hart Crane, Wallace Stevens vocabulary, zany.'[8]

These were not common influences on English poetry of the time. The 'Movement', as it came to be called, included widely disparate poets such as Philip Larkin and Donald Davie, who were subsequently collected in Robert Conquest's *New Lines*, anthologies that were published by Macmillan between 1955 and 1963. It was a group that could be identified chiefly by what it was *against*: namely anything that could be identified as pretentious, with particular suspicion reserved for the use of the old 'myth kitty'. Dylan Thomas, the most celebrated poet of the preceding generation, was felt to depend far too much on rhetoric to be trusted. Many Movement poets were old enough to have fought in the Second World War and liked to use language cautiously, as if a rash word could betray them into fascism.

Formally, they favoured rhyme and structured verses. Indeed, the tradition of English poetry had scarcely been affected by the modernism of Pound and Eliot. The latest representatives of the mainstream were on their guard against both inappropriate emotion and lyricism, defending themselves by an ironic tone and phrases such as 'I suppose', 'almost', or 'perhaps'.[9] Many – though not Davie – were as impatient with the influence of Continental Europe as, say, Nancy Mitford's Uncle Matthew from the novel *The Pursuit of Love*.

Although Hughes had determined to dedicate his life to writing, his inner certainty of success in the first year after he graduated should not be exaggerated. He was still within the period he described to the *Paris Review* as his 'years of devastation at University'.[10] John Honey, who met

Hughes in the street near Fitzbillies some time in 1954–5, remembers that he was not only seriously considering emigration to Australia – which he continued to do – but also working there as a school teacher.[11] At the time, Australia was so anxious to bring in immigrants from Great Britain that he would have been given a virtually free passage. He could also have got a job teaching in a school in England even without having a teaching qualification. However, he was attracted to Australia not only by the unfamiliar landscape, so memorably described by Lawrence, but by the hope of joining his childhood mentor, his brother Gerald, with whom he remained in close touch by letter. This Australian option was at the back of his mind for two years after his graduation.

Hughes was putting no effort into self-promotion, no thought into marketing what he wrote, and he made no attempt to ingratiate himself by spending money on clothes. Myers remembers him wearing a brown leather greatcoat which had been issued to an uncle in the First World War. Modestly, he continued to publish in university magazines rather than sending out his work to London journals, although the calibre of the poems so placed may be judged by the fact that both 'The Jaguar' and 'The Casualty' – later included in *The Hawk in the Rain* – appeared in issue 7 of *Chequer* in November 1954. 'The Jaguar' is one of Hughes' most anthologized poems. Even before his readers reach the cage where the animal paces, they are transfixed by the pungent stink left by all the other creatures on their straw. The poem is a physical assault on the senses, as well as a description of a restless animal longing for freedom. 'The Casualty' is a poem about an airman who has fallen, burning, out of the sky. His allegiance is immaterial. He is, like one of Goya's victims of war, too damaged to be helped, and the whole poem confronts an extremity of experience deliberately kept at bay by most of Hughes' contemporaries.

In other ways Hughes was still close to being a naughty schoolboy. Boddy records a discreditable poaching expedition to kidnap one of the geese presented to King's College by the People's Republic of China, although he cannot put a precise date to the episode: 'We waited for a moonless night and after the pub closed we slipped a punt at The Anchor and coasted off down the Cam towards King's.' Another friend, whom Boddy has left unnamed, was with them. 'Ted stood at the back, a huge black figure against the sky and used the pole.'[12] They had little difficulty finding the geese, but catching one was another matter. It was Boddy who succeeded, and stunned the bird before breaking its neck as he had learned to do with the geese that his family kept back home. The next day, Ted asked Boddy's girlfriend to cook the bird, but she refused.

During the time they were together, the two young men talked a lot about themselves and their lives 'as in a barrack-room friendship that ends as soon as the necessity for being together ceases'.[13] Soon after the incident with the goose, police came to question Boddy about Hughes, presumably because the college bedders had reported Hughes as an illicit guest, and Boddy was banished as a result to lodgings outside college.

After meeting Myers, Hughes often stayed with him in his hut at St Botolph's Rectory on his return visits to Cambridge. Myers had advertised in the university newspaper *Varsity* for some kind of shed and had been answered on 12 October 1955 by Mrs Helen Hitchcock, the widower of the former rector of St Botolph's. She had been allowed to remain in the rectory after the death of her husband and lived by letting rooms to four or five student tenants, and an au pair. She was able to offer Myers the hut in her garden rent free, with light, an electric fire and a radiator, in return for the stoking of two fires – an Aga cooking stove and a Sentry boiler.[14]

Unlike St Botolph's Church, which is close to Pembroke, the rectory itself was not in the centre of town. It also lacked the comforts of college life, but it offered a freedom not to be found in any college room. Although Myers washed the hut out and painted it, the floor still retained some of the odour of its past use as a chicken coup. The first time Hughes stayed in the hut, he insisted on sleeping on the floor, despite Myers urging him to use the only bed. Hughes admitted no discomfort at the time, but he later spoke of the impossibility of getting the smell of chicken droppings out of his green jumper. The arrangements were entirely informal. A note from Hughes left outside Myers' hut in 1955 announced his intention of staying in Cambridge for two days, and a scribbled reply from Myers confirmed that he would return about nine-thirty. As there was a large garden filled with fruit trees, Hughes soon bought a tent and pitched it there.

Another close friend of the period, David Ross – a cool, good-looking public schoolboy who had shared rooms with Nathaniel Minton for a time – also chose to live at St Botolph's. Minton, a medical student, had been at St Paul's – a prestigious London fee-paying school – with Daniel Weissbort. He went on to become a Jungian psychoanalyst, much in sympathy with Hughes' vision of the human inner landscape. Ross had gone up in September 1953 to read History, which meant he was two years behind Hughes and four years younger, and he, too, thought of

Ted as an older brother. For a time he edited a fortnightly magazine of criticism called *Broadsheet* with Daniel Weissbort, to which Michael Boddy also contributed. At this time Ross was writing poems himself and was eager to learn all he could from Hughes; he was impressed by Hughes' knowledge of primitive legends and was attracted to his notions of shamanism, as practised in primitive societies. Those chosen for the role of shamans enter their deeper selves and, having wrestled with their own personal demons at the risk of self-destruction, are able to return and bring healing to their tribe. It is not a process necessarily confined to poets, but Hughes came to find this way of thinking a fruitful means of releasing his own imagination. Ross also shared Hughes' enthusiasm for Graves' *White Goddess*. In his introduction to that book, Graves suggested that there was a struggle between Socrates' philosophical distrust of myths and ancient beliefs, and Hecate, the goddess of all that is hidden and secret, who supposedly took a terrible vengeance on Socrates by giving him a shrew for a wife and arranging his death by hemlock. Graves describes this magical power as 'the White Goddess, or Muse, the Mother of All Living, the ancient power of fright and lust'.[15] No doubt part of the excitement of these ideas lay in their licence of eroticism, in a period when sexual attitudes had reverted towards repression in the aftermath of war.

Ross found Ted's knowledge of astrology intriguing:

> We were both interested in astrology at that time. And Helga – who became Daniel Huws' wife – is someone who's always interested in Tarot cards and those sort of things . . . I was interested in astrology, but not to the point of studying it. Earlier I wasn't particularly convinced by it, although I did work out a theory as to why astrology should work, but that's really as far as it went. What astrology does, it places you in space and time – that's what you're doing when you draw up a chart for somebody – and that was my explanation as to why it might be rational, but I don't think Ted was very interested in rational things anyway.[16]

This interest in the non-rational world was attractive to Hughes and to all his close friends, although Michael Boddy remembers attempts at hypnotism, levitation or holding a seance at St Botolph's Rectory as no more than part of the general horseplay between volatile young men. Because Graves traced the links between Celtic and Roman myths, he opened the door to Jung and Jungian psychology for Hughes. Lucas Myers, for all his wry, laconic manner, was equally ready to explore Hughes' arcane knowledge, although since Myers was fortunate enough to be taught by the distinguished mathematical anthropologist Edmund Leach, he was under no illusions about the historical accuracy of Graves' theories. Myers continued to take astrological advice in correspondence with Hughes in later years. Like Hughes, he was in search of some metaphysical vision of the world that could replace the Christianity of his childhood.

According to Myers,[17] it was Olwyn who had first aroused Ted's interest in astrology, but by the time Myers knew Hughes, he was an expert in his own right: 'He responded to requests of friends to cast their nativities or those of their girlfriends, and he was marvellously entertaining in explaining their significance.' Nevertheless, Hughes did not see astrology as a science, more 'as a vivid expression of intuitive insights'.[18]

When Al Alvarez, poet, critic and literary editor of the *Observer*, came to describe Hughes' interest in astrology, primitive religion and black magic, he wrote, 'it was almost as though, despite all the reading and polish and craftsmanship, he had never been properly civilised – or had at least never properly believed in his civilisation'.[19] The last suggestion makes some sense, if we think less of Hughes' attempts to civilize *himself* and more of the distrust he felt for the supposedly civilized world as he witnessed it in the aftermath of the Second World War. An awareness of human brutality permeated the culture of late 1940s and 1950s.

Hughes was less enthusiastic about Graves' poetry than his study of myth. Weissbort remembers eagerly attending Graves' Clark Lectures, one of the most important series of Cambridge lectures in the 1950s. Hughes, however, disliked Graves' rejection of 'alien stowaways, namely Eliot and Pound', and thought Graves 'a learned champion' of that British tradition, which he described memorably as 'defensive'.[20]

The group of friends continued to meet, most often in the private bar of The Anchor – the scruffy, down-at-heel little pub that had been a favourite when Ted was at Pembroke. About once a week they drank mild-and-bitter there, sang Irish and Scots ballads and took a Celtic pride in not being part of the Cambridge literary world. Among them, rather surprisingly, was Harold Bloom,[21] who was to become a distinguished American critic. Although few poems were discussed on these occasions, Harold Bloom had already read some of Hughes' work and had been favourably impressed.[22] 'All of us knew,' Daniel Weissbort once remarked, 'that Ted was the best of us.'[23] The group, in turn, were amazed by Bloom's formidable memory for poetry, which he could recite from every period. Philip Hobsbaum, still at Downing, regarded the group with a mixture of alarm and disdain:

> Ted ran with a rough crowd. They inhabited an abandoned rectory which had been attached to St Botolph's Church ... At this time, and I am speaking of the mid-fifties, there were poets such as Redgrove and myself who wore suits and ties, and poets such as Hughes and his associates who, to put it mildly, did not. Among these charmers [*sic*] were Joe Lyde, Michael Boddy, Daniel Huws and Luke Myers ... In spite of the fact that Daniel Huws had written a vituperative review of my magazine (*Delta*), I welcomed him to a party [held] in honour of the *Delta* he had maligned. That was for Ted's sake rather than his own. What I was not prepared for was the ruck of gatecrashers that followed in his wake.[24]

Hobsbaum then describes a character whom he does not name, who went around his party splashing drink everywhere and narrowly missing Hobsbaum's 'then girlfriend's rather elegant white ballgown'. Hobsbaum ordered him to leave. The interloper, however, soon returned to the party, this time with a bottle with which he threatened to hit Hobsbaum over the head. This was prevented by Hughes, who gripped his wrist, saying, 'Don't hit Hobsbaum, he's a good man'[25] – a rare example of Hughes using his strength and size.

The great advantage of living in St Botolph's was the sexual freedom afforded by living out of college. Nevertheless, undergraduates remained under the jurisdiction of the Proctor. One evening an undergraduate from Peterhouse had invited a female friend to stay for a few days and, perhaps imagining that Daniel Huws was away since his bed was empty, had allowed her to sleep in Huws' college room. Unfortunately a Peterhouse porter opened the unlocked door and saw long blonde hair on Daniel's pillow. So porters were waiting for Daniel as he climbed into college by the usual route. Although he was not responsible for the girl's presence, the porters told him that they had no choice: his tutors would be informed the next morning. Meanwhile the girl, forced to leave Peterhouse, made her own way to St Botolph's; Hughes and Myers found her there and organized sleeping arrangements 'as reputably as the circumstances would permit'.[26] Myers, implicated by the Peterhouse undergraduate, was himself called before his own tutor at Downing the next morning. Daniel Huws was sent down for the rest of the term: a relatively light sentence.

Myers was forced to leave the hut in the garden of Mrs Hitchcock's rectory, although the following autumn she allowed him to rent her dining room. This change brought him into contact with Helga Kobuszewski, 'a dark and intense girl from Bonn',[27] with whom he made common cause against the other inhabitants of the kitchen. An even closer friendship was subsequently forged between Helga and Daniel Huws, who took her back to Wales with him.

Since Hughes was known to be sharing Myers' living quarters, he was forbidden to return to Cambridge – that is, to set foot within three miles of St Mary's Church in the centre of town, an area over which the university had jurisdiction – but he ignored the prohibition. Whilst his quiet dedication to his writing did not waver, his other plans changed constantly. He was attracted by the possibility of teaching English abroad – in Spain, possibly, before emigrating to Australia. Perhaps he still hankered after the freedom he would have had if he had followed his brother's path as a gamekeeper, rather than putting himself in the 'cooker' of grammar school and university. Something made him hesitate to set off, however, and it may have been because he had begun, unmistakably, to discover his own poetic voice.

For all the schoolboyish glee of his Cambridge exploits, Hughes had begun to reach for that inner understanding that is the source of his finest poetry. He returned to London. Alone there, away from friends and distractions, Hughes started to brood over the dream that had led him to change his Tripos from English to Anthropology. The poem that grew from these reflections was 'The Thought-Fox'. Hughes imagines a living fox somewhere outside his room, putting delicate footprints in the snow, before entering his poem as an embodiment of the animal world that his critical work ignored. 'The Thought Fox' may seem gentler than the dream, yet something of the sheer physicality of the vision is caught in that sudden 'hot stink', which transforms the fox from an ethereal phantom into a real presence:

> Across clearings, an eye,
> A widening deepening greenness,
> Brilliantly, concentratedly,
> Coming about its own business
> Till, with a sudden sharp hot stink of fox

It enters the dark hole of the head.
The window is starless still; the clock ticks,
The page is printed.[28]

Writing in the 1970s to Mrs Aurelia Plath about the alternative routes
that he and Sylvia might have taken, Hughes conjectures that if he had
indeed followed his impulse to go to Australia, he 'might have been lost
altogether'.[29] As he wrote to his brother in 1956,[30] he felt unhappy at the
thought of spending his important years of growing up as a writer far
away from Europe.

While Hughes was in London, he attended a few meetings of
Hobsbaum's London group, held in Philip's bedsitter off the Edgware
Road, perhaps with the thought in mind of such a growing up, although
on the evidence of 'The Thought Fox' he had already found an entirely
new voice of his own that no one in the group around Hobsbaum could
equal. Hobsbaum remarks, 'Ted was the lyric poet par excellence and we
all knew how good he was,' but he reserved judgement on any possibility
of Hughes' further development.[31] In the Edgware Road bedsitter,
Hughes scandalized Hobsbaum's South African landlady by frying black
pudding for his supper and singing ballads with his girlfriend Rosemary
Joseph, whom Hobsbaum considered a likely model for an early poem,
'Secretary'. Hobsbaum particularly remembers Hughes' top G in 'Lord
Randall, My Son'. Hughes enjoyed reading verse aloud and on one
occasion read several of Gerard Manley Hopkins' poems with such intensity that another listener took the poems for Hughes' own.

For a time he worked as a reader of novels for the film company J.
Arthur Rank. This job was arranged for him by Philip Hobsbaum, who
had written a letter of reference to Joyce Briggs, then story editor at Rank.
His task was to write summaries of novels and plays so that the directors
had some idea of their possible use as films. Hughes was more or less
forced to use a typewriter and he disliked the effect on the structure of
his sentences. He decided then that he much preferred the natural resistance set up by the effort of writing with pen and paper. In the event, the
job only lasted seven weeks; according to Hobsbaum, because Hughes
found the pressure of reading so much junk was affecting his faculties.[32]
Another account suggests that Hughes was discovered reading Shakespeare and that he walked out when rebuked.

Hughes was still a hidden figure, and there were aspects of this that he
liked. He speaks of his preference for not 'being and working in the public

view',[33] although he was very noticeable as a human being. Rosemary Joseph, a school teacher, described by Philip Hobsbaum as 'a very shy girl', was already part of his life, as were some good-looking nurses from Addenbrookes hospital; Michael Boddy recalls a nurse called Christine. Hughes was an attractive man, never likely to be short of female company, even in Cambridge. Antonia Byatt (née Drabble) saw Hughes on the day of the St Botolph's party, standing across the street with a group of friends, and thought to herself, 'He looks *real*.'[34]

In the summer of 1955 he used a little of the money he had saved to visit Paris. In those untrammelled, carefree days he relished French claret and Gruyère cheese, and was moved by the bullet-pocked walls, which represented the courage of the French Resistance and the German defeat. In a poem in *Howls and Whispers*[35], 'Paris, 1954', he marvels at the simplicity of his world before Sylvia Plath entered his life and how unable he was to hear 'the scream' approaching him.

The idea of starting a magazine had first surfaced among the group of Hughes' disconsolate friends as they sat drinking wine in Lucas Myers' hut, waiting to hear the outcome of the fiasco over the blonde girl caught in Peterhouse. The name came quickly, since all of them regarded St Botolph's as their 'spiritual home'.[36] David Ross agreed to pay the print bill, and the contributors were to be Daniel Huws, Daniel Weissbort, his brother George – who was a painter, David Ross, Lucas Myers and Ted Hughes. In the event, the *Review* looked rather like a pamphlet, in a card binding, but magazines in those days were frequently flimsy and badly printed. Once finished copies were available, teams of friends set off around the streets in February to sell them, and a party was arranged to launch the *St Botolph's Review* on 26 February 1956.

A hall was hired on the second floor of the Cambridge Women's Union in Falcon's Yard, off Petty Cury. A jazz band, with Joe Lyde[37] on trumpet, Michael Boddy on trombone and Daniel Weissbort on piano, were ready to play. Michael Boddy helped lift the piano up the stairs. Like most parties of the 1950s, the main euphoriant was alcohol, and that was planned to flow freely. David Ross recalls that he was already rather drunk before the party started. Lucas Myers writes in his memoirs that enough copies must have been sold to pay the print bills, but David Ross was well aware that this was not the case. He had spent the day touting the *St Botolph's Review* around Newnham and Girton, partly in the hope of meeting attractive girls, and was disappointed to find 'all these young women hunched over desks, working like barmy'.[38] Peter Redgrove, who was, as it happened, already involved with the woman who would become his future wife, was more successful.

One Newnham girl, however, had already bought a copy of the *St Botolph's Review*. Even as the party got under way, she was sitting in Millers Wine Parlour on the King's Parade, nervously drinking whisky macs with a young man called David Hamish Stewart, a Canadian reading English at Queens' College. She was Sylvia Plath, known to Ted and his friends as a good-looking American Fulbright scholar whose poems had appeared in several university magazines. One of these, 'Three Caryatids', had appeared in *Chequer* and had been subsequently singled out for a savage attack in *Broadsheet* by Daniel Huws.

Both Lucas Myers and Ted Hughes brought girlfriends to the party. Myers' girlfriend, Valerie, was black-haired and pretty, a 'sweet flower of London's bohemia and a good painter'.[39] Ted Hughes arrived with a girl whom David Ross remembers incorrectly as a nurse.[40] Myers confirms in his memoir her name was Shirley and describes her as 'a sensitive, handsome, light brown-haired and deep-eyed woman, quite English, quite reserved and the polar opposite of Sylvia',[41] but he points out that, far from being a nurse, she shared a weekly supervision with Jane Baltzell (later Kopp) another American postgraduate student living in Whitstead,[42] whom Sylvia regarded as a rival. Hughes was sufficiently involved with Shirley at the time to have taken her to stay for a weekend with his parents in Yorkshire, where he introduced her to his sister Olwyn. Myers attributes the origins of 'Fallgrief's Girlfriends' to Shirley, and confirms that it was written before Hughes met Sylvia Plath:[43]

> The chance changed him:
> He has found a woman of such wit and looks
> He can brag of her in every company.[44]

Everyone was dressed with deliberate informality; Myers was wearing black and white checked baggy pants and a loose, swinging jacket. Hughes had ignored ominous astrological portents to be at the celebration. As he remarks in *Birthday Letters*, Chaucer would certainly have stayed at home with such an astrological chart. The party was both noisy and drunken and so thoroughly out of control that by the end 'the windows of the Women's Union Building were smashed'. Ross himself may well have been involved with this. He reports[45] that quite early in the evening he hit Jerry Plumb[46] for no more than coming up to him and saying, 'You're supposed to be a poet – give me a poem.' Hughes was by no means as drunk as most of his friends.

Sylvia Plath entered the party 'with brave ease':[47] a tall, slender girl with long legs, blonde hair falling loose over her face, and a mouth painted with thick crimson lipstick. She was dressed in red and black. She approached Daniel Huws with animation almost at once, and challenged him about his criticism of her poem. As she spoke, she gestured with 'balletic, monkey-elegant fingers'[48] and when she laughed her eyes became as bright as 'a crush of diamonds'.[49] Myers pays tribute both to her red shoes and her 'flash'.[50] Ted Hughes noticed her at once. That 'flash' was rare among Cambridge girls of the period.

Lucas Myers, already drunk, was dancing – his own version of jit-terbugging – with a girl in a green dress, but quite soon Sylvia also began to dance with him, quoting some of the verse he had published in the *St Botolph's Review*, while he smiled in a way she described in her journal as 'satanic'.[51] For all her evident interest in Lucas, she was curious about Ted Hughes even while she was dancing with Myers. By this time her vivacity had interested Hughes enough for him to approach her. Although she had picked out Myers first, Plath had already asked the name of 'that big, dark, hunky boy, the only one there huge enough for me',[52] and she knew by heart the poems of Hughes from the *St Botolph's Review*. The excitement of this encounter enters the wild syntax of the journal entry itself. The noise level of the party was shattering, but they shouted at one another 'as if in a high wind' nevertheless: 'I started yelling again about his poems and quoting: "most dear unscratchable diamond" and he yelled back, colossal, in a voice that should have come from a Pole, "You like?" and asking if I wanted brandy, and me yelling yes and backing into the next room.'[53]

For a time they talked about the review Daniel Huws had written of her poem, with Hughes claiming that Daniel knew she was beautiful and would not have written as he did about a cripple. Her reply seems to have convinced him that she was 'all there'. They spoke about the job he was doing in London and then, though he explained he had 'obligations in the next room', he kissed her, 'bang smash on the mouth', as she describes it in her journal, then ripped her hairband off and her favourite silver earrings. The journal entry continues with him 'barking' his intention to keep what he had taken, and kissing her neck. In response, Plath bit him so long and hard on his cheek that blood was running down his face when they returned to the other room. Myers, who had not seen anything of their violent encounter, nevertheless saw the swelling of tooth marks on Hughes' cheek later. In *Bitter Fame*, Anne Stevenson writes of Hughes being taken aback by this 'energetic, extremely excited, very drunk American girl', but Hughes' own snapshot memory of the occasion in *Birthday Letters* shows how very intensely both her energy and her excitement attracted him:

> And the swelling ring-moat of tooth-marks
> That was to brand my face for the next month.
> The me beneath it for good.[54]

When he returned to Cambridge on 9 March, he found out Sylvia's address from Luke's cousin, Bert Wyatt-Brown, and he and Luke tried to wake her that night by throwing stones up at her window in Whitstead. He went back to London without seeing her, since they had been throwing stones at the wrong window, but Sylvia continued to occupy his thoughts. A letter to Myers, then living in Barton Road, makes clear that he felt an attraction strong enough to interfere with most of his other plans.

Ted had been given an ultimatum by the Australian immigration authorities. His application had been approved two years earlier, but he had deferred the date of his departure. Now, they pointed out, if he did not take up their offer he would lose the chance of a free passage. It would have made sense for him to go as soon as possible if he planned to join Gerald in Australia and did not wish to pay the full fare. Instead, he wrote to Lucas of postponing his departure for as long as nine months, and made a point of asking Myers to give Sylvia Plath his London address, as well as arranging some free lodging for her. Ted observed the confusion in his own letter with some amusement, but returned to his desire to see Plath in the last sentence: 'Don't forget Sylvia and discretion.'[55]

In a note appended to this letter in the Hughes archive at Emory University, Lucas Myers observes: 'Ted almost never asked me to do anything for him ... this is the only instance I can remember in which he asked me to do something for him I didn't want to do.'[56]

FOUR

Plath

Myers' uneasiness about furthering the relationship between Ted and Sylvia did not prevent him from taking a hand in doing so. His cousin, Bert Wyatt-Brown, took him over to Whitstead to meet the American girls living there and Myers invited Sylvia to have supper with him at his new lodgings on Barton Road[1] so that he could find out more about her. There was much to like, he discovered. He recognized her neat, well-groomed appearance, carefully made-up lips and Hollywood hairstyle – which put off many of her fellow Newnham students – as typical of the college world of the United States. She had a marvellously smooth complexion; she was tall and pretty, and in these respects she was 'a little like one of my sisters'.[2] Quite as much as Daniel Huws, however, he found her poems too well made, and disliked her 'bourgeois values and commercial instincts'[3] and what he saw as naked ambition. He registered her effusiveness and her enthusiasm for Wallace Stevens – which he shared – but there is no suggestion in his disapproval of her wishing to publish in magazines like *Mademoiselle* and *Seventeen* that he intuited the presence of genius. Myers kept his word to Ted, gave Sylvia his London address, and invited her to meet Ted and himself for a drink in London at The Lamb, a public house in Conduit Street.

Sylvia Plath was then only twenty-three but her inner life was already marked with the extraordinary intensity that was to put her among the greatest poets of the twentieth century. Candid, passionate, self-critical, self-admonitory, Plath's journals hold the molten lava of all the emotions concealed by the seemingly extrovert personality that she had presented to Myers. It was an appearance in several ways misleading. Her hair looked blonde, the glamorous colour of the period. In reality, it was mousy-brown. Myers found her good-looking, but it was animation that gave

50

her face its attractiveness; in repose her face looks different in every photograph. Her whole manner was designed to mask her formidable intelligence, as her American college education had taught her to do.

Sylvia Plath was born in Boston on 27 October 1932 to parents of German extraction. Her father, Otto, had emigrated to America from Prussia at the age of sixteen; her mother, Aurelia, was a second-generation Austrian, twenty-one years younger than her husband. Otto, who had been married before, held a doctorate from Harvard University in Entomology, although when he first met Aurelia he was teaching German at Boston University, where she was his student. Photographs suggest that he was a very handsome man. Once married to Otto, Aurelia, whose one aim had always been to get herself a good education, devoted herself entirely to her home, her husband and soon her two children; Sylvia, the first-born, and Warren.

Otto proved a domineering husband, whose work had to come before anything else. His *Bumblebees and their Ways* was published in 1933, and he contributed an essay on insect societies to *A Handbook of Social Psychology*.[4] The dining table was his desk. If Aurelia Plath wanted to entertain friends, she had to choose a night when he was out teaching. She would also have to memorize the position of all his books and papers so that they could be returned to their correct places. Her own wish to study had to be abandoned, and she transferred her ambitions to her clever daughter, Sylvia.

It was Aurelia who provided the idyllic childhood that Sylvia remembered with nostalgia, taking her children to the beach and arranging toys in their bedrooms. It was Otto, however, who was idolized by his daughter. In 1940, when Sylvia was eight, Otto began to feel the first symptoms of what proved to be diabetes. Obstinately suspicious of doctors and fearing a diagnosis of incurable cancer, he allowed his illness to go untreated, until he stubbed his toe and the minor injury led to violent inflammation of his leg. Gangrene followed, for which in those days there was no treatment but amputation, whereas diabetes was even then a manageable disease if caught early. Less than a month after the amputation of his leg, Otto was dead. From now on, it fell to Aurelia to support two children single-handed, scrimping and saving to give them piano lessons and send them to college. The family was forced to move away from their home near the Atlantic Ocean to Wellesley in Massachusetts.

Sylvia's pain is vividly caught by her childish words when she heard from Aurelia of her father's death: 'I'll never speak to God again.' She was not present at her father's funeral. It would nowadays be regarded as a mistake to deny her the chance of mourning at her father's graveside, but Aurelia's decision was conventional enough at the time. It may be that the loss of a loved father at such an early age marked Sylvia's whole life with a fear of abandonment and an inability to cope with rejection.

Her intellectual and literary aspirations, however, ranged widely. She was not only precocious and prolific in writing poems and stories, she was also academically competitive and unusually successful. Her energy is staggering. While excelling across the board at Bradford Senior High School, she was sending her work to magazines far outside the usual expectations of a schoolgirl. By the time she graduated from Bradford in 1950 at the age of eighteen, she had sent forty-five stories to *Seventeen* magazine. The first to be accepted was 'And Summer Will Not Come Again', which appeared in August of that year. In the same month her poem 'Bitter Strawberries' was accepted by the *Christian Science Monitor*. Writing had already become an integral part of the way Sylvia judged herself.

She was nevertheless healthily eager to be accepted as sexually desirable by the opposite sex, and many boys asked her out on dates. These followed the acceptable rules for sexual behaviour in the 1950s between middle-class young couples. Intimate petting on couches or in the back of cars was expected, without any particular emotional engagement; but there was little risk of full sexual intercourse. Her journal records the mingling of fascination and revulsion when a boy exposed himself so that she could masturbate him. Some of her frustrations she expressed to Eddie Cohen, a boy who had written to her as an admirer of her first story in *Seventeen*. Most of the knowledge she acquired about orgasms and contraception she received from this admirer at a safe distance.

In 1950 Sylvia entered Smith College, supported by a $850 scholarship that was funded by Olive Higgins Prouty, a romantic novelist who had created the successful radio serial 'Stella Dallas'. At Smith, Sylvia was lonely at first, and her relationship with a young Yale boy, Dick Norton, a son of a friend of her mother, was already making her wonder whether she really wanted the life of a conventionally married woman. In correspondence with Eddie Cohen, and above all in her journal, she lamented the misfortune of being born female, unable to satisfy her normal lusts without taking on all the restrictions of married life. She recognized that, despite the high academic standards of Smith, the students there were not encouraged to have ambitions beyond those appropriate to wives and mothers. From Eddie himself, however, she wanted no more than sympathy. When he showed up at her house unexpectedly, fired by her wistful letters, Sylvia was horrified by his unkempt appearance and dismissed him with cursory rudeness.

In her sophomore year she was elected to Alpha Phi Kappa Psi, an Honours Society for the Arts, and was appointed to the editorial board of the *Smith Review*. This was the year that Dick Norton smuggled her into his hospital to see foetuses in bottles, a film about sickle cell anaemia, and the birth of a baby, some of which went into passages about Buddy Willard in *The Bell Jar*. In the summer of 1952 she won $500 from *Mademoiselle* magazine for a story, 'Sunday at the Mintons', and spent the following summer in New York working for the magazine as part of her prize. Her uncertainties, and the lack of pleasure she was able to take in this experience, are given slangy vitality in her novel *The Bell Jar*, which was written towards the end of her life.

Sylvia returned home from her spell in New York to a disappointment. Aurelia had typed up Sylvia's stories for submission to Frank O'Connor's summer writing class at Harvard, but she had not been accepted. Alongside a casual dismissal of her poetry in the spring term by W.H. Auden, who was on a brief visit to Smith, Sylvia took this second rebuff as evidence that her chances of becoming a serious writer were slender. Her reaction was out of all proportion to the rejection especially when set against her previous history of success. It was a sign that Sylvia had been investing far too much of her own sense of identity in the public acknowledgement of her talent. Her mother reported witnessing a great change in her behaviour: 'All her usual *joie de vivre* was absent';[5] instead, a quite uncharacteristic lethargy possessed her. One morning, Sylvia appeared with purple gashes on her legs and replied when questioned: 'I just wanted to see if I had the guts! ... Oh, Mother, the world is so rotten! I want to die! *Let's die together!*'[6] That she intended this literally is confirmed in an unsent letter to Eddie Cohen in which she writes: 'Pretty soon, the only doubt in my mind was the precise time and method of committing suicide. The only alternative I could see was an eternity of hell for the rest of my life in a mental hospital, and I was going to make use of my last ounce of free choice and choose a quick clean ending.'[7]

Sylvia was twenty-two. This hell she was living in sounds like the onset of clinical depression, as described for instance by Lewis Wolpert.[8] On 24 August 1954 she broke open her mother's drug cabinet and stole sleeping pills, taking as many as she could carry before hiding in a hole under the porch of the house. She was missing for three days and only survived because the pills she had swallowed had caused her to vomit. This was no cry for help that had gone wrong; it was her survival that was unexpected. Her brother Warren heard her moans and discovered her.

Her recovery from these three days so close to death was slow, and she was very lucky not to be physically damaged by dehydration. Funded by the generosity of Olive Higgins Prouty, who had herself suffered a nervous breakdown in her youth, Sylvia was given the best treatment known at the time, in the privately run Maclean Hospital (in which Robert Lowell was a later inmate, and to which Anne Sexton would return periodically). A psychiatrist at Maclean prescribed a course of electro-convulsive therapy, which filled the sensitive young girl with terror. Anne Stevenson speculates[9] that the hidden menace that was to haunt so many of her poems might be attributed to that course of ECT. Whilst the voltage of ECT has now been dramatically reduced, it still remains one of the most effective ways of treating severe depression even in the age of Prozac. Half a century later no one is certain about the sources of depressive illness, for which pharmacology may well turn out to provide a better therapy than any talking cure. Depressed people however, are no longer described as psychotic and their suffering is far more widely understood.

Sylvia was living in a period when psychological illness was assumed to turn on the discovery of a key childhood trauma, as suggested by the 1964 Hitchcock film *Marnie*. Freudian analysis, at its very high watermark of acceptance, was on hand to interpret her violent mood swings and self-destructive impulses in terms of an Oedipus complex. Some of our certainties about Freud's reading of the world have wobbled since then, but several of Plath's most extraordinary poems use the story of her childhood loss as their central myth.

A Freudian analyst, Ruth Beuscher, was chosen to probe Sylvia's mind for clues as to why such a seemingly fortunate young girl should try to take her own life. The early loss of her father, and the possessiveness of her mother, were soon brought into focus. As Sylvia recovered from her near-comatose state to her former self, she was given an explanation of her inner distress that was to prove highly dangerous. She did not return to Smith until February 1954.

Sylvia was welcomed back there as a golden girl, but she must also have been recognized as a fragile one. Partly through her old friend Marcia Brown and a new best friend Nancy Hunter Steiner,[10] Sylvia met Richard Sassoon, then a Junior at Yale, in April 1954. She found his slender sinuous body, dark eyes and air of European sophistication altogether compelling. He was a distant relative of Siegfried Sassoon, the First World War poet, and although three years younger than Sylvia, he had decadent tastes, European assumptions and a wide-ranging literary intelligence. His attitudes were exactly calculated to impress Sylvia, who was soon in love with him, even while acknowledging that the solid Gordon Lameyer,[11] who was well on the way to regarding himself as engaged to her, would have made a socially more acceptable match. Perhaps as a result of her therapy, she had decided to experiment sexually, but she seems to have been afraid to bring her untried virginity to Sassoon's bed. Instead she chose a minor figure in her life, a young scientist called Irwin, as her first lover. In the process, Sylvia suffered a vaginal tear and a haemorrhage of such terrifying enormity that she had to be admitted to hospital to have the flow of blood assuaged. It says something for Sylvia's health and resilience that her eager interest in sex should continue unabated after that frightening experience.

All through her Senior year she continued to see Sassoon, sometimes spending weekends with him in New York, while working on her thesis about Dostoevsky's use of the double, taking entrance examinations for Oxford and Cambridge, and applying for a Fulbright scholarship. About this time she shed Eddie Cohen altogether, to his great indignation. Once again, fortune seemed to be smiling on her. She won the Alpha Phi Kappa Psi award, and was given an Alpha for Creative Writing. News of a Fulbright award, which gave her the chance to study in Cambridge, reached her in May 1955.

A turbulent history, then, lay beneath the image of academic achievement, physical health and supreme confidence that Sylvia Plath presented to Lucas Myers. Her journals record insecurities and frequent black unhappiness, even allowing for the natural human tendency to turn to a diary when things go badly. Her first term in England was marked by a desperate loneliness, although she was soon pursued by several eager young men in Cambridge. Towards the end of that first term, Richard Sassoon flew in from Paris to see his English relatives and took Sylvia to lunch. They arranged to meet again in Paris at Christmas, and Sylvia travelled there with Jane Baltzell,[12] a fellow American student from Whitstead. Sassoon took her to Notre-Dame, the Comédie Française and Montmartre, where Sylvia was particularly fascinated by the 'painted whores' on the Place Pigalle. Then she and Sassoon took a train south together to visit the Côte d'Azur and the Matisse chapel at Vence. But she was beginning to recognize that the attachment she had formed to Richard Sassoon was not reciprocated. He was neither faithful nor committed to keeping their relationship alive. He continued to live in Paris, but made no move to encourage her to visit him. Her obsession with him remained so strong, nevertheless, that she had to force herself not to write him beseeching letters when she returned to Newnham. Indeed, Richard remained her dominant preoccupation even after her first encounter with Hughes.

Her journals reveal both the intensity of her sexual arousal by Hughes and the limits of the relationship she anticipated. Learning that Ted had returned to Cambridge, she implored on 10 March: 'let me have him for this British spring. Please please ... Oh, he is here; my black marauder; oh hungry, hungry. I am so hungry for a big smashing creative burgeoning burdened love: I am here; I wait; and he plays on the banks of the river Cam like a casual faun.'[13] Yet even as she is waiting 'in hell' for a footfall on the stairs that might be Hughes, another part of her is hatching a plan to travel to Paris to look for Sassoon. Nor did she give up that plan even after Sassoon wrote her a letter saying their relationship was at an end.

Ted had not yet become the fixed star in Sylvia's life. She longs for him, certainly, but it is interesting to read in her journals that after their first encounter she climbed into Queens', with Hamish and made love to him in his college room, even though she later regretted her sluttish behaviour. And even when she travelled to London to visit Hughes at Myers' suggestion, she was on her way to Paris, where she hoped to find Richard. The misery of that search and the hopelessness of it were not known to Hughes until he read her journals after her death. As he saw the matter, however, there was an oracular destiny in their meeting.

Ted was still living at 18 Rugby Street, a small Georgian house in Bloomsbury, where he occupied a living room with two windows facing south. There was a tiny kitchen and a small bedroom, but no running water, and the only bathroom was three floors below, beneath the street pavement. Grimy and inconvenient as the run-down building was, it was hardly 'daunting for somebody who had been through National Service or the English public school system ... you had to bang the knocker twice for Ted, who would then throw down the key'.[14] It was Myers who brought Sylvia there. Hughes heard her running up the stairs to his room and, more than fifty years later, could recall, writing *Birthday Letters*, her exhilaration, her cobalt-blue aura, her sparkling eyes and her effervescence.

In '18 Rugby Street', he evokes her physically: the 'aboriginal thickness' of her lips, the rubbery, changeable quality of her 'roundy' face.[15]

Michael Boddy, who occasionally stayed with Hughes at Rugby Street, interrupted them – not, as has often been suggested, already on a bed, but with Plath sitting, legs drawn up, in an armchair, close by the entrance to the bedroom:

> They took no notice of me. He was sitting on a chair facing her, close to her, leaning forward, knees touching her chair. There was a table lamp at the back of them, and between them. It lit them in the manner of a La Tour painting, from behind with faces half in light. They were whispering together, she with her hands to either side of her face, focusing on his ... I had no intention of getting involved and they were virtually oblivious of me.[16]

Ted walked Sylvia back to her hotel in a trance. Somehow she smuggled him into her hotel room near Fetter Lane and there he was able to marvel at her naked beauty for the first time. In three lines, Hughes calls up one of John Donne's most celebrated lyrics and gives them a contemporary meaning:

> You were a new world. My new world.
> So this is America, I marvelled.
> Beautiful, beautiful America![17]

It was on this, only their second meeting, that she explained to him how the scar at her temples was a result of her attempted suicide and subsequent ECT treatment; an inner voice, which he ignored, warned him to 'stay clear'. When he returned to Rugby Street in the early morning, he kicked Michael Boddy awake in a state of high excitement, needing somebody to talk to:[18] 'I had not seen him in an agitated state before. He was always pretty calm. But he was restless, couldn't settle ... I got up and went into the little kitchen, lit the single gas ring, and started to fry sausages. He was in the main room, moving about, saying things I couldn't catch.'[19] Hughes sat down to eat four sausages and bread. It was almost morning.

Plath did not yet regard herself as bound to Ted. However, she revelled in his strength and passionate lovemaking. Erica Wagner conjectures that the 'sleepless holocaust night', despite the purple bruise on her cheek and her raw neck, had not involved full sexual intercourse: 'Plath was forthright to herself about achieving practical satisfaction while maintaining "technical virginity". She was, after all, a child of 1950s America.'[20] Michael Boddy's memory of Hughes' words suggests otherwise. Plath wrote her notes about her night with Hughes while she was in Paris in anguished search for Richard Sassoon. His flat was empty; he had not only provided no clues as to his whereabouts but had also left behind a pile of her letters to him, all unopened. The concierge of number 4 Rue Duvivier blandly told her that Sassoon was not expected back until after Easter. Plath sat down in his living room and wrote an incoherent letter, with hot and scalding tears falling on the paper. Unreasonably, since her arrival was not expected, she regarded Richard's behaviour as a total betrayal.

Yet her young, healthy body took the rejection less seriously than her tears and words suggest. Quite soon she perked up enough to enjoy a little flirtation with a young journalist who was sketching at a café. As she began to remember her night with Hughes, she wondered whether she might not move in with him at Rugby Street, although she was a little put off by her memory of there being no place to wash. She was tempted to telegraph and ask if she could stay there until she had to return to Whitstead at the beginning of term. As for Hughes, he had fallen in love for the first time in his life. Lucas Myers, too, soon made out as much, but more gloomily.

In the event, Plath decided against returning to England. She made do instead with a friendly American Fulbright, Gary Haupt. He had already helped her at Cambridge by holding her hand when she had to have a splinter of grit taken out of her eye in Addenbrookes. She also took solace in a young man called Tony, with whom she got into bed in the Hotel Bearn; however, he seems to have changed his mind about lovemaking.

Having run into her old boyfriend, Gordon Lameyer, by chance in the Paris offices of American Express, where perhaps she had been hoping to find a letter from Ted, she settled for a week of travel to Munich, Venice and Rome. She sent a postcard to her mother, and another – a card of Le Douanier Rousseau's 'Snakecharmer' – to Ted. Her trip with Gordon Lameyer did not prove very successful, however. They argued from the first moment they got on the train until five days later when they separated in Rome, with Gordon generously buying Sylvia an air ticket to Heathrow. She told her mother that Sassoon had gone off to Spain where he had been miserably lonely, writing long letters that she did not receive until too late.[21] At the same time she began to describe Ted to her mother as 'the strongest man in the world with a voice like the thunder of God'.[22]

Hughes had already decided that Sylvia was to be part of his life. He put his Australian plans on hold. When Sylvia returned to Whitstead in mid-April, they walked in the fens, talking avidly. His circle of friends were less enthusiastic about this new relationship, perhaps because it excluded them, perhaps because they resented his taking on any commitment other than poetry. Myers, particularly, feared that marriage would draw Hughes into a struggle for all the suburban goods of the American way of life, but he recognized how ardently Ted now cared for Sylvia. When Myers suggested that the university magazine *Varsity* had commissioned a piece of Sylvia's about Paris chiefly with the intention of bringing out her American, gushing quality, he observed that Ted's eyes 'took on a protective, hurt expression at the thought of Sylvia being set up for mockery'.[23]

Myers disputes Erica Wagner's conjecture in *Ariel's Gift* that Hughes felt any jealousy over his own friendship with Plath,[24] but in conversation with Drue Heinz[25] Hughes describes his awareness of Sylvia's continuing interest in Lucas, quoting her dreams from later on in their relationship in which he recognized the figure of Myers. Hughes seemed to feel no rancour about this.

What was most important to him was their close reading of each other's work. Ted wrote to Gerald that Sylvia's intelligent criticism of his own poetry was wonderfully helpful, that he was now writing freely every day, and that two of his poems, sent out by her, had already been accepted in America. In the same letter he explains, with enthusiasm, his plan to marry her and go off to the United States at her side. Hughes, unlike Myers, was far from repelled by a dedication that he accepted as equal to his own. Sylvia had written far more verse than he had. Her fellow American graduate student Jane Baltzell condescendingly described Plath as 'someone very capable. I sensed ... a stubborn even stolid capacity for perseverance.'[26] Hughes, in contrast, understood the value of the woman he had discovered:

> Once I got to know her and read her poems, I saw straight off that she was a genius of some kind. Quite suddenly we were completely committed to each other and to each other's writing ... I see now that when we met, my writing, like hers, left its old path and started to circle and search. To me, of course, she was not only herself: she was America and American literature in person.[27]

59

To be near Sylvia, Ted gave up his work in London, and was happy to hang around Cambridge. He lived in the top room above Alexandra House, a restaurant off Petty Cury that was run by the Women's Voluntary Service, where he was able to borrow a mattress. By this time he was so much in love with Sylvia that infidelity was out of the question, even though he slept in the same bed as a woman who had recently left her husband. He also resisted sexual advances from a wilder girl, who was plump and pretty with a gap-toothed laugh.[28] He spent May and June at Alexandra House, while Sylvia read Plato and wrote essays for Dorothea Krook, a personable young Jewish Fellow of Newnham who was warm and generous towards her.[29]

What Sylvia and Ted both had in mind was not a settled existence, but a vagabond life not unlike that of Frieda and D.H. Lawrence, though in their plans it was always clear that they would *both* dedicate themselves to writing. Even though on 29 April 1956 her maternal grandmother, to whom she had been much attached, died after a long battle with cancer, the tone of Sylvia's letters to her mother through April and May is close to ecstatic. By 18 May Sylvia was taking responsibility for their future movements. At twenty-five, Hughes might well not have considered matrimony, since he had no means of supporting a wife, but he was altogether committed to remaining at her side.

The vitality and sexual voracity that Hughes found in Sylvia might have been overpowering to someone with a less assured centre, but he adored those very qualities. When Mrs Aurelia Plath was putting *Letters Home* to press in 1975, Hughes wrote a letter explaining that marriage was originally Sylvia's suggestion: 'Did she sacrifice anything in marrying me? She wanted to teach, I wanted to go off round the world. I didn't even ask her to marry me. She suggested it as a good idea and I said OK, why not?'[30] This letter, however, was written at a time of considerable acrimony, and sounds curmudgeonly, while the poem in *Birthday Letters* is filled with joy at the memory of Sylvia's eyes overflowing with emotion on their wedding day. On the night before the wedding, he stayed with Michael Boddy and Joe Lyde in their lodgings at Park Street, Cambridge, but said nothing of his marriage plans when he left for London the next day. He was keeping his word to Sylvia that their marriage must be secret, even from his close friends and family. Only Plath's mother had been told. So it was that on 16 June – on Bloomsday – in 1956, with Sylvia in a pink woollen suit bought for her by her mother, and Ted in new shoes and trousers for the occasion, they were married in the eighteenth-century church of St George of the Chimney Sweepers in Bloomsbury, although not without a struggle to get a special licence. Then Ted arranged to move his books and other property back to Yorkshire.

Ted believed that his marriage had to be kept secret in case it put Sylvia's Fulbright scholarship at risk. Lucas Myers is sceptical about this explanation, pointing out that there was only an old regulation that made it necessary for her to ask her tutor's permission, which turned out later to be a formality. Myers believed he was detecting an early sign that Sylvia wanted to keep Ted very much to herself. As I cast my mind back to those days, however, I am not sure that – whatever the regulations say – his conclusion is the right one. Newnham undergraduates certainly *believed* they risked a serious penalty if they chose to get married. Several girls who were forced to seek illegal abortions would have chosen matrimony if they had seen that as an option.

Sylvia showed her mother London and then they flew – as a threesome – to Paris. There, Sylvia was entranced by every sign of the literary legends around Hemingway and Scott Fitzgerald, but for Ted the wartime reality of occupied Paris remained palpable, even in the pavement cafés where he still sensed the presence of the SS and their collaborating mannequins.[31] He saw the recent history of Paris as she did not, but was quite unaware either of the misery of her own recent trip there or of whom she might be fearing to encounter as they strolled, fingers linked, round the streets. He writes in *Birthday Letters* of walking at her side, like a dog, protecting her. When Lucas Myers met Ted and Sylvia in Paris on their honeymoon, after Mrs Plath had returned to America, he found them both happier than he had ever seen them before.

FIVE

Marriage

There can be few marriages between poets of such equal gifts in English literature. Their temperaments, however, were markedly disparate. Ted was quiet, self-contained and easygoing; Sylvia was animated, articulate and emotionally volatile. She could sob with joy when things went well, but readily succumb to terror when, for instance, Ted failed to appear at a projected meeting place. When she found him at King's Cross, rather than at a bus station, on the occasion that Ted records in *Birthday Letters*, he 'knew what it was to be a miracle'.[1] Their love at the outset was both equal and passionate.

One of Ted's plans before meeting Sylvia had been to go to Spain and teach English there for a year before leaving Europe behind. In those days, Spain remained one of the most primitive countries in Western Europe, and its ancient traditions excited him. At first Sylvia seemed willing for him to explore alone while she remained at Cambridge to finish her degree but neither of them could bear the thought of separation. They settled instead on visiting Paris and Spain during the long vacation in 1956, and set off in a shared euphoria.

Although Ted had taken his belongings from London back to Yorkshire the week after the wedding, he had not yet mentioned his marriage to his parents. It was from Benidorm that he wrote to announce it.[2] Benidorm was no more than a fishing village in the 1950s. They stayed at first with the widow Mangada in a house on the seafront facing a sandy beach, choosing her smallest room, which had french windows opening on to a terrace where they planned to write. There was only an antique petrol stove to cook on, no hot water, no refrigerator and ants in the kitchen. Rashly, they both drank water from the tap before Señora Mangada revealed the cistern by the sink from which she drew water for her own use. The possibility of new lodgers arriving to share their accommodation decided them to move on, after only a week. Further away from the beach, they found a whole, bright house to rent for no more than they had been charged for one bedroom and the use of a dirty kitchen.

They were delighted by the cheapness and abundance of fruit, vegetables and local sardines, and they both experimented with cooking. All their mornings, however, were dedicated to writing. In a letter to her mother, Sylvia describes her joy at living with someone as committed to work as she was – with Ted at the big oak table writing the stories that went into *How The Whale Became* and Sylvia at the typewriter from eight-thirty till noon, planning future stories and making detailed diary entries: about the women dressed in black, going with their wicker baskets to the market with the yellow plums and peppers, and huge wreaths of garlic. Neither then, nor at any other time, did Sylvia show Ted her diary, although he liked to read her the animal fables that he was writing. She seemed most relaxed, Ted observed,[3] while making detailed pen and ink sketches of the village.

The advice that Plath gave herself so often and so poignantly in her journal – particularly on 16 April 1956, where she vowed to 'never complain, be bitter or ask for more than normal human consideration'[4] – proved hard to follow in practice. Some time in July she and Ted had a quarrel, the source of which hardly matters. Both were devastated. Sylvia gives a brilliant description of the way their separateness infected the whole house.[5] Most damaging was Sylvia's retreat into a sulk. a spoiled child's means of punishing a parent, which is always painfully self-destructive. Hughes, bewildered to know what was wrong, decided to take a walk in the darkness; Plath went with him because she was afraid to be left alone. Then they both sat silent and apart under the glaring Spanish moon. In her journal Plath noted the merciless quality of that moonlight, which would return again and again to haunt her poems.

Somehow that particular quarrel resolved itself, and they were soon planning a visit to Alicante. Sylvia's journal, quite as much as the letters home to her mother, records the relish with which they enjoyed their life together. Since they were short of money, their only way of getting around Spain was by hitchhiking, a safe enough mode of travel for the young in those unsuspicious days. They ate almonds from trees at the roadside while they waited for cars to stop, and were finally given a lift by a French couple with a poodle. Back in Benidorm for Ted's birthday, they cooked beans in a cream sauce. The next day Ted lit a carbon fire in their back oven and they cooked a dish of beef and vegetables, with red wine added at Ted's insistence.

Yet the memories of Spain that fire two poems in *Birthday Letters* dwell on Ted's realization that her 'bobbysox' education had not prepared her for a land of blood and death unless it was made over into literature. 'You hated Spain,' Hughes writes, recognizing that the very primitive qualities of the place which intrigued him appalled her. She would not be the only tourist disgusted by bewildered bulls and a grey-faced matador vomiting with fear, but when he came to write *Birthday Letters* Hughes guessed that she was peopling Spain with the terrors she found in her own dreams. Ted himself was fearless in a landscape of unfamiliar nocturnal shadows. It took all Sylvia's courage to put aside the safety of American comfort and follow him into a world with 'African black edges'.[6] What was important for the moment was that his presence stilled her panic.

There was another crisis when Sylvia caught a stomach bug. Hughes nursed her admirably through this, taking some pride in making a huge soup out of carrots, tomatoes, peppers and onions as his mother would have done, but he was a little impatient with her anxiety at being so far away from doctors able to diagnose and prescribe. Sylvia had grown up in American comfort with good medicine readily available; Ted had learned to be stoical from childhood. He found her fear of dying excessive. As he writes in *Birthday Letters*, he remembers how he 'recoiled, just a little',[7] with a chilly fear that she might be crying wolf, which could prove dangerous in the future. The true pathos of the poem comes from a sense of how little, in her happiness, Plath found anything seductive in death.

Towards the end of August they returned home through Paris, where Ted met Sylvia's brother Warren for the first time. He had spent the summer in Austria, and was now on his way home to Wellesley and his final year at Harvard. Ted and Sylvia were by then virtually penniless and travelled north to stay at The Beacon, Ted's parents' house, just outside Heptonstall in West Yorkshire. Even though Edith had been hurt not to have been told of her son's wedding, she and William received Sylvia warmly. Photographs show Ted looking relaxed and happy, and proud of his new wife, while Sylvia sits smiling with open-faced charm, her waist belted in tightly in the fashionable 'new look' shape. Edith felt warmly towards her daughter-in-law, both then and later,[8] and Ted was pleased by her approval. Sylvia found the gnarled old stone houses of Heptonstall, along with the narrow cobbled main street and the wild, bare landscape in which the village was set, altogether romantic. At the same time, writing to her mother, she described Ted's mother and father as 'dear simple Yorkshire folk' and she exaggerated Uncle Walt's affluence as a prosperous factory owner.

While in Heptonstall, Sylvia received a cheque for $50 from *Atlantic Monthly*, which had accepted her poem 'Pursuit', and Ted heard that the BBC, perhaps at the suggestion of Peter Redgrove, wanted him to audition for a job reading poetry on the radio. Nothing could have seemed more auspicious, although it has to be said that 'Pursuit' is a strange poem. It was written after Plath's first drunken encounter with Hughes, and was recited to him on their first night of lovemaking in Rugby Street. The 'black marauder' of her poem is an erotic fantasy, which declares Plath's masochistic longings with almost embarrassing explicitness:

> There is a panther stalks me down:
> One day I'll have my death of him;[9]

It should be noted that it was after only one brief encounter that Plath intuited – or, more exactly, projected – an image of her own desires on to Ted. Nothing in Ted's own life had prepared him for being perceived in such a role. His girlfriend at the St Botolph's party may have hissed with jealousy, but he had left no throngs of unhappy women devoured or abandoned behind him as 'Pursuit' suggests:

> Charred and ravened women lie,
> Become his starving body's bait.[10]

The poem should have alarmed Hughes, but instead it may have excited him; he enjoyed the force of Sylvia's verbal exuberance. And the poem has a disturbing authenticity. Edward Butscher recalls that George MacBeth, who had hired Plath for Radio 3 in spite of disapproving of her gushing manner, mentioned in conversation a remark arising from Plath's reading of his own poetry. She said: 'I see you have a concentration camp in your mind too.'[11]

On 30 September Sylvia returned to Cambridge while Hughes remained in Yorkshire. In October she had a letter from *Poetry Chicago*, accepting six of her poems – a coup that allowed her to begin the new academic year with great confidence. Meanwhile, Ted heard that the BBC wanted him to record a number of Yeats' later poems. This new income, and the propinquity of Cambridge to London, made it only sensible to consider living there together. The only difficulty lay in tackling the Fulbright Committee in London, and finding a helpful ear among the Newnham dons. Sylvia therefore approached her favourite supervisor, Dorothea Krook. Permission to continue as a married undergraduate turned out to be far easier to arrange than she had feared. Dr Krook, who had already noticed an unusual ferocity in Sylvia's attention in lectures, was frankly relieved to hear that the confession Sylvia came with such anxiety to make was of nothing more damaging than marriage. Miss Morris, Sylvia's tutor,[12] also raised no objections. It was only necessary for Sylvia to give notice to the college so that another affiliated student could occupy her room in Whitstead for the following two terms.

So Ted found a flat on the ground floor of 55 Eltisley Avenue, a street of rather ugly Victorian terraced houses close to Grantchester Meadows, and moved into it alone in November 1956. As they were very short of money, particularly that month with the expenses of Sylvia's Newnham College room as well as the new flat, he took on a job in a secondary modern school. This involved teaching English to children who had failed to pass the eleven-plus examination, which at that period segregated the abler children for grammar schools. Most of the boys in a secondary modern would leave school at fourteen or fifteen without qualifications. Some of them were unable to read.

Sylvia moved into Eltisley Avenue with Ted in the middle of November. While they had been enveloped in their own happiness, however, the world around them had suddenly turned dangerous and unpredictable. It was the autumn of the Hungarian Revolution, when voices from Budapest pleading for help from the West could be heard on the radio, and there were fears of a third world war. Refugees lucky enough to escape Hungary, before the Russian tanks moved in to crush the rebellion, poured into Cambridge. In one large house in Adams Road, Dr Alice Roughton housed about twenty of them. The Suez crisis, too, had horrified both Ted and Sylvia, with the crass imperialism shown by Britain and France in their invasion of Egypt.

Officially, Sylvia retained her room in Whitstead until 7 December. Olwyn, who was on her way south from a visit to her parents before returning to her job in Paris, remembers being entertained to tea in that room, with Sylvia curled up on the window-seat in tartan slacks and a roll-neck sweater. Olwyn, at twenty-eight, was a strikingly handsome woman, and at five feet nine inches she was as tall as Sylvia. She had been finding life in Europe altogether more congenial than Britain. After university she had taken a job for a time near Wimbledon in South London, editing a scientific journal, before leaving for Paris in 1952. There she worked first as an au pair for the Bejessey family in the fashionable *seizième arrondissement* then moved on to secretarial jobs first in embassies and finally for NATO. She had been away when Ted and Sylvia had travelled through Paris on their way to Spain. On their first meeting the sisters-in-law scrutinized one another carefully.

The two women had very different expectations from life. Olwyn had a ready, throaty laugh, a casual zest for living, and a European irony and sophistication. She had no particular wish to settle down into matrimony. She was an excellent reader of literature in both French and English, and had considerable literary talent of her own, but she felt no ambition to become a writer. Sylvia recognized a forceful personality and recorded her impression of Olwyn in a letter to her mother, admiring her beauty, her amber-gold eyes and hair, but nevertheless indignantly complaining how she wasted money on cigarettes and clothes, which had been borrowed from Ted without repayment.[13] For her part, Olwyn observed the intensity of attention Sylvia brought to spending her generous Fulbright book allowance in Heffers: 'It was my first glimpse of her thus totally engaged, curiously impressive, as though she'd switched to some private, highly efficient gear. The implication of my perception was that she had *not* been so engaged up to this point.'[14] Olwyn found Sylvia poised and controlled, with a hint of reserve or constraint,[15] and admired her fair skin, brown eyes and the casual ease of her American clothes; Sylvia took some trouble to welcome Olwyn with a roast beef dinner in Eltisley Avenue. In their after-dinner conversation, when Sylvia spoke with her usual animation about writers and places she had visited, and was scathing about the 'nunlike bigotry' of the dons, Olwyn privately found the 'primary colours' of Sylvia's style disconcerting,[16] but she spent the night on their shabby sofa without fuss.

When Olwyn had left for Paris, Ted and Sylvia returned to work. Sylvia continued to keep Ted's manuscripts circulating, even as they jointly painted the yellow walls of their new flat a gentle grey, and put their books in bookcases. She had promised to get at least fifteen of his poems into print within a year;[17] although forty of the poems that were to go into *The Hawk in the Rain* had already been written, only five had so far been accepted: two each by *Poetry* and the *Nation* and one by the BBC. Sylvia was impatient for his recognition. In November, at a party, she approached John Press, then working for the British Council, and asked if he had heard of the poet Ted Hughes.[18] He said he had not; nor had he, although he was taken by the eager young American girl and invited her home to supper with his wife. There she asked his advice about getting Ted's poems into print; he gave her a leaflet from Harper Brothers Publishers, in New York, who were sponsoring a poetry competition through the New York Young Men's Hebrew Association Poetry Centre for the best first book of poems. It was to be judged by Marianne Moore, Stephen Spender and W.H. Auden. Sylvia typed up forty of Ted's poems and sent them off under the title *The Hawk in the Rain*.

In the context of the poetry being written in 1957, these first poems of Hughes' are truly remarkable. It is not only a question of subject matter. The whole urbane tone of the Movement has been jettisoned, as if Hughes had found some mainline access to far earlier roots of the language. The distinctive voice can be heard in the first lines of the title poem, with their alliteration, pounding syllables and physical density:

> I drown in the drumming ploughland, I drag up
> Heel after heel from the swallowing of the earth's mouth
> From clay that clutches my each step to the ankle.[19]

There are half a dozen equally successful poems, notably 'Wind', 'Pike' – which evoked the pond he fished on the Crookhill estate in his childhood – and 'The Thought-Fox', written before his meeting with Plath and one of his most anthologized poems. There are quatrains in 'The Thought-Fox' certainly, but the half-rhymes are nearly inaudible, and it is the daring of the central image that is memorable. Hughes had brought together his twelve-year-old encounter with a fox in the countryside around Mexborough and his dream of a fox entering his college room. In the dream, the bloody human hand placed on the essay that Hughes had been writing becomes a signal for him to abandon the English Tripos. In his poem, an inviolate fox wanders off and leaves behind a completed page.

In most of the poems it is the quality of observation that is striking; the craft is almost invisible. Consider his meeting with a mountain goat, for instance, with its 'square-pupilled yellow-eyed look' or the lovely image of a glass of wine left out overnight in 'October Dawn' that has a premonition 'of ice across its eye'. Perhaps best of all is 'Wind', where the length of the lines seem to feel the brunt of the wind as much as the man attempting to walk into it:

This house has been far out at sea all night,
The woods crashing through darkness, the booming hills,
Winds stampeding the fields under the window
Floundering black astride and blinding wet[20]

The first line of this verse is iambic, but the lines have an underlying trochaic beat, held in place by alliteration more than metre. Where there is metaphor, Hughes uses it with a recklessness that has no fear of mixing 'stampeding' with 'floundering' in a context where land and sea are so mingled in his imagination. It is as if years of Leavis have been overthrown in a moment. The wildness of the moorland and its stone remain present even when the family is sitting by the blazing fire in the last verse.

The craft in 'The Horses' lies in the evocation of the world of frost before dawn and the patient creatures in a strange silence. Hughes wishes to remember 'Hearing the horizons endure'.[21] The book also contained poems about young men killed and the destruction of a whole generation during the First World War, with his father and uncle as fortunate survivors.

The voice is so fresh that it is hard to identify a source. There seems little resemblance to John Crowe Ransom, whose poems we know Hughes had been reading with admiration. Nevertheless, Hughes confessed to Ekbert Faas that it was American literature that had woken him from his six years of bewilderment, mentioning a Penguin anthology of American poets that came out in 1955, which included work by Karl Shapiro, Robert Lowell, W.S. Merwin and Richard Wilbur, as well as Crowe Ransom.[22]

It was a period when Sylvia's own acceptance as a poet was growing. She had had several poems published in *Granta*, one of which – 'Spinster' – had even been reviewed in the *Sunday Times* by their distinguished theatre critic, Harold Hobson. He was brought round to Eltisley Avenue on 17 March 1957 by Wendy Christie (later Campbell) who shared Sylvia's supervisions with Dorothea Krook. There was no way, of course, that Hobson could have realized at the time how much the diction of that poem owed to the unknown Ted Hughes.

Ted and Sylvia spent the Christmas vacation in Yorkshire, although Sylvia was studying intensely for her examinations and Ted was writing most days. Both Edith Hughes and Aunt Hilda continued to like and approve of Sylvia. Olwyn, too, was impressed by her, but this was the occasion when she first heard about her attempted suicide and the resulting shock treatment. For all the dramatic detail with which Sylvia told her story, Olwyn remained unaware that the episode had lasted for several months, and imagined it had something to do with a boyfriend. She thought that Ted knew as little then about Sylvia's long stay in hospital as she did herself; if he knew more, he did not enlighten her.

The magnificent landscape of Yorkshire delighted Sylvia, who wrote happily to her mother, declaring, 'I have never been so happy in my life: it is wild and lonely and a perfect place to work and read. I am basically, I think, a nature-loving recluse. Ted and I are at last "home" '[23] The idea of living in Yorkshire was never to be taken up. It would have been, to say the least, ill-advised. Plath could never have thrived in so unpeopled a landscape, and Ted guessed as much about her, even as he wondered 'What would stern/Dour Emily have made of your frisky glances'.[24]

With Ted's Uncle Walter, they walked across the moors to Top Withins, usually taken to be the setting for Emily Brontë's *Wuthering Heights*. Sylvia's health, freedom and the athleticism with which she climbed a tree had little in common with Emily Brontë, nor was she – as she recognized herself in her poem, 'Hardcastle Crags' – at home among hills of indifferent iron. All she shared with Emily was her passionate literary ambition. Ted already knew a good deal by now of his wife's inner world. He knew that she was superstitious, apprehensive and bewildered by his mother, father and sister.[25] Writing to Gerald and Joan to thank them for letters to Sylvia in 1957, he acknowledges the unease Sylvia had felt in meeting his family. He could understand and accept her view of their domestic behaviour without sharing it. It does not appear to have led to any quarrel. And on one point he was emphatic to Gerald: Sylvia was his own 'luck'.

When they returned to Cambridge, Ted continued to work in the secondary modern school. He was a naturally good teacher, and boys who were often eager to leave school and earn some money responded with unexpected enthusiasm to his reading of Auden's ballads. A liberal head teacher gave him the freedom to educate the children in general knowledge, particularly the history of the Russian Revolution, the rise of the Nazis in Germany and what had happened to the Jews. He did not dislike what he was doing, but he soon perceived that teaching drained very much the same energies as did writing, and he had long ago opted for freedom even with the attendant discomforts of poverty. Eltisley Avenue was cold, and would have been colder still without the gift to Sylvia of a paraffin heater from Dorothea Krook.

It was in Eltisley Avenue that Hughes wrote 'View of a Pig' and

'Thrushes', both of which were to appear in *Lupercal*. 'Thrushes' is one of the most extraordinary of Hughes' early poems, opening with a vision of evolutionary continuity between the adaptive perfection of birds and the genius of human invention:

> Terrifying are the attent sleek thrushes on the lawn,
> More coiled steel than living –[26]

To yoke together such seemingly commonplace agility with 'Mozart's brain' was a fancy that John Donne might have essayed, using the geography or alchemy of his own day, just as Hughes was using Darwin.

The poems of Ted's that Sylvia continued to send out to American magazines came back with dispiriting frequency, however. Sylvia minded far more than Ted; she wanted to prove she could be of help to him. In his *Birthday Letters* poem, '55 Eltisley', Hughes remembers being more preoccupied with the unexpected isolation he now found himself in. To someone as deeply superstitious as Hughes, the discovery of a bloodstain on a pillow at their new home, and his imagination of the dead husband and bereaved wife whose senile lives were haunting their damp little flat, were troubling omens and led him to reflect that

> His death and her bereavement
> Were the sole guests at our house-warming.[27]

He had returned to a suburban Cambridge, as far from the St Botolph's chicken shed as could be imagined. His circle of friends had dispersed. Even those who had come up to Cambridge two years after him had now gone down; David Ross and Lucas Myers had taken a villa in Italy during the summer and their freedom seemed enviable. As if to bait him, about this time Myers wrote a satirical poem attacking the institution of marriage but, as Hughes later noted with amusement, both David Ross and Dan Huws had themselves got married within a year of the St Botolph's party.

Other friends who occasionally looked in were unpopular with Sylvia, who had never had much time for Joe Lyde or Michael Boddy. Daniel Weissbort thought she 'did not find him interesting enough'[28] even to resent. The life Ted had imagined did not include setting up a *House and Garden* apartment, which one part of Sylvia kept as a dream.

In Erica Wagner's reading of '55 Eltisley', Ted already feels Sylvia's nervous insistence on keeping him apart from any other women as oppressive, and the poem certainly refers to Sylvia's 'delirium of suspicion' and the 'pack-ice' she set up against any mention of earlier girlfriends. But even more strongly does it suggest his own horror of the plodding suburban safety in which they were encased, which Keith Sagar, describing Sylvia Plath's childhood, calls 'a landscape from which disturbing wildness had been effectively removed'.[29] Hughes had already written poems that suggest the kind of freedom his nature craved. Sylvia provided instead a context in which the purpose of life is measured in fame and money. At least he took these to be Sylvia's values, as one of the most unsettling of the poems in *Birthday Letters* illustrates.

Ted had given Sylvia a present of tarot cards on 28 October 1956, and all through their time in Eltisley Avenue they turned for amusement and instruction to the Ouija board. That this may have been only half serious is suggested by a description in *Letters Home*[30] of the questions asked of the spirit they invoked, whom they invited to predict results which might have led to a win on the football pools. And the spirit in Hughes' poem jokes too, until Ted asked: 'Shall we be famous?'

In asking a question so far from his own concerns, he intended to go along with Sylvia's – and her mother's – ambitions. To his astonishment, she became furiously tearful, almost as if, the poem concludes, she had clairvoyantly guessed the posthumous nature of her own worldwide acclaim:

> 'Fame will come. Fame especially for you.
> Fame cannot be avoided. And when it comes
> You will have paid for it with your happiness,
> Your husband and your life.'[31]

This is written in an odd tense, a hindsight that throws its own light forward. It is a note of the determinism that goes to the heart of Hughes' own late perception of the world, and gives it an ominous, brooding tone.

Even if Hughes' own close friends had left Cambridge, there were still parties to which Ted and Sylvia were often invited. Karl Miller remembers meeting Sylvia and Ted together at one just opposite Pembroke College, at which his wife, Jane, recalled that Ted was rather tongue-tied and shy.[32] Hughes had never been at ease among a Cambridge set whose background and social skills gave them a different speed of conversation. Not everyone remembers him in the same way. Wendy Christie for instance, the slightly older woman who had been invited to share supervisions with Sylvia Plath by Dorothea Krook, remembered seeing Ted and Sylvia at a party in her own rooms: 'smiling and smiling and incandescent with happiness ... They seemed to have found solid ground in each other. Sylvia had found a man on the same scale as herself. Her vividness demanded largeness, intensity, an extreme, and Ted was not only physically large, he was unafraid: he didn't care, in a tidy bourgeois sense, he didn't care a damn for anyone or anything.'[33] Nor did he. He was not waiting for every post, as Sylvia so often came to do, or feeling low because of frequent rejections. However, when the telegram arrived on 25 February 1957, announcing that Ted's first book of poems – *The Hawk in the Rain* – had won the Harper first publication contest, they rejoiced in it together. Both of them were excited enough to let their breakfast burn while they phoned their mothers with the news: Ted's in Yorkshire as well as Sylvia's in the United States, although Anne Stevenson only mentions the need to phone Aurelia Plath. That evening they dressed up and had a splendid celebratory supper at the King's Parade Restaurant. In her journal Sylvia notes, like a true 1950s wife, her delight that Ted was the first to make his name, but the next morning they woke to a silly argument and Sylvia made a rather grim entry in her journal that she had not had an acceptance of any kind herself since October of the preceding year.

She was having to work extremely hard. She already held a degree and was therefore taking Part Two of the English Tripos in two years instead of the usual three. For this she had to sit six three-hour examinations. The compulsory subjects were the Tragedy paper, an essay and passages of English verse and prose for comment. This last paper was a problem for her, since the practice of dating passages in a literary historical context was not something she had needed to master at Smith. Indeed, she had far less knowledge of the body of English Literature than Ted, for all her alpha grades. To help her he made a map of the key figures in English literature, which she put up on the wall so that she could learn the dates. The other papers she had chosen were: the Moralists, including a compulsory section on Plato and Aristotle, which she studied with Dorothea Krook; the history of English literary criticism: and Chaucer. She also submitted a manuscript of her poems, now called 'Two Lovers and a Beachcomber'.

The first poem that Lucas Myers saw of Ted Hughes' began 'Money, my enemy' and, although it was never to pass the first draft, it was passionately felt. The need for money endangered time and energy, and Hughes hoped to devote both wholeheartedly to poetry. Poets in the past who had achieved this had had private incomes to support their dedication. Hughes had none. Yet he was adamant on the necessity of gambling on a full-time writing life. Plath wanted the security of an academic job while she was finding her literary feet and so, when in March 1957, the offer of just such a post at Smith arrived, she was relieved as well as flattered. The job had been arranged for Sylvia by her most enthusiastic supporter on the Faculty at Smith, Mary Ellen Chase. Sylvia would be an instructor, with three classes of three hours each per week at a salary of \$4200.[34] Northampton, Massachusetts, was not perhaps the adventure of exploration they had both planned when they talked of Lawrence and Frieda, but Sylvia was excited at the prospect, and Ted went along with it. It had always been her dream to teach at an important university. Ted was equally adamant that this was not the road he wanted to take. Sylvia tried to explain to her mother without much success how wasteful it would be for Ted to aim at such a way of life himself.[35]

Immediately after the examinations, in which Sylvia got a respectable, if not dazzling, 2.1,[36] the Hughes returned to Yorkshire. Ted was correcting the American proofs of *The Hawk in the Rain*; both of them worked in the mornings and walked together in the afternoons. Olwyn, on a visit from France, saw that they only joined the rest of the household in the evenings, though she also observed how much pleasure Sylvia took in cooking meals, and particularly remembered her fish chowder as excellent.

One afternoon John Fisher, Ted's old English teacher, and his wife drove over from Mexborough to visit Ted and meet his new wife, as well as to see the rest of the family, who were old friends. Sylvia, knowing how important Fisher had been to Ted, was particularly animated, but whether or not her manner 'disconcerted' the Fishers, as Olwyn suggests, or whether Sylvia began to feel excluded from a conversation which turned on reminiscences she could not share, she suddenly got up and left the room. In Olwyn's words: 'When she didn't return after about ten minutes, during which time Ted had become rather silent, he rose in turn and said he'd better go and see where she was. Quite a while later they returned, Sylvia rushing straight upstairs.'[37] Olwyn felt this behaviour was so embarrassing that Sylvia ought to have apologized. If Ted found his sister's opinion unwarranted, he made no issue of it. Some weeks later he gave Olwyn a variety of explanations in a letter written en route to America from the *Queen Elizabeth*. He attributed Sylvia's rudeness to her nerviness after the stress of the examinations. Then, thinking about it as he wrote, he pointed out that much of Sylvia's behaviour was an attempt to disguise her panic when meeting people she did not know well: 'Only this American stereotyped manner keeps her going at all. She says stupid things then that mortify her afterwards. Her second thought – her retrospect – is penetrating, sceptical and subtle.'[38] Ted understood how highly strung Sylvia felt outside her own territory. He had not yet grasped how far he was about to leave his own world behind.

SIX

America

F ew Britons of Ted's generation knew much about America, except
from the way of life presented in Hollywood films and whatever
they had seen of American GIs. Americans were perceived as
wartime allies, liberators, relaxed, easygoing democrats. The old colonial
powers – France and Great Britain – who had invaded Egypt in 1956,
were regarded with far more suspicion by the young and liberal. More
ambitious literature was being written in the States than anything in Great
Britain in the immediate post-war period. And it was not only American
poets such as Lowell, Wilbur and Crowe Ransom who had helped Hughes
to find his voice; it was in America that he had achieved his first recognition
and was soon to see his first book of poems published. So setting out on
20 June 1957 with Sylvia to cross the Atlantic on the *Queen Elizabeth*
was an exciting adventure. For him, Sylvia personified America and the
challenge of American literature. They were very close. As Ted put it, 'our
minds became two parts of one operation. We dreamed a lot of shared or
complementary dreams.'[1]

What Ted meant to Sylvia we can read in her journals. He was someone
who could give her passionate sexual love and the protection of a male
parent; who spoiled her with coffee and orange juice in the mornings,
and yet was a genius already acknowledged by the world she longed to
impress. Neither of them was troubled in the least by the fact that they
were about to live on Sylvia's earnings. In their own minds they were
footloose wanderers whose only bond was to one another. It was an image
of the good, creative life that influenced many who fell under Lawrence's
spell at the height of his reputation in the 1950s. Al Alvarez has described
the power of the legend on himself in *Where Did It All Go Right?* There
is some irony then in their humiliating experience with Customs officials

on arrival in New York. When they burrowed into Sylvia's trunk, they discovered a copy of *Lady Chatterley's Lover*, and officials interrogated Sylvia so tenaciously about her courses at Smith – where she intended to teach Lawrence – that she burst into tears. Such an entry into America foreshadowed much of the small-town bigotry that Ted was to experience in the United States and came to hate passionately.

By 29 June 1957, Ted and Sylvia were in Sylvia's home town of Wellesley, Massachusetts, at a garden party of seventy relatives and friends. Ted was at first delighted by Mrs Plath's thoughtful wedding present: a rented cottage at Eastham, Cape Cod, where the couple could stay for seven weeks, swimming, fishing and writing without interruption. He described it to Lucas Myers as a little wooden house in a Christmas tree forest.[2] In a letter to Gerald, however, he confessed that when he discovered the expense of renting the cottage, he was so irritated by the waste of money that he found it impossible to write anything while he was there, for at least three weeks. Both of them were paralysed by a life of sitting around on a beach, and Sylvia soon fell into a helpless depression. Given their joint unease, Ted's recollection of the Cape Cod holiday itself in 'Flounders' in *Birthday Letters* is unsurprisingly ambiguous. The poem opens with a telling question: 'Was that a happy day?'

At first it looks as if the doubt refers to no more than a narrowly averted accident. The tide dragged their small rowing-boat inexorably out to sea, and they were lucky to be rescued from a sandbar by a motorboat. Later that day they caught a wonderful haul of flounders, which they must have enjoyed cooking and eating, although the poem does not mention it. Frieda described Lawrence as always bringing pleasure to daily chores in her autobiography *Not I But the Wind*. Hughes calls it the 'thrill-breath' of what most people live by, ordinary human joys that might have bonded Sylvia and himself together.

But in several respects they were not like Lawrence and Frieda. Sylvia and Ted were *both* dedicated to the creation of literature, whilst Frieda was far too lazily self-indulgent for any such disciplined effort, although she sometimes claimed a hand in the writing of Lawrence's novels. Moreover, Sylvia had an anguishing insecurity, which made it difficult for her to enjoy life without a constant stream of reassurance from the literary world that she longed to enter. Part of the determinism of *Birthday Letters* comes from the sense, with hindsight, that the service of poetry had to take some of the blame for what happened to their love. At the end of the poem, 'Flounders', Ted reflects:

It was a visit from the goddess, the beauty
Who was poetry's sister – she had come
To tell poetry she was spoiling us.
Poetry listened, maybe, but we heard nothing
And poetry did not tell us. And we
Only did what poetry told us to do.[3]

In an unpublished chapter from a forthcoming book, Professor J.B. Beer writes tellingly of a component in Sylvia's attraction towards Hughes, which he calls a 'hunger for being', felt all the more strongly in 'a passionate fragmentary girl' as she describes herself. In contrast, Beer finds that for Hughes 'being was identified with physical life'.[4] That summer, Sylvia's need to bolster her own belief in herself was intense. Her manuscript came back unchosen for publication in the Yale Series of Younger Poets, although she had already written to her mother that she had heard it was a contender. Most writers are sensitive to rejections, but for Sylvia they went painfully to the heart of who she was, as if she could not believe she existed without recognition. Her response was to change the direction of her energies towards prose. Most of that summer she was gloomily trying, and failing, to write stories. Those who have doubted whether Plath could have become a successful novelist,[5] since she so commonly depended on the material from her own life in her prose work, have perhaps forgotten how often Lawrence, for instance, commonly made a practice of it. The detailed observation of the journals suggests that she might have become a sharp, witty novelist if she had allowed herself to work without aiming at specific magazine markets. Ted saw her attempt to write stories as a threat to her finding the true voice of her poetry, which it surely was, although her need to target her writing was equally damaging to her prose.

In fact, neither Ted nor Sylvia had a very productive summer and there were two weeks of genuine panic when she thought she might be pregnant. The only poem that Sylvia began became 'Mussel Hunter at Rock Harbour', a remarkable poem that she could not yet push through to completion. Unable to use free time when it was available, Sylvia was looking forward to the start of term and her teaching of Hawthorne, Henry James, Lawrence and Virginia Woolf.

By the end of August, Ted and Sylvia had moved into a pleasant flat, at 337 Elm Street in Northampton, Massachusetts. It stood next to a park and five or six acres, and looked into treetops from every window. Ted was still optimistic about the United States. He was cheerfully anticipating a chance to meet American poets of some stature at Smith, and to Lucas Myers he mentioned Anthony Hecht,[6] whom he thought Myers would know. Yet there were already signs of unexpected difficulties. The plan was for Ted to write while Sylvia was teaching at the university, and he had not yet understood how much of a strain this was for her. All he perceived was that in this new world he was finding it difficult to function himself. He wrote to Lucas Myers in the autumn of 1957, apologizing for his failure as a correspondent and saying that this was only part of his seeming inability to write anything, almost as if he had neither head nor hands: 'I sit for hours like the statue of a man writing ... I have never known it so hard to write ... I shall get a part-time job, I think.'[7]

Ted did not blame his marriage for this unexpected block, but he certainly remembered the state of being unmarried with some regret as he advised Myers not to take on more work than will feed him, and to compose, behave and fornicate for Dan, David[8] and himself since they were all by now so 'wived, ringed and roofed'. Ted was at pains to point out that this new world he found himself in was 'Not worse, but different ...' In the same letter, Ted reflected grimly, rather as a prisoner might, that his 'stretch' in America was to last for two years. He had little contact with Smith, and he described such contact as he did have as 'old mushrooms to my left nostril'. He longed for news of his old friends: 'You must write and give details of your days. You cannot be too detailed. Until I can fasten some associations into this place, my days are dull as an empty house.'[9]

Both Ted and Sylvia were already unhappy in America, but for very different reasons. Since Ted scrupulously never read Sylvia's journals, he had no conception of how much her desire to excel made the experience of teaching a nightmare. The polish of her appearance fooled him. 'I had supposed/It was all OK,' he wrote in *Birthday Letters*.[10] Even so, he could see that the energy she put into preparation for her classes had to be taken from her writing. By November, Sylvia had come to agree with him, and when she sent a Christmas card to Lucas Myers – still in Italy – to compliment him on a poem appearing in *Poetry*, she wrote rather as Ted might have done: 'Teaching is no job for a serious writer. We hope to set up shop on the slummy side of Beacon Hill next year ... Will you ever come home?'[11] Ted added his own modification, which makes clear just how unhappy he was with their life in America: 'She doesn't mean

"will you ever come home", she means "will we ever get back to Europe"
... Our hope.'[12]

Small-town America was not then, and probably is not now, very
hospitable to the idea of a writing life. The Hughes were poor, in a world
where an affluence unimaginable in post-war Britain was commonplace.
Their ordinary living expenses consumed the whole of Sylvia's salary.[13]
Ted adjusted to new social circumstances slowly, as he had in Cambridge,
and made friends at the same pace. Sylvia at least had gone back to Smith
in part to realize an ambition. A great many people knew her and were
eager to greet her as a celebrated graduate of the college. Few people had
any idea what Ted might be trying to achieve.

Clarissa Roche, for instance, the wife of the poet Paul Roche, who had
modelled in his youth for the painter Duncan Grant and was subsequently
the inheritor of his paintings, spoke of Hughes with little respect.[14] Her
own English family had connections with Smith which made it possible
to arrange a teaching job there for Paul, who was by that time an admired
figure on the campus. Clarissa herself had never been a student at Smith,
although her connections made her rather more than a Faculty wife. She
nevertheless made it plain from her first meeting with the couple that she
was only interested in Sylvia: 'As far as I know, or could see, Ted was just
there – nobody made any great fuss about him. I think he had won the
Harpers prize – or his book was about to be published – but every year
somebody won that prize, and because there were so many poets – names
one doesn't even know any more – people weren't impressed.'[15]

This is far from an accurate description of Hughes' perceived stature.
On 6 October 1957, W.S. Merwin had hailed the distinction of *The Hawk
in the Rain* in the *New York Times Book Review*. W.S. Merwin was a
formidably gifted poet, whose work Ted already admired. Three years
older than Ted, Merwin had graduated in 1947 from Princeton University
where he was taught by John Berryman. During the early 1950s he made
a living, translating from Latin, French, Spanish and Portuguese, on the
island of Majorca, where he was tutor to the children of the poet Robert
Graves. He had already received the Yale Series of Younger Poets Award
from W.H. Auden for 'A Mask of Janus' in 1952, and went on to win
every major literary prize America had to offer, including the Pulitzer. In
Boston he was already a notable figure.

In late 1957, John I. Sweeney – then director of the Woodberry Poetry
Room at Harvard's Lamont Library – arranged for a meeting between
Ted and Sylvia and W.S. Merwin and his wife Dido. Dido, a personable,

aristocratic Englishwoman – whom Ted once described as a young Lady Bracknell – was often wittily judgemental, and always had the confidence that comes from a sense of belonging to what Anne Stevenson characterizes as 'the English intellectual squirearchy'.[16] Her uncle was Lascelles Abercrombie, a poet who had known Robert Frost.

Ted may have been rather shy on that first meeting. 'He didn't say much, and appeared to be watching attentively from the touchline,' Dido Merwin wrote later,[17] but all four liked each other and met again quite soon in the Merwins' flat on West Cedar Street. It was the most important new friendship that Ted made in his two years in America, apart from his companionable rapport with the artist Leonard Baskin and his first wife Esther, whom Ted did not meet for another year.

The Merwins encouraged Ted and Sylvia to believe it was possible to live as freelance writers without teaching jobs to supplement their earnings, and suggested that Ted and Sylvia rent their flat when they moved to Boston the following year. The trouble with such a plan was the necessary downpayment of two months' rent in advance, and in the end the Hughes decided to gamble on finding somewhere suitable when they arrived.[18]

By March 1958, Ted was finding his situation in Northampton intolerable. Sylvia quotes him in a journal entry of her own as saying, 'I want to get clear of this life: trapped.'[19] Some part of his depression may have been due to a virus infection he suffered that month, but life in the suburbs was certainly a major factor in his low spirits. This was compounded by their financial situation. As the first semester finished, it was already clear that – far from saving money – they were spending a few dollars more each month than Sylvia earned. Ted decided to take a job, with the hope that the extra money would help get them back to Europe the following summer. He arranged to teach for fourteen weeks, that is, half an academic year, at the University of Massachusetts.

As he put it to Myers,[20] Ted had taken a job as a teacher only because no more dignified job was possible. There was a slump and many people were out of work in the town. He taught a 'Great Books' course, which involved two classes three times a week, and also a class of freshmen twice a week – as heavy a load as Sylvia's. He enjoyed teaching Milton but, as he wrote to Myers: 'To tell the truth, Lucas, I am a little weary of this place.'[21]

Ted tried to find some comfort in the way Sylvia's unhappy year at Smith had helped her to see through the glamour of a university teaching life, and there were other compensations. The University of Massachusetts might not have the social cachet of Smith, but the girls he taught were attractive, as he confessed to Myers, and in spite of their wealth, 'not bitches'. Their presence alleviated Ted's boredom.

However, Ted's sombre mood did not lift and Clarissa Roche gave a hostile portrait of his behaviour at a dinner party just after Easter that year, at which Sylvia was the animated star: 'After dinner Ted just went completely silent, and it *filled* the atmosphere, just made the atmosphere so heavy. Sylvia was talking more and more quickly, louder and louder. She was sitting on the floor, which we often did, and he literally snuffed out the evening. And apparently he often did that – Sylvia called them "white hot silences".'[22] As it happens, Sylvia had described that very dinner at the Roches in her journal, stigmatizing the occasion as *dull*: in passing she excoriates a woman scientist, Dorothy Wrinche, who was also present. Observations in her journals of Paul and Clarissa are generally spiky: she saw the 'gilding and curling'[23] of Paul's hair as the work of a hairdresser, and noted that Clarissa liked to slouch about in a baggy white sweatshirt and could sometimes be found recovering from sulky tears herself.

Whether or not Sylvia confided in Clarissa Roche after this occasion, by now both Ted and Sylvia were grumpy with one another and occasionally quarrelsome. Ted, for instance, thought Sylvia had thrown away his old cufflinks because she disliked them, and also a book on witches, which she could never bear because of the descriptions of torture. It was usually Ted who did the washing up, but for a time greasy dishes piled up in the sink and the rubbish bin overflowed with coffee grounds and rotting fruit rinds.[24] In April 1958, Sylvia was altogether dispirited when her poems were rejected by the *New Yorker*. Only the thought of Henry James' failure to win readers in his own lifetime consoled her.

Ted had been asked to give a reading at Harvard, for which he was paid $100. On 11 April they drove down in a car borrowed from Sylvia's brother Warren, who was in Austria at the time on a Fulbright scholarship. Although it was already April, a winter storm had brought snow and sleet to the streets of Boston. Plath was afraid that the bad weather would mean no audience at all, but there was a responsive, if not huge, audience, which included Sylvia's mother, Gordon Lameyer, Mrs Prouty and Adrienne Rich, whom Sylvia had long envied as a more successful woman poet and whom she memorably described in her journal as 'round and stumpy with vibrant, short black hair, great sparkling black eyes and a tulip-red umbrella'.[25] They went out to dinner afterwards with Adrienne Rich, her husband – the economist Al Conrad – and John and Marie Sweeney.

For all the gaiety of that episode, Ted was still writing to Myers in May 1958 about the natural starch in the New England air and of feeling as he used to on Sundays when in chapel. Sylvia herself was strung 'tight as a wire'[26] – which Ted attributed to the Moon and Saturn – and his own inertia continued.

One happy occasion, on 4 May 1958, however, was their meeting with the Baskins. Leonard Baskin was eight years older than Ted and, although not yet the public figure he would become, with paintings and sculptures in all the major art galleries of the world, he was already formidably assured and often searingly abrasive in his judgements. He took an instant liking to Ted, whose integrity was transparent. Baskin's influence was to be in several ways decisive in Ted's development. They were to collaborate all through Ted's life in illustrated books for Baskin's Gehenna Press,[27] and in conversation with Baskin Ted learned a great deal about Jewish scholarship. Baskin, the son of a rabbi, was well educated in Hebrew mystical traditions and fascinated by all forms of religious experience. These questions were a matter of particular urgency to him. He and his wife Esther, who had a small child, Tobias, had to confront the fact that she was developing multiple sclerosis, and Baskin was never free from the knowledge of the human evil committed in the European death camps. The birds that haunt Baskin's sculpture and painting alike offered images that Ted was soon to use, first on his own book covers and later in his poetry. Sylvia, too, loved the Baskins for what she calls 'their lack of smarm'.[28]

In several letters to Myers, Ted describes his difficulties in mustering sufficient concentration to write anything, when so much of his psychic energy was being stolen by his students: 'This teaching of mine is death. I have a lot of ideas – more than I could use if I had all day, and it is the best season of the year.'[29] Yet many of the poems that were to go into *Lupercal*[30] were being published in 1958 and they were Hughes' finest work to date. In *The Hawk in the Rain* the landscape is the mud and blood of a vast no-man's-land. The poems in *Lupercal* give a sharper sense of the vitality and animation to which Hughes was always drawn.

In 'Snowdrop' as much as 'Hawk Roosting', the poems have an unmistakable signature. 'Snowdrop' reveals a continuity between the winter that holds the animals in a grip of semi-hibernation and the rest of the cosmos. The flower is part of the same continuum:

> She, too, pursues her ends,
> Brutal as the stars of this month,
> Her pale head heavy as metal.[31]

The surprise of 'brutal' as a description of so delicate a flower is picked up by the rhyme of 'metal' in that last line; the word 'metal' suggests the force needed by vegetable life to break through hard soil, while the weight gives an especial fragility to the stem bent over by a white flower. For the most part, these are poems from an English landscape, which he imagined all the more intensely in being far away from it.

'Hawk Roosting' was to prove controversial. Hughes imagines the long creative process that has gone into producing the perfection of the hawk's feet and feathers, and he takes on the voice of the hawk to do so:

> Now I hold Creation in my foot
> Or fly up, and revolve it all slowly –
> I kill where I please because it is all mine.[32]

Audiences listening to Hughes read that last line aloud may mistake a delight in the long vowels for the poet's own glee. In an interview with Ekbert Faas, Hughes explained that in writing 'Hawk Roosting' he did not have in mind 'the symbol of some horrible totalitarian genocidal dictator. Actually what I had in mind was that, in this Hawk, Nature is thinking.'[33] In evoking the power that, as he wrote in 'Crow Hill', he feels in the whole universe, there is something related to Wordsworth's vision:

> What humbles these hills has raised
> The arrogance of blood and bone,
> And thrown the hawk upon the wind,
> And lit the fox in the dripping ground.[34]

In May 1958, Paul Roche directed a public reading of his translation of Sophocles' *Oedipus* and asked Ted to read the part of Creon, 'out of courtesy', according to Clarissa. Anne Stevenson reports Ted as agreeing to do so 'somewhat grudgingly'. Clarissa suggests that Ted deliberately tried to wreck the play in order to humiliate Sylvia, who had enjoyed a burst of creativity over the Easter holiday: 'Every time Creon[35] came on, Ted mumbled.'[36] Now Ted, who had already read several of Yeats' poems on the BBC, was always a marvellous reader, so Clarissa's account of him deliberately muffling his lines is surprising. It is possible that Ted was embarrassed at taking an acting role. Michael Boddy thought he was always too much himself to make an actor.[37] And it may be that Ted did not admire Roche's version. His less than enthusiastic participation did not help Paul Roche's play, but it is altogether far-fetched to explain Ted's poor performance as a way of punishing Sylvia.

Ted had particularly asked Sylvia not to come to the play, but she went nevertheless, and her journal confirms that Ted performed badly. She, too, detected *something* wrong on that occasion. Worse, from the point of view of their relationship, was her finding Ted afterwards sitting at a piano 'with a mean wrong face' and 'banging out a strident one-finger tune … I'd never heard before'.[38] She was convinced he was ashamed of something. The simplest explanation, that he had disliked his own performance, did not occur to her. The hint in the 'tune [she had] never heard before' is of some other life apart from the one they shared, and it brought out in her an anxious insecurity that was always waiting and which was soon to find dramatic expression.

Classes ended in May, and Sylvia had examination scripts to mark. After her final lecture she hurried to meet Ted as they had planned and, although their car was in the parking lot, Ted was not in it, nor was he in the library either. Much has been made of Sylvia's description of him

> coming up the road from Paradise Pond where the girls take their boys to neck on weekends. He was walking with a broad, intense smile, eyes into the uplifted doe-eyes of a strange girl with brownish hair, a large lipsticked grin, and bare thick legs in khaki Bermuda shorts … his smile became … too white-hot, became fatuous, admiration-seeking. He was gesturing, just finishing an observation, an explanation. The girl's eyes souped up giddy applause.[39]

Hughes' own version of this incident is given for the first time in a draft letter to Janet Malcolm[40] – whose *Silent Woman*, published in 1993, Hughes admired. That handsome, fair-haired girl whom Sylvia saw approaching with Ted up the path from Paradise Pond was a student in his creative writing group, and Ted was being particularly friendly to her because a couple of days earlier he had snubbed her offer of a farewell glass of red wine at the end of his last class. The reason he gives Janet Malcolm for refusing to stay and drink with the girl and her friend is an illumination: he was anxious not to be late for a meeting with Sylvia. For all his apparent granite assurance, Ted was seriously worried about antagonizing his wife.

Ted made no attempt to explain his behaviour to Sylvia. There was little enough to explain in any case, and he went off to sleep easily while Sylvia remained insomniac and furious. All the same, Ted was angry too. Sylvia's journal records a quarrel on 17 June, with Sylvia throwing glasses and Ted slapping her face. On that occasion there was some kind of resolution, probably sexual, and the 'Air [was] cleared'.[41]

Nevertheless, on 7 July Sylvia registers a certain restlessness of her own, which in the light of her usual neediness is worthy of remark: 'I enjoy it when Ted is off for a bit. I can build up my own inner life, my own thoughts, without his continuous "What are you thinking? What are you going to do now?" which makes me promptly and recalcitrantly stop thinking and doing.'[42]

In early September 1958, Ted and Sylvia moved from Northampton to a two-room apartment at 9 Willow Street, on Beacon Hill in Boston. For his part, Ted was glad to see the year at Northampton coming to an end. Moving to a freelance life in Boston was a step in the direction of a less conventional life. Sylvia was more ambivalent. Although the chance of writing full time was exactly the reason they had chosen to move to Boston, Sylvia found this very freedom put a new pressure on her. Always less sanguine than Ted about making do on little money, she could see that they had saved only enough to live on for a few months and had no certain prospects of any income thereafter. She wrote rebelliously in her journal: 'What is so terrible about earning a regular wage?'[43] Her decision to take an ill-paid job at Massachusetts General Hospital, typing, filing and editing, was motivated by several kinds of terror. Among these, the odd blank within was the most significant, although financial insecurity played a larger part than Ted was perhaps willing to acknowledge when he claimed[44] that she took the job mainly to gain some experience of the real world. Ted disliked her nagging anxiety. He approached the problems of making a living by writing with equanimity, indifferent to the ragged holes in his sweater elbows or the fact that his shirt showed through them and, as Sylvia observed in her journal, he took 'no interest in TV boxes, iceboxes, or dishwashers ... Only in writing'.[45] Sylvia might care equally about writing, but she felt panicky and empty while trying to write, and at first the decision to work outside the house seemed an excellent one.

By 16 December 1958 Sylvia had already completed 'Johnny Panic and the Bible of Dreams', which is by far her most original story. But 'Johnny Panic' was also peculiarly disturbing; and though it signalled creative vitality, it also suggested the dangers of gaining access to Sylvia's innermost being. It is told through the mouth of a typist who falls under the spell of the dreams of patients, called up as if by a single supernatural force that she names Johnny Panic. Anne Stevenson in *Bitter Fame* called the last scene pure nightmare; but there is a surreal logic in giving the inhabitants of the asylum a vision of Johnny Panic as Lord of this world. And the story concludes memorably: 'He forgets not his own.'

Sylvia knew exactly how strange her own vision had become and had already sought help. By 12 December 1958, she was back in the hands of Dr Ruth Beuscher. The analysis seems to have taken a fairly orthodox Freudian path, although many analysts would surely have drawn back from Sylvia's need to be given permission to hate her mother. Sylvia loathed the burden her mother's heroic efforts to bring up her children had always placed on her. And she recognized, too, all the forces of American conformity that judged Ted for having no more than his talent and energy to support a wife. It was presumably Sylvia's own internalized voice of her mother that her analyst knew she needed to reject. In the Plath *Journals*, what comes out about her father is equally interesting: she reports her mother's description of Otto as such a brute that she was unable to love him, even hated him, and that Otto had given the salute, 'Heil Hitler,' in the privacy of his home.[46]

When Ted recalled their life in 9 Willow Street, Boston, he remembered their closeness as more destructive than supportive. They were entering a difficult period of their relationship, in which Ted, for all his sympathy, had begun to feel that Sylvia's desperation to write, and her inability to cope with rejection, was too much for him. There were some pleasures. Lucas Myers visited them on his way from Tennessee back to Paris. And Ted was reading widely for himself: Huxley's *Heaven and Hell*, for example, which he thought a scatty sequel to *The Doors of Perception*, Huxley's account of the effects of mescaline. However, he admired it for the author's attempt to reach an understanding of the human mind by means other than introspection.

For all the problems in their relationship, Plath was struggling slowly towards a vision of 'the poems I would write, but do not'.[47] Between February and March 1959, she had begun to discard the evasions pre- viously offered by myth, and to explore her own inner experience. 'Suicide off Egg Rock' belongs to a small batch of poems that confront the subject matter that was to go into *The Bell Jar*.[48] It was a poem Ted Hughes described as being her first attempt to work out what it was that hurt her. Not all the poems that follow make use of the same grittily realistic landscape.

Famous poets lived all round Boston: Richard Wilbur, for one. Archibald MacLeish was Professor at Harvard; Robert Frost lived in Cambridge on Brewster Street. These were almost too grand to be a source of contention, but Sylvia was very conscious of Anne Sexton and Maxine Kumin, and visiting poets such as Donald Hall, Kenneth Koch and John Ashbery. At twenty-six, Sylvia Plath was perhaps a little afraid that once outside the academic world of Smith, she might be perceived as no more than Ted Hughes' wife. She had wanted him to succeed first; but, for her to be happy, her own success had to follow his.

Ted saw the situation differently. In a box of photocopies of Hughes' letters at Emory[49] there is one to Peter Davison, the poetry editor of *Atlantic Monthly*. This was in response to a draft chapter of Davison's *The Fading Smile* (published in 1994), sent to Hughes for comment, which dealt with Ted and Sylvia's Boston year of 1958–9. Davison remembered Sylvia then as always standing a little behind Hughes perhaps even hiding behind him. Ted points out that, in his memory, he felt rather like the mute child, Kaspar Hauser, and altogether dependent on Sylvia to interpret the local American signals. Davison's reply, also in the box of photocopies, insists that in Boston it was taken for granted, nevertheless, that Ted was the more powerful poet and that Sylvia knew as much. Did Sylvia admit some envy to Davison, as he claims in this note? If so, it is a fact he chose to omit from his chapter as it appeared in *The Fading Smile*. In any case, Ted's marriage was to founder more dangerously on Sylvia's need to have him belong only to herself than on any rivalry between them.

Sylvia continued to worry about money even though Ted earned $1000 in September by selling poems to magazines and by winning the Guinness Poetry Competition. In her anxiety, Sylvia began to nag Ted about his dirty hair and ragged fingernails. They began to fight quite often, sometimes quarrelling over very little: when Ted, for instance, spoke to friends in public about her never sewing on buttons and in private spoke of a resemblance to her mother. For her part, she was sensitive to people thinking of Ted as lazy or shiftless. As a sign of how terrifying Sylvia now found it to rely on writing alone to give her a sense of identity, she had even begun to imagine that studying for a Ph.D. would satisfy her.

On 9 March 1959 she went with Ted to visit her father's grave. This visit she records in her journal eleven days later as being very depressing. There were three graveyards, separated by streets, and 'ugly crude block stones, headstones together, as if the dead were sleeping head to head in a poorhouse ... I found the flat stone, "Otto Plath: 1885–1940," right beside the path, where it would be walked over. Felt cheated. My temptation to dig him up.'[50]

This episode appears both in *The Bell Jar* and in a poem that Sylvia herself afterwards rejected: 'Electra on Azalea Path'. It is a significant poem which, even as it notes 'I borrow the stilts of an old tragedy', nevertheless brings her own family history into the myth. Tim Kendall argues that these references are not wholly successful, but the colloquial last line seems to me well on the way towards the voice of *Ariel*:

It was my love that did us both to death[51]

Ted continued patiently along his own track, rereading Ezra Pound's *Cantos*, for instance. While he admired what Sylvia was struggling to achieve, he was beginning to fear that she shared the oppressive American urge to conform, which he so disliked. He was even afraid that something was happening to himself that would not be easily reparable. As he wrote to Myers: 'My devils seem to have been in Sunday lock-up ... My emotional life has been like a dead man's over here. I don't think it's America. I think it's just me. I recognise it.'[52]

By 11 January 1959 they had both decided that the only answer was to return to England to live. It was a move that Ted had been determining for some time was what he needed, although by February 1959 Sylvia had found a shape for her own life that might have cured her situation: she had decided to join Robert Lowell's writing class. Lowell himself was a poet with a gigantic reputation, whose *Life Studies* – a volume of confessional poetry about relationships within his own family – was to influence a whole generation. Plath admired the 'tough, knotty' language he had perfected. His class had several distinguished students in it, notably Anne Sexton, with whom Plath has sometimes been compared.

They were not truly alike. Sexton had lived, and would continue to live, a much racier life; Sylvia had a far more highly trained intelligence. Sexton was a beauty. Adrienne Rich, for whose three books of poems Plath had occasionally expressed some envy, remembered meeting Sexton at a party given by Lowell and Elizabeth Hardwick in June 1959, and feeling a twinge of jealousy herself: 'I didn't expect her to be such a knockout – tall, tan, wearing white and looking very gorgeous.'[53] Sexton was flamboyant, while Sylvia was never more than attractive and sharp. However, the meeting was a stimulating experience for both poets and they gradually moved into a warm friendship, which was probably closer than Sylvia formed with any other woman poet of comparable stature. There were things they had in common. Sexton was also a daughter who had problems in her relationship with her mother, as well as with being a mother herself.

Also in Lowell's class was George Starbuck, a talent scout for the Boston publishers Houghton Mifflin, who was already Sexton's lover. He went along in Sexton's battered Ford to drink at the Ritz and listen to the two women poets talk about their psychotherapy, their early attempts at suicide, and death. When Sylvia, Sexton, George Starbuck and Maxine Kumin habitually had an evening out drinking together, there is no sign that Ted joined in these occasions any more than in the writing classes. As Sexton put it, she and Sylvia 'talked death with burned up intensity, both of us drawn to it like moths to an electric light bulb. Sucking on it.'[54] A remark such as this suggests in both women a longing for death independent of any external circumstances, as if death had a secret glamour.

That year Lowell suffered a manic episode which took him into Macleans Hospital, but he was back in Boston by June. In one of his first classes after returning, Lowell delighted Sylvia by setting her up alongside Anne Sexton, which Plath found an honour, although she also felt 'there is a lot of loose stuff' in Sexton's poetry.[55] Yet the class was giving her some confidence and, fired by two acceptances from the *New Yorker* of 'Watercolor of Grantchester Meadows' and 'Man in Black', she began putting together a manuscript of forty poems, which she submitted to the Yale Series of Younger Poets. Ted was quietly getting on with the poems that were to go into *Lupercal*, and in April 1959 his calm persistence seemed to be totally vindicated: he was awarded a Guggenheim Fellowship of $5000. Suddenly the worst of their financial insecurity seemed to be over. As he wrote to Olwyn, this not only removed their money worries for the coming year at a stroke, it also meant his exile was at an end: 'The chance to come to Europe – with all the usual worries etherised – overpowered me when I got the letter.'[56]

Although the new Boston friendship with Anne Sexton had opened up the situation a little for both of them, Ted knew that Sylvia still needed endless cosseting in the face of rejections. When on 20 May she heard that Anne Sexton's book of poems had been accepted by Houghton Miffin rather than her own, he found it almost impossible to console her. Perhaps, for all his understanding of her, he was so free from her habit of pacing himself against his contemporaries that he could not give enough weight to her sense of defeat. He was studying both cabbalistic and Hermetic mysticism, which offered him little encouragement to think of human life in terms of winners and losers.[57]

The ways in which he was assessing his own work are apparent in his correspondence, particularly with Lucas Myers. He was feeling his way towards a language that would break the taboo against dialect,[58] a poetry that would be concrete and honest. What he wanted to avoid above all was 'gesture'. At the same time he continued to read widely: classical Latin poets such as Petronius (whom he admired), William Carlos Williams (whose *Paterson* he found pretentious) and Hart Crane (behind whom he found no human being, only an 'electronic noise').[59]

All the previous year Sylvia had been terrified of pregnancy. It may be that it was the relief from financial anxiety provided by the Guggenheim that made her suddenly decide that what she wanted next was a baby. It had not been part of their original plan, and Ted was initially opposed to the idea,[60] but Sylvia was so heartrendingly set on it that he agreed. At once Sylvia felt calmer than she had for months.

Just before they left Boston in July, however, Sylvia visited the hospital and was told that she was temporarily infertile. With horror she confronted a possible future of never being able to bear children, a state she described in her journal as being 'part of the world's ash'.[61] She was given treatment before they set out on their travels and – as it happens – was already pregnant when they left. But she did not know that, and her fear of being a woman from whom no life could ever grow must certainly have polluted her mood on the trip.

During the summer of 1959 Ted and Sylvia decided to drive across Canada and the United States to visit Plath's aunt, Frieda Plath Henrichs, and her husband Walter J. Henrichs, in California. Their journey, which covered thousands of miles, took them twice across the American continent. They travelled through Ontario, Wisconsin, the Dakota Badlands, Montana and Yellowstone Park to the Pacific Ocean at San Francisco, before turning south to Los Angeles and then east again through the Mojave Desert and the Grand Canyon to New Orleans. They even took in Washington before going home to Boston. The vast skies and wild landscapes revealed an America that was new to both of them, and for which the eastern coastal seaboard of the United States was no preparation.

A few days spent fishing on the Wisconsin Peninsula proved enjoyable, though Sylvia was frightened in Yellowstone Park – first when they almost ran out of petrol and again when she heard that a bear in a neighbouring campsite had killed a tourist. When they reached the Pacific, they found it exhilarating to sleep under the stars on Stinson Beach, even though they woke to a cold fog. Then they relaxed for a few days with Sylvia's Aunt Frieda – Otto's sister – at Pasadena, California, before setting off to cross America once more on their return journey. The dry, dangerous emptiness of those deserts revealed themselves later in the surreal landscapes of Plath's *Ariel* poems.

Ted decided their journey across the Badlands was a quest for Sylvia's true self, that central part of her which her cosy New England upbringing had repressed. That self was to become the savage creator of her *Ariel* poems, with their stark colours echoing the bleached bright landscape of the American West. However, long before that, she wrote about Yellowstone Park in a story she herself described as a 'stiff artificial piece'.[62]

The picture Sylvia paints of the husband in her story 'The Fifty-ninth Bear' is peculiarly unlike Ted, who was resourceful, sensible and courageous in situations where Sylvia was often close to panic. As in the poem from *Birthday Letters*, which describes their travels, Ted was if anything far too sanguine in imagining that a hatchet would be some use against an aggressive bear. It may be that what led Sylvia to imagine the death of the husband at the hands of the fifty-ninth bear was no more than a failure of invention; but it suggests an aggression towards him that was probably hidden from herself. Unsurprisingly, it was read as such by Olwyn and Ted's friends when it appeared in the *London Magazine* in 1961. It would lead Olwyn to think of her sister-in-law in a new and even worse light.

From 9 September to 19 November Ted and Sylvia were guests at Yaddo, an artists' community at Saratoga Springs in New York State. For Ted, this was a revivifying experience. He was given a studio like a conservatory deep in the woods, and Sylvia had a workroom on the top floor of an annexe to the grand mansion, furnished with great beauty. Breakfast and dinner were served in the mansion's dining hall under a beamed ceiling; lunchboxes and thermoses were provided so that artists could arrange their own work schedules.

Both Ted and Sylvia did a great deal of work at Yaddo. Ted wrote 'Things Present', the poem that would complete the manuscript of *Lup-*

ercal, and he worked particularly with the Chinese composer Chou Weng-Chung, a fellow guest at Yaddo, on a libretto for *Bardo Thodol (The Tibetan Book of the Dead)*. Although nothing ever came of this project, Ted learned an enormous amount from it – not only about Eastern mysticism, but also about theatre, music and, perhaps most important of all, the pleasures of collaboration with artists in different fields. Lucas Myers, who was already beginning to think of himself as a Buddhist, understood more than most what made *Bardo Thödol* important for Ted. The words 'Bardo Thodol' translate as 'a liberation through hearing of the sacred texts'[63] and the work uses an Indian form of Buddhism which is closely linked with magic.

Sylvia, too, worked well at first: almost a third of the poems that went into *The Colossus* were written at Yaddo. On 6 October, when she wept at receiving a rejection of her poems from Henry Holt, Ted suggested simply and sensibly that she start another book. She found herself able to write well for a time – completing twenty-one poems for *A Birthday* – but she could not help envying how easy Ted found it to work. From now on, she would always take for granted that he could write under any conditions. For herself, the privileged peace of Yaddo meant that she depended more and more on reassurance from Ted. On 13 October 1959, Sylvia wrote sadly in her journal, 'Ted is my salvation. He is so rare, so special, how could anyone else stand me!'[64] By 11 November Sylvia was longing to leave Yaddo, since she had begun to feel that she had no life separate from Ted's and hated the thought of becoming a mere accessory.

For his part, Ted was returning to England with a wife five months' pregnant, not much money and uncertain prospects. He knew that the responsibility of a child would put a stop to any dream he might still have of freely exploring the world, and it would certainly make it impossible to live as modestly as he had hoped. He was still very much in love with Sylvia, however, and he wanted her to be happy.

Their ship left America on 9 December 1959 and docked in Southampton on 14 December. They set off directly for Heptonstall and a Yorkshire Christmas.

SEVEN

A Family Man

C hristmas in Heptonstall was cheerful enough and Ted enjoyed coming home to his family and the Yorkshire landscapes. It was rainy and windy, however, and, although Ted and Sylvia took short walks, they spent most of their time working. During the day Sylvia typed up the manuscript of the poems she planned to send to James Michie, an editor at the London publisher, Heinemann, who had admired poems of hers that had appeared in the *London Magazine* in the autumn.

Olwyn came home from Paris, looking far younger than her thirty-one years. She dressed with simple French chic and had been enjoying her Parisian life far more than Ted had enjoyed his two and a half years in the States. From her secretarial job at NATO she had moved to a Hungarian theatrical agency and was living with a Hungarian journalist. She still had local friends in Yorkshire and, while she was out dining with them, Ted's mother and father dozed in front of a roaring coal fire. Ted could soon see tensions developing between Sylvia and Olwyn. Indeed, they were apparent when Olwyn first appeared in the sitting room at Heptonstall and commented on the colour of Sylvia's hair, which she had failed to realize before was not naturally blonde.

Some evenings Ted and Sylvia played cards with Olwyn and Vicky, their cousin of twenty-one, who was an art teacher. Sylvia taught them all the game of tarok, learned from her grandmother, which was played with tarot cards. She played with gusto, and there was much convivial laughter for a time. One evening, Sylvia explained that gambling (even for sixpences) made her 'too strung up to sleep' and when she wanted to withdraw from the table Ted supported her. Olwyn was irritated by this.[1]

Among the letters from Ted to Gerald,[2] there is by chance a touching note from their mother, written after that family Christmas, describing

Sylvia's resentment of the easy intimacy between Ted and Olwyn and the strain this produced in Ted. Neither Edith nor Ted himself thought of Olwyn as intrusive, though Ted recognized Sylvia's need to be the most important person in his life. In later years, he came to believe that, if he had not nursed and coddled her like a child, she might have grown up more happily. 'He regretted not having carried on just as he was instead of wrapping his life up in a cupboard while he tended her.'[3] Explaining Sylvia's exceptional dependence to Olwyn, however, would only have exacerbated her growing anxieties over his choice of a wife, and he just wanted everyone to get on pleasantly together. His mother tried to defuse one absurd incident[4] over a mauve dressing gown. It had been made using the material of an abandoned blue dressing gown of Sylvia's, and Mrs Hughes had lent it to Olwyn. When Sylvia seemed to take offence, Edith suggested she could make Sylvia a new one as a replacement. The offer calmed the situation, but Ted could see that the sisters-in-law had begun to look askance at one another.

If Olwyn was beginning to voice criticism, so was Sylvia. She complained in a letter to her mother about Edith's kitchen, which she called 'dirty', and her cooking, which she described as so unpalatable that she found it hard to eat and was worried about the damage to her unborn baby's health. When Ted read this letter in the manuscript of *Letters Home* many years later, he asked Aurelia Plath for it to be cut, pointing out that his mother's cooking – whilst far simpler than Sylvia's – was not that bad.

When Ted had first won the Guggenheim, there had been plans of going to Italy and renting a house on Corsica, where Lucas Myers was then living, but with a baby imminent this was now impossible. Ted and Sylvia planned instead to live in London, although Ted remembered with some repugnance the literati at Cambridge who were now running the metropolitan literary world. In *Birthday Letters*, 'Stubbing Wharfe'[5] suggests that he was himself drawn to the large houses then going very inexpensively in Yorkshire but he could see that Sylvia had no wish to live so far away from London.

In 18 Rugby Street once again, where Dan and Helga Huws were now living in a third-floor flat with a baby, Sylvia and Ted made do with a sagging bed on the second floor. Rugby Street still had only one lavatory – several floors down – and no bathroom, and Sylvia found it squalid. Nevertheless, it was an essential base and they put in a gruelling fortnight searching for somewhere to live. Daniel Huws remembers Sylvia as indefatigable in her house-hunting, but his wife Helga watched her becoming visibly more downcast and tired as the search produced nothing suitable. She was, after all, six months' pregnant and was hoping for a flat with central heating, or at least hot water, and enough space to accommodate a child.

Such expectations soon had to be modified. Flats of any kind were hard to find. On the point of giving up, they were directed by their Boston friend, Dido Merwin, to an unfurnished flat that they could afford at 3 Chalcot Square, NW3. Nowadays this is one of the most expensive areas in London, but then it was a little seedy and the flat cost no more than six guineas a week. It was quite close to the far grander house in St George's Terrace where Dido and her husband Bill were living. Although there was one room less than they needed in Chalcot Square and it had appalling wallpaper, Ted and Sylvia settled on it with relief.

The Merwins were able to contribute several pieces from their attic to help furnish it. Dido found Sylvia's reluctance to buy a second-hand bed rather than a new one, along with her extravagance in purchasing a refrigerator, bewildering. Sylvia, rather like any woman of the present day, took a refrigerator for granted as part of a normal way of life, especially with a baby expected. She was well aware of Dido's attitude towards her, and in turn described Dido in a letter to her friend Lynne Lawner[6] as Merwin's 'older, very energetic, very British, *very thrice-married wife*'. (My italics.)

Merwin introduced Ted to Douglas Cleverdon, the influential BBC producer of Dylan Thomas *Under Milk Wood*, originally written for radio as a play for voices. Cleverdon had made BBC Radio a reliable source of income for Merwin and was soon to do the same for Ted. On 10 February 1960, Sylvia signed her contract for *The Colossus* with James Michie of Heinemann.

As Sylvia waited to give birth, Ted painted the living room walls white, and they decided to hang an engraving of Isis from one of Ted's astrological books on the living room wall. Builders were dealing with a new boiler. There were floors to be sanded and shelves to be made. Ted often cooked so that Sylvia could lie in bed and recover from the strain of the last few months. In the evenings, they sometimes went with the Merwins to the cinema – to see *Ivan the Terrible*, directed by Eisenstein, for instance. They also saw many new plays, including Brendan Behan's *The Hostage*.

The flat in Chalcot Square was so small that Ted borrowed a card table from the Merwins and set up a workplace in the hallway by the entrance door, where he managed to work well enough. Indeed, in a private letter to Anne Stevenson,[7] he describes it as one of the best places he ever found to write in. Altogether, he was much happier than he had been in America. His old circle of friends had begun to gather round him. Sylvia had always disliked some of them – for instance, Joe Lyde – and had been unwilling to entertain them at their flat. Ted's friend Michael Boddy had left for Australia as a migrant in 1959, but on 27 February there was a reunion in the flat of several of the *St Botolph's Review* group who were in London. Unsurprisingly, Sylvia found visitors a strain, particularly when they stayed for a long time, smoking and talking. She preferred to go with Ted to a local pub with a group of them – Daniel Weissbort, Dan Huws and David Ross, for instance. David Ross knew Ted and Sylvia well when they lived in Chalcot Square, since he and his first wife were living not far away. Ross was at pains to stress that he never saw any sign of Sylvia's over-possessiveness or resentment of Ted's earlier friendships: 'I certainly didn't sense this, and we got on well – we'd chat together.' But he remembered Sylvia as 'one tough lady'.

> We went to see them one afternoon. And Sylvia was going on about her Olivetti 22 typewriter, and how she'd worn out the roller in a year. Now the roller on my Olivetti 22 never showed the slightest sign of wear, even after many years of use. Sylvia was absolutely determined to make her mark on the literary world, and also that Ted should. Sylvia was really doing the pushing that was necessary for it. So, as I say, my impression was of someone who was determined, strong...[8]

Peter Redgrove, already himself enjoying success as a poet of some standing and an established radio dramatist, found no sign of tension when he visited Ted and Sylvia at Chalcot Square. He had liked Sylvia in the early days of the marriage and, far from finding her in any way threatening, he was very interested in her: 'I remember looking very deeply into her eyes.'[9] However, after the Hughes returned from America, Redgrove thought her attitude had changed and 'was bright and ebullient but rather false, like Doris Day. She had a Doris Day mask.'[10]

Daniel Weissbort has often said that Sylvia did not find him interesting enough to bother about, but it is Weissbort's style to be self-deprecatory. He has always avoided flamboyance in any form, although he was able to play a good jazz piano with Joe Lyde at Cambridge. Ted valued very highly Weissbort's wry, ironic lyrics, which described the twists and turns of his own experience. And for Weissbort, his relation to Ted was probably the most important friendship of his life. He took little interest in Sylvia, whose early poems he had not much admired.

One evening Lucas Myers, who had recently returned from Paris, arrived as Sylvia was preparing supper. Lucas suggested that he and Ted go out for a drink. In the pub, as Lucas confided some of his own troubles, Ted mentioned to Myers that he was finding it difficult to work in the flat because Sylvia interrupted him so constantly. Lucas reports that on that particular morning Ted had decided to count, and Sylvia had called out 104 times.[11] Any writer would have found this distracting. This is noteworthy as one of the few examples of Ted talking about his relationship to Sylvia with anyone, except in order to explain or excuse.

When Ted and Lucas returned after about forty minutes, they were confronted by a furious, glaring Sylvia and three half-filled bowls of clam chowder.[12] Myers reports that he and Ted ate their soup and cleaned away every sign of supper in an attempt to make amends, but Sylvia remained sulky. She specialized in fish soups and had probably put rather more time into preparing this one than Myers appreciated. She was also only one month away from giving birth. Pregnant women often feel a need for protection, which makes them dislike being alone, although this is usually offset by relief when company returns. Myers gives the impression that Sylvia's chief concern on this occasion was to ensure that her displeasure was made known.

A few weeks before giving birth it is normal to tire very easily, so Sylvia was relieved to hear that Olwyn, who was coming to London soon after this, had arranged to stay with a former colleague of the NATO typing pool rather than at Chalcot Square. Nevertheless, she put herself out to make a meal for her. On 5 March 1960 Olwyn arrived at Chalcot Square a little late for lunch, and bringing her friend, Janet Crosbie-Hill, with her. Since Lucas was also present, this means Sylvia was involved in preparing a meal for six people, which must have been exhausting. Their kitchen was 'so small that it seemed to fit only one person at a time'.[13] The impression Sylvia gave, however, was of someone seething with fury simply because her guests were late. Janet Crosbie-Hill, in a letter to the *New Review*, recalled the occasion with that as the chief emphasis: 'As Olwyn had spoken only with affection of both brother and sister-in-law, I was totally unprepared for the resentment our visit seemed to cause Sylvia.'[14] From Olwyn's point of view, Sylvia's rudeness lay in totally ignoring Janet. Indeed, Sylvia only became her usual warm and animated self when Bill Merwin arrived, as if to point up the selective nature of her antagonism. Lucas Myers records: 'It was the only time I ever saw Olwyn disconcerted.'[15]

After this encounter, Olwyn decided that Ted was altogether too tolerant of his wife's rudeness. She simply could not understand how her handsome, good-natured brother could be so passive. Walking with him to the Underground afterwards, Olwyn suggested that Ted should at least tell Sylvia how much he disapproved, but Ted only 'replied with a helpless gesture'.[16] It seems unlikely Ted could have succeeded in explaining the two women to one another. He knew that reproach of any kind made Sylvia feel emotionally insecure and was likely to generate hysteria rather than an apology. He also knew that his easygoing sister meant no slight in being late.

Edith, too, had been worrying a little, whilst hoping that Ted and Sylvia got on well enough when they were alone. She observed in a letter to her elder son that they were 'more sombre' than Gerald and his wife Joan, 'who always seemed to have sunshine around you'.[17]

Olwyn had no idea of the vulnerability that Sylvia's ferocity disguised. She was aware of her literary aspirations, but not yet of her genius, although she would not have excused her incivility in any case. She minded very much being frozen out of her brother's life; they had always been close, and Ted continued to admire her. He does not seem to have resented Olwyn's comments, or thought of her as a bossy elder sister. Indeed, he reported to his brother Gerald that Olwyn was in very good form, looked about nineteen, and was enjoying her Paris life, where she and the Hungarian journalist lived in a large top-floor room on the Boulevarde Garibaldi.

Ted tried to make peace the next day by telephoning Olwyn and asking her to come round so that Sylvia could explain. Olwyn duly appeared but Sylvia did not refer to the matter when she and Olwyn were alone. Lucas Myers, who had learned to know Olwyn well in Paris as both tolerant and generous, did what he could to heal the situation in a letter, which sensibly reminded her of the limits of what she could change: 'Ted suffers a good deal more than he would ever indicate or admit, but he also loves her and I think it is best to assume he will stay with her.'[18]

These domestic tensions aside, March 1960 proved an amazing month for Ted. *The Hawk in the Rain* won the Somerset Maugham Award on 24 March. He had expected a quieter fate for his second book, but

Lupercal, which came out in the same month, went on to win the Hawthornden. On 27 March, the influential critic Al Alvarez devoted a column and a half in the *Observer* to *Lupercal*. He had expressed reservations about *The Hawk in the Rain*, but he saluted *Lupercal* confidently: 'Hughes has found his own voice, created his own artistic world, and has emerged as a poet of the first importance. . . . What Ted Hughes has done is to take a limited, personal theme and, by an act of immensely assured poetic skill, has broadened it until it seems to touch upon nearly everything that concerns us.' In three years Ted had transformed himself from a writer submitting his work to small Cambridge magazines into a formidable presence on the English literary scene. And he was not yet thirty.

He was soon to find his life transformed in another way by the arrival of a child. Sylvia had been afraid of the ordeal of giving birth, mainly because she thought it would involve going into hospital, but they discovered that it was possible to have the baby at home. On the recommendation of her GP, Dr Horder, found for Sylvia by Dido Merwin they had the help of a midwife. It was not a hugely sensible decision at a time when one in a thousand women died in childbirth, but fortunately Sylvia was strong and healthy. Ted gave her several sessions of hypnotism to make the birth easier, and this worked so well that Frieda Rebecca Hughes was born after a labour of only four and a half hours and no analgesics. Ted was present at the birth, which was uncommon in those days.

For a week afterwards Ted did all the housework and Dido Merwin kept up a supply of hot casseroles so that Sylvia was able to rest with her new child in a state of euphoria. It was a period when fathers ordinarily felt little responsibility for the care of their children. Right from the start, however, the work of looking after Frieda was shared equally between the parents. Ted was determined that Sylvia's talents should continue to develop to the full. He did not simply free her from time to time as a favour but regularly looked after Frieda every morning from 9 a.m. to 1 p.m. while Sylvia worked. He did his own writing in the afternoons. When the Merwins left London in May for a house in France, Bill – who had always felt concern when he thought of Ted working in a corridor – offered him the use of his study. This too was a privilege Ted shared with Sylvia. Such consideration for the writing life of a partner was almost unique at that period.

In the weeks after the birth of their child there was a period of enforced sexual abstinence. Whilst showing no sign of post-natal depression, Sylvia did find her jealous suspicions returning, rather as they had in her last term at Smith. In particularly she began to suspect that Ted was attracted to Dido Merwin, whom she knew he admired. When Sylvia heard that Ted was to accompany Dido to meet Bill Merwin as he arrived at Trafalgar Square on the last stage of the Aldermaston March against nuclear arms, she determined to be there too. It was only three weeks after the birth, and it says much for her health and vigour that she was able to do this. Peter Redgrove, who loaned her a carrycot, helped her to carry the baby in it to Trafalgar Square. When Ted got back to the flat, she had not yet returned, and he had no idea where his wife and child might be.

Sylvia's behaviour, though impulsive, sprang partly at least from a genuine opposition to nuclear weapons. She was frightened by the thought of radioactive fall-out and appalled by the possibility of the annihilation of the planet. She and Peter waited with Frieda on the grass near the National Gallery while Trafalgar Square filled with a seven-mile-long column of marchers, who had walked from the atomic bomb plant at Aldermaston, carrying banners inscribed with 'Ban The Bomb'. Her presence was a declaration that maternity had not put her out of communal action. She wanted to be part of London activity of all kinds.

Ted had ambivalent emotions about social occasions but Sylvia enjoyed without qualifications her sense of being at the very heart of London literary life. She delighted in dressing up for a Faber cocktail party, for which they had to employ a babysitter for the first time. She also relished a party of John Lehmann's, where they met the English poet Elizabeth Jennings. And they both enjoyed the many new friends they began to make as Ted's reputation grew. Among these was Al Alvarez, who has given a vivid account of their acquaintance in both *The Savage God* and *Where Did It All Go Right?*

In 1960, Alvarez occupied a role that is now virtually non-existent on the English poetry scene: he was a kingmaker. What he said in his column of the *Observer*, and the poems he selected to print in that paper, defined what was important on the literary map. It was when he was invited by the editor of the *Observer* to interview Ted that the friendship began. The two men liked each other. Ted realized that Alvarez was quite different from himself: quintessentially North London, Jewish, academically sharp and streetwise. For his part, Alvarez recognized and admired another kind of powerful presence in Ted. As so often, Emily Brontë supplied his first image: 'He reminded me of Heathcliff – another Yorkshireman – big-boned and brooding, with dark hair flopping forward over his craggy face, watchful eyes and an unexpectedly witty mouth. He was a man who seemed to carry his own climate with him, to create his own atmosphere, and in those days that atmosphere was dark and dangerous...'[19]

Alvarez noted the black corduroy jacket, black trousers,[20] black shoes and socks, but he also admired Ted's genuine self-possession, his quiet-spoken shrewdness, and the fact 'you could never predict what he would say; his reactions to people, places, books were always his own.' Alvarez was critical of much of Ted's belief system – of astrology, Celtic myth and Jung – but he saw how it made sense for Ted and got him where he needed to be to write his poetry. He was knowledgeable enough about Yeats and Graves to understand that other poets had found the same traditions valuable. In describing Ted as 'Lawrence without the nerves and the preaching, but also without the flowers and the tenderness', he was perceptive enough to see that Hughes' methods of getting through to his 'creative underlife worked for him because, among other reasons, he was a man of unusual inner strength and assurance'.[21] He was at this juncture much more interested in Ted than Sylvia, but later on he came to reflect on the precise dangers that Ted's interest in the occult presented to Sylvia with her altogether more delicate psychic make-up.

Ted remained intensely preoccupied with astrology. In mid-May 1960, he laid out instructions for Lucas Myers' actions, based on his own calculations, which there is every reason to believe that Myers took seriously. Merwin also often asked for astrological advice. Hughes obligingly, and without the least irony, suggested good days in August for new ventures: '17th would be very near your ascendant. Avoid 18th ... the 17th would get Venus right on your Venus and I shall have to try to fix something for that day too, since it is my birthday...'[22]

On that first meeting, walking together on Primrose Hill in north-west London, Alvarez did not at first recognize in the pleasant-seeming, housewifely figure of Mrs Hughes, the poet Sylvia Plath, even though he had already accepted one of her poems for the *Observer*. And his interest remained focused on Ted for most of the time that he was in touch with the couple. He formed a strong impression of Plath's trained intelligence, however, and saw that, almost as much as Lawrence, Ted was essentially an autodidact, with all the advantages that accrued from such a situation and some of the residual shyness.

A sign of Ted's acceptance in literary circles was an invitation to dine with T.S. Eliot and his wife on 26 April 1960. Unsurprisingly, Ted and

Sylvia were rather overawed, and it was just as well that Stephen Spender was also present to fill in the gaps of conversation, although he wrote to apologize for chattering too much. Sylvia wrote a good deal about this encounter to her mother, who must have been bemused at so rapid a translation of her son-in-law into an acclaimed major poet.

While enjoying the opportunity to explore the world of London now open to them, Ted was beginning to be almost as critical of the prevailing English mood as he had been in the States of the American way of life. In this, too, there is a passing resemblance to Lawrence. All his life Lawrence believed that there was a 'somewhere else', which, once reached, would prove a good and rich society such as he had failed to discover. Acknowledging the sharp wit in Harold Pinter's *The Caretaker*, Ted saw in the depleted experience of the characters an English spirit still not recovered from the war and content to inhabit a dingy, shabby world.[23] Merwin, by now in France, had written a *New Statesman* article on the Aldermaston March, which Ted praised warmly, although he added his own opinion: that Shakespeare and 'my Blake' would have demanded bloody rebellion.

Lupercal went into a second printing in June 1960. Ted was beginning to receive fan mail and was enjoying the hours he spent in Merwin's study, where Popo, the Merwins' cat, had become a passionate friend. Popo slept most of the day on Hughes' desk, but could have been more useful in Chalcot Square, where Ted had discovered there were mice, which had to be caught alive and thrown out on Primrose Hill, since the only alternative was to poison the creatures and then leave them to decay under the floorboards.

Ted spent most of 1960 writing plays for the BBC, which were among his most important radio work, but he was restless in Chalcot Square. He continued to work on his unperformed libretto of *Bardo Thödol*, whilst coping with the problems of a boiler and defecting heat engineers, but there was nothing to explain the ominous note to his friend in mid-June: 'If I were a loyal astrologer, I would retire to the country for the next two years.'[24] As for Sylvia, she began *The Bell Jar* in the Merwins' study, and found it rolling along with surprising fluency in the four hours every morning while Ted looked after the baby.

The Chalcot flat was naturally made to feel even smaller by the presence of Frieda, although Hughes enormously enjoyed the hours spent playing with her. At the end of the summer of 1960, the Merwins returned from France, so Hughes needed somewhere to work. He arranged with the woman who lived above them that he could work in her flat during the day while she was employed as a translator for the telephone company. It was not a very successful arrangement – partly, it is suggested in *Bitter Fame*, because Sylvia was suspicious of this middle-aged woman, but mainly because Ted felt he was intruding – and he did most of his work in their own flat in any case.

The Colossus was published in Britain by Heinemann just before Sylvia's birthday on 27 October. It gathered a few respectful reviews but did not command the attention she hoped. No wonder Sylvia felt a dispiriting sense of anticlimax, as she had written almost no new poetry between 'Mushrooms' (11 November 1959) and 'The Hanging Man' (27 June 1960).

As Ted and Sylvia drove up to Yorkshire for Christmas that December in their new Morris car, Ted could not but wonder how this visit would go. There was much to share with his family that was encouraging. He now had an assured series of commissions from the BBC, which meant that he and Sylvia could begin for the first time to save money, and he had so many invitations to read that he had begun to refuse speaking engagements. When he turned down a request from the BBC to appear as 'Poet of the Year', this especially disappointed his mother.

There were enjoyable walks on the moors, and Edith's delight in her young grandchild, but Sylvia was no longer on her best behavior with the Hughes family, particularly Olwyn. The visit was spoiled by another flare-up between them, which seems to have arisen over very little. As the story is told in *Bitter Fame*, a malicious remark of Sylvia's about someone Olwyn did not know sparked Olwyn's incautious response: 'I say, you're awfully critical, aren't you?' Sylvia immediately drew Ted away, Olwyn lost her temper and the damage was done. The baby had been sitting on Olwyn's knee throughout and when Olwyn said, 'But we shouldn't talk like this over her sweet head,' Sylvia silently seized the child, took her off to bed and did not reappear. In Sylvia's account of this episode to her mother, Olwyn called her 'Miss Plath', as if refusing to acknowledge that she was even married to Ted, and accused Sylvia of treating The Beacon as if it were *her* house, whilst declaring that *she* was the daughter of the house.[25] This makes the whole occasion sound like a dispute over territory.

Sylvia, however, decided it was something far more sinister, something closer to her own sexual possessiveness, as detailed in a letter to her mother, dated 1 January 1961. Perhaps that explains her behaviour on the two earlier occasions that she had met her sister-in-law. At any rate, at dawn the next morning, Ted, Sylvia and Frieda set off back to London several days earlier than planned, without more than mumbled farewells. Whatever Ted felt about the shortening of his visit, he yielded to Sylvia once again for the sake of peace.

Brian Cox recalls that it was in January 1961 that he invited Sylvia to edit an American supplement to his influential *Critical Quarterly*. In the same month she was invited to take part with Ted in a series of programmes by the BBC in a radio series called *Two of a Kind*. However, Sylvia was troubled by colds, a general lowering of spirits and a grumbling appendix as the year began.[26] Ted agreed to look after Frieda during the afternoons so that Sylvia could take a temporary job with the *Bookseller*, the publishing trade journal, which took her into the outside world, always a warning sign of failure in her self-confidence. Early in February, she unexpectedly miscarried their second child. Soon afterward her appendix was removed, although the stay in hospital seems to have restored her spirits and her vision of Ted as heroic. It also produced some remarkable poems.

'Tulips', a poem Sylvia wrote on 18 March 1961 about this experience, takes off from a gift of flowers from Edith Hughes. It has the unmistakable rhythms of her late poetry and the memorable finality of her strangest propositions. She is enjoying the hospital whiteness, 'learning peacefulness' as the nurses 'pass and pass' and rejects the red life the flowers suggest:

> I didn't want any flowers, I only wanted
> To lie with my hands turned up and be utterly empty.
> How free it is, you have no idea how free —[27]

Even though her journal records her delight in Ted's hospital visits and the steak sandwiches he brought to supplement the poor hospital food, there is enough in the organization of this poem to suggest that Sylvia had begun to prefer a dangerous withdrawal from her ordinary life, which felt like 'a country far away as health'.[28]

The marriage was by now taking too much out of both of them. It is not clear whether Ted realized as much at the time, but he did so with hindsight, in 'Epiphany' from *Birthday Letters*. This recalls the time, just after the birth of Frieda, when Ted, still light-headed from lack of sleep, met a young man on Chalk Farm Bridge with a fox cub under his coat, which he was selling for a pound. Ted knew that no such creature could be fitted into their cramped living quarters and yet he was tempted to buy it. Walking on, 'As if out of my own life', he wonders what his own responses to the fox cub signified:

> If I had grasped that whatever comes with a fox
> Is what tests a marriage and proves it a marriage –
> I would not have failed the test. Would you have failed it?
> But I failed. Our marriage had failed.[29]

It is impossible not to read that poem without questions. Was this a sign that Ted had already begun to recognize too much of his spirit was being sacrificed to placate Sylvia? Or had he come to see that something in his own nature was incompatible with domestic life? In a letter to me of 4 April 2000, written after reading my review of Erica Wagner's *Ariel's Gift* in the *Times Literary Supplement*, Olwyn questioned both these interpretations. The Fox's 'small woebegone eyes were those of Sylvia herself', she felt. It is a possibility reinforced by Ted's letter to Anne Stevenson, which compares protecting Sylvia Plath's legacy to someone holding a fox cub to protect it from hounds, allowing himself to be bitten in the process.[30] All the same, the thread of the poem in *Birthday Letters* suggests that it was his own life that he felt he was abandoning with the fox cub, and that it was Sylvia who had not been put to the test.

The strain of living in a small flat, with both of them thrown together every hour, must have made them wonder whether London was the right place to be. A growing child would need space and a garden. They could not afford to rent a large house in London; to buy a house on a mortgage would have involved Ted in taking a full-time job, probably teaching, and he remained opposed to any such commitment. The decision therefore was made to leave the London literary milieu and look for space and beauty in the countryside. At some point they decided to go south rather than north, even though trains were expensive, and they knew that they would need to go some distance from London to take advantage of lower prices. This made the move even more decisive.

Alvarez describes Sylvia as that time as 'effaced, the poet taking a back seat to the young mother and housewife ... Her brownish hair scraped severely into a bun'.[31] He saw Ted as very much alive and vigorous and although he already had sufficient respect for Sylvia's talent to publish a poem of hers, she did not yet exert the same fascination.

Sylvia was no early feminist but she was ready enough to fall in with the idea that men were taken more seriously than women in the literary world, and she sometimes talked in this way with her new friend, the poet Ruth Fainlight, wife of Alan Sillitoe. Alan had been given the Hawthornden Award for *The Loneliness of the Long Distance Runner*, and the custom was that the holder of the award pass it on to the winner the following year. As Fainlight remembers:

> So we went to some building on the left hand side of St James's Square ... the opposite side to the London Library ... one afternoon and that was where I and Sylvia and Ted met. And after the ceremony was enacted we went to a café for a cup of tea or something, I think, and we arranged to see each other. It was shortly before they went down to Court Green and they were living in Chalcot Square. And we went and saw them there, and they came to see us in our little flat ... not far from here ... a childless young couple's flat. And they had one baby ... All of us ... had a lot in common ... you know: *not* Southern English, *not* public school, working class Northern, you know ... Alan was a public figure. And Sylvia and I were both American, both wrote poetry, and were both nobodies. She had a baby already. She had a book which was about to be published, but she didn't figure ... Immediately, there, we were sister souls but they were about to leave [for Devon] in a month or two months ... Sylvia had Frieda and this arrangement with Ted ... Alan didn't have to do that because we could afford an au pair.[32]

Despite the fellow feeling generated between the two women poets by their sense of living at the side of far more successful men, the 'lack of acknowledgement' that Plath was receiving should not be exaggerated. For instance, it is worth noting that, the day before Ted received the Hawthornden prize, Sylvia had recorded a twenty-five-minute programme of her poems with Marvin Kane for the prestigious BBC *Living Poet* series.

It may be that one of the pressures on the marriage was Sylvia's insistence that Ted should at least write *commercially* if he was determined to do nothing but write. It is an opinion offered by Suzette Macedo, who met Ted and Sylvia at the house of Sylvester and Jenny Stein some time in June 1961, shortly after Ted had won the Hawthornden prize.

Suzette had grown up in Mozambique in East Africa, which was then a Portuguese colony, although her first language was English, and she taught at the University of Witwatersrand. She was married to Helder

Macedo, a Portuguese poet, now a Professor of Portuguese Literature at King's College, London. She and Helder had run away together from Portugal, then under the dictatorship of Salazar. Both of them were very impressed with Ted, who seemed willing to listen to what everyone said; he showed a particular interest in Helder's poetry and in Portuguese poetry in general. The Macedos felt that they had a great deal in common with Ted and Sylvia, being at once literary and poor. Suzette, who was always elegantly dressed herself, remarked that on the first occasion they met Sylvia was dressed very smartly. She 'wasn't beautiful but had a bright animation'. While Helder and Ted talked, Suzette asked Sylvia about Ted and was told: 'Ted is a *genius*.' Asked about what she did herself, she said, 'Oh well, I write a bit ... but I'm not in the same league.'[33]

Sylvia spoke of writing short stories for a woman's magazine and then confessed that she also wrote poems. When Suzette asked her if she had had any published, she discovered that Sylvia wrote under her maiden name and Sylvia was pleased to find that Suzette had read some of her work. The two women met several times after that, on occasion exchanging recipes. In an account of a dinner at the Macedos, which Sylvia describes to her mother, Suzette's culinary skills are highly praised. Since Suzette had lived in South Africa, with its high standard of living, she was also able to share Sylvia's astonishment at the dinginess of English bathrooms.

Ted put Helder in touch with George MacBeth, who was in charge of poetry at the BBC. His quiet presence, and his wish to encourage everyone to write as well as possible, impressed both the Macedos. Visiting the Hughes' flat, Suzette was amazed by Ted's readiness to help with the cooking and do other household chores, including nappy-changing. Suzette had no children, but would not have expected such collaboration from Helder in any case. 'Of course, in South Africa, everyone had servants.'[34]

In speaking of Sylvia's managerial skills, in promoting and sending out Ted's work, Suzette formed the impression Ted 'did not altogether like that about her'. She was emphatic that Sylvia, for all her inner drive, had no more idea than any other 1950s wife that her own career should be central. She might indeed, Suzette thought, 'have settled for something quite second rate if Ted had not encouraged her'. Sylvia had a huge respect for him as a mentor and felt that he knew far more about literature than she did. 'Her adoration of Ted was unmistakable. She had Wagnerian fantasies about Siegfried and Brunhild.'[35]

Although Suzette is reporting accurately how Sylvia spoke to her, it is hardly an adequate description of the Hughes' working relationship. Ted did not perceive Sylvia as a typical 1950s' wife, putting her husband first and accepting a subservient role. He repudiates that vision of her explicitly in a letter to Aurelia, knowing that Sylvia saw neither cooking – which she often liked to do to relieve other tensions – nor housekeeping as 'subservient' activities. She was 'Laurentian', not women's lib.[36] And Ted usually did the washing up, at least until the last two months of their living together. Writing to Aurelia Plath in 1975, Hughes pointed out that the question of whose writing took priority was a complex one. The problem was that Sylvia needed four hours every morning to write in; otherwise life felt unmanageable to her. For both of them the key issue was the way to ensure that she at last began to write as well as she wanted: 'We assumed my writing would carry on anyway somehow. Our great anxiety was for hers. And that dated from 1956 . . . Our main programme was her writing. That was absolutely the dominant theme – it was our big invalid. She thought as I did that mine could look after itself.'[37]

Sylvia wrote to her mother about a meeting with Theodore Roethke, who gave Ted a nod that he could have a teaching post in Washington any time he wanted. But another drama, which she did not unfold to her mother, concerned Ted's BBC producer Moira Doolan, and it suggests that Ted was once again distrusted by his wife. Hearing Moira's lilting Irish voice on the phone inviting Ted to a meeting at her office, Sylvia immediately intuited that she had a rival. When Ted was not back by lunchtime, Sylvia's jealous premonitions escalated. Moira Doolan was approaching fifty, that is, almost twice Ted's age, and there is no suggestion that there was any sexual involvement. When he returned with the good news that Moira had agreed to produce the series of programmes that he had suggested, Ted found all his work in progress – his plays, poems and even his precious Shakespeare – had been torn to shreds in Sylvia's rage. Any writer would feel indignant on Ted's behalf, but in fact, although he was upset, he never held that act of destruction against her. He saw it as a passionate act that did not go to the heart of his marriage, as he explained to Mrs Plath.[38] What he minded, and found, soon enough, bewildering, was the use Sylvia now began to make of difficulties between them as occasions for poems.

In mid-June 1961 Mrs Plath arrived in London and stayed in the Merwins' flat. She babysat for Sylvia and Ted, enabling them to take a fortnight's holiday in France, five days of which were spent with Bill and

Dido. The visit did not go well. Anyone curious about the largely petty incidents that turned Dido from someone who had been a helpful and supportive friend into a savage critic of Sylvia Plath can consult her vividly written, but hostile, memoir of Sylvia in Appendix II to Anne Stevenson's *Bitter Fame*. As they left, Dido asked, as Olwyn had on an earlier occasion, why Ted put up with Sylvia's moods with so little protest. The answer has the ring of truth: '[H]e told me that it would only make things worse, that "she couldn't be helped that way." '[39]

When Ted and Sylvia got back from France, with Mrs Plath still baby-sitting, they set off once more to explore Devon and Cornwall and to look for somewhere to live. Sylvia had only just begun to taste a little of the excitement London had to offer, but had convinced herself that a move to the country made sense. Devon was Sylvia's preference, once the decision had been made to leave. She stressed that preference to Suzette Macedo, even mentioning rather implausibly that she might look for a house on the tourist routes where she could run a bed-and-breakfast hotel.

In Devon they fell in love with Court Green, North Tawton, at first sight. To enable them to buy it, they received £500 from Edith Hughes as a gift and a loan of the same amount from Aurelia Plath. With their $6000 savings, they had enough to buy the house outright without a mortgage. Ted wrote to the Somerset Maugham trustees to explain that he would not now be able to go abroad, as the Award required all recipients to do, since there was so much work involved in the house move; all that remained was to sublet the remaining three years on their lease of the Chalcot Square flat.

This was no problem. Indeed they found a tenant almost at once, who wrote them a cheque for the key money. When two other applicants appeared – the gentle Canadian poet David Wevill and his lovely wife Assia – the Hughes so much preferred them that they tore up the first cheque and allowed the Wevills to move in as their new tenants. About the same time, the Wevills and the Macedos became close friends. It was August 1961. Sylvia had finished *The Bell Jar* and was once again pregnant. They were about to make yet another new start.

EIGHT

Devon

The village of North Tawton is about an hour's drive from Exeter, in the heart of lush Devon countryside and, at the time, it was on a direct route to London. Court Green, which Ted and Sylvia purchased from the Arundell family, stands on one of the main streets, although only the thatched roof can be seen from the road. The house, which had once been a rectory, was detached and substantial: it had nine rooms, a wine cellar and an attic, all in considerable need of repair. Three acres of land and an apple orchard came with the property, and there was also a run-down cottage and a stable that could be used as a garage. Court Green stood next to the church and its garden shared one wall with the churchyard. Three huge wych elms, on the edge of a prehistoric mound, could be seen from the large upstairs room chosen by Sylvia for her study.

Ted and Sylvia took all their furniture to Devon in a small builder's van and moved into Court Green on the last day of August 1961. They were soon unpacking and scrubbing vigorously, as Sylvia described in a letter to Ruth Fainlight: 'The days have flown over our heads in an aroma of death-watch-beetle-killer and drying paint ... Ted has made shelves; I have whitened them.'[1] He also made a six-foot table for Sylvia to work at, using a broad elm plank two inches thick. Sylvia painted little hearts on the furniture, and was stalwart and practical enough – in Peter Redgrove's memory – to clamber up and fix the ballcock of a recalcitrant lavatory that refused to flush.[2]

On 29 September Sylvia wrote to Ruth Fainlight that after all their hard work they were at last able to begin writing. And 'The Table' in *Birthday Letters* gives a portrait of Sylvia drinking Nescafé happily at her desk,[3] as Ted continued to act as midwife to the poems that followed the

111

completion of her first draft of *The Bell Jar* on 22 August, just before the move.

Sylvia's poems are filled with images of death, and not always her own death. In 'Widow', the 'bitter spider' makes out the husband as 'prey she'd love to kill'. On 23 October 1961, immediately after 'The Moon and the Yew Tree', where she spells out the bleakness of 'the light of the mind, cold and planetary', she wrote 'Mirror', which reminds us that we still read Sylvia Plath because her gifts were extraordinary and they included intelligence and wit. Despite all the assurance of the language at the heart of her poetry, there is always a sense both of danger and of some price to be paid for aspiration. What makes her poetry overwhelming is the way she ruthlessly exposes her own terrors. For all her stern intelligence, Plath had only superstition to help her transcend her everyday desperations. Hence all those fantasies of witchcraft; the imaginary powers of wax images; the mental image of herself with a doll's body, or some forbidden act of burning.

Now writing was becoming her only religion – confession, discipline, consolation and immortality. It is a dangerous faith, which Ted shared and encouraged. Poetry was a way to gain entry to one's innermost being; an alternative mirror, or perhaps a mirror of another, less helpless self. There are a great many mirrors in Plath's poems. In 'Mirror', the voice is that of the reflecting glass itself. The commenting voice of the mirror has 'no preconceptions' and tells no more than the truth. When the woman comes to consult her:

> Each morning it is her face that replaces the darkness.
> In me she has drowned a young girl, and in me an old woman
> Rises toward her day after day, like a terrible fish.[4]

Ted carpentered and gardened in the morning, while looking after Frieda; he then gave the child lunch and put her to bed before retiring to his attic study, just under the rafters, to work. He had several commissions from the BBC, and had taken on some reviewing for the Third Programme. On 31 October Sylvia was asked to read out her prize-winning poem 'Insomniac' at the Guinness Prize ceremony in Goldsmiths' Hall, to an audience that included Robert Graves. Sylvia stayed overnight in London with the Sillitoes, while Ted remained in Devon looking after Frieda. As Sylvia's letters to Ruth Fainlight show, Sylvia was eager to make the most of her time in London and asked whether she might possibly stay a second night, to give her time to see a play at the Royal Court Theatre.

The friendship between the two women poets was developing as no other relationship had that Sylvia had formed in England so far; three weeks before the London visit, on 6 October, Sylvia wrote a compassionate note about Ruth's recent miscarriage, showing an awareness of her friend's possible feelings and needs that gives the lie to the portrait painted of her as wholly egotistical.

Ted, too, found the work of moving into Court Green was more onerous than he had expected. He now thought it would take them a year or two to really get possession of the house. In a letter to Merwin in late 1961 he describes the age of the house, the eleven apple trees and the many robins, noting that Court Green's 'virtues are taking effect' and 'certain symptoms' – presumably of their London life – were disappearing.[5]

Yet something was seriously wrong, something in Ted as well as in the hidden underworld of Sylvia's being; something that convinced Ted it had been an error for them both to come to Devon. Ted's own splendid physique suddenly seemed less reliable than he had always imagined. After a few hours' digging, as he records in 'The Lodger', he felt an unnatural perspiration and, in lines whose awkward rhythms mime his lurching heart, he describes

> The pangs. The poundings.
> At night on my pillow the syncopated stagger
> Of the pulse in my ear.[6]

An unlikely hypochondriac, he became conscious of every irregular heartbeat and took the faintness that came over him when his heart slipped out of gear as evidence that he must soon be going to die. In the poem he speaks with a chill certainty of being 'already posthumous'. His heart had developed arrhythmia, a recognized symptom of stress. What then were the stresses that had provoked such a change in his robust physiology?

Lucas Myers, to whom Ted made no mention of any such symptoms in letters at the time, sets down – after first reading *Birthday Letters* – his speculations about a conversation he remembered having with Ted in 1963 when he mentioned his heart problem of two years previously: 'He had thought the fibrillations were going to carry him away. One day he decided not to die. The fibrillations stopped immediately. I did not question him about this further. The meaning I thought was clear. My guess is that the fibrillations began in earnest in 1961, and he decided not to die in the winter and spring of 1962.'[7] Lucas, as he explains a page earlier, saw Ted 'as a sort of prisoner in his own marriage. He was mostly a willing prisoner, but Sylvia did not want him out of her sight at all . . . and sometimes his position made extraordinary demands even on a person of his substance.'[8]

Myers is guessing that the agitation of Ted's heart was connected to his confinement in Sylvia's world. Yet Sylvia and Ted were far from isolated. Sylvia's brother Warren had come on a visit almost as soon as they moved in; Helder and Suzette Macedo spent a weekend at Court Green only a few weeks later, and heard Sylvia declare herself 'blissfully happy'. Ted was less bound to Devon than Sylvia, since his work with the BBC involved him travelling to London and the BBC would have paid his expenses for such trips.

Sylvia herself, five months' pregnant when they moved to Court Green and close to delivery as the year changed, was far less sanguine than she appeared to visitors. Much of her performance of euphoria was just that: a performance. She feared that the villagers regarded her with suspicion, partly because she was a foreigner and partly because she received letters addressed to 'Miss Plath', which led to rumours that she and Ted were not really married. The midwife sometimes appeared unannounced when Sylvia had not yet tidied the house; this would fluster her, although she had an excellent and friendly cleaning woman in Nancy Axworthy, who came in two mornings a week and also did all the ironing.

Sylvia felt the loneliness of her situation enough to join for a time the Anglican congregation in the church next door, even though she loathed the rector's reactionary politics. She tried to make friends with other mothers through the pre-natal clinic. At North Tawton, however, there was very little distraction of any kind. In the evenings Ted usually read to Sylvia while she sewed or did something with her hands: 'She never sat doing nothing. And she never read in a leisurely way.'[9] Hughes enjoyed reading Conrad to her while she worked; at one point he remembered, she was making a rag rug. Reading her journal after her death, he discovered how ferocious were some of the emotions she knotted into that rug – or 'bled into'[10] it, as 'The Rag Rug' in *Birthday Letters* has it. He was appalled, with hindsight, and came to wonder whether her seemingly peaceful work had not been closer to weaving a curse. Although he had no access during her lifetime to her journals, from her poems he understood the gallantry of her immense struggle to cope.

Both Ted and Sylvia were conscious of being four hours away from new friends like the Sillitoes and Ted's old Cambridge network, which they had left behind. Perhaps Ted was more alert than Sylvia to the dangers for her in this. He registers pungently in 'Error' how they lay together, with the rain drumming on the roof, listening

> To our vicarage rotting like a coffin,
> Foundering under its weeds.[11]

As far as her own work was concerned, however, Sylvia seemed liberated. It could be said that, almost for the first time since her marriage, her writing block had mysteriously lifted. She was beginning to write great poetry, and Ted knew as much. From 'Blackberrying' onwards, Plath's own idiosyncratic voice had begun to speak: sensual and alert to the richness of berries growing in profusion, yet imagining menstrual blood in their juices and living corruption in the flies gathering around their ripeness. Bleakly, in the orange rock face at the cliff end of the lane, she saw

> nothing but a great space
> Of white and pewter lights, and a din like silversmiths
> Beating and beating at an intractable metal[12]

Yet, though he himself had set 'The Moon and the Yew Tree' as an exercise for Sylvia one night when she could not sleep and was staring out at a full moon, he was deeply alarmed by the poem he had triggered: the obsession with her dead father as much as the cold light that infused the moon's 'O-gape of complete despair'. It depressed him greatly. They had both worked very hard to get her poetry airborne, but he was nonetheless horrified when he saw in 'which way [her imagination] wanted to fly'.[13]

In the last month of her pregnancy, Sylvia took on a serenity that precluded either travel or writing, and she gave birth to Nicholas Farrar Hughes on 17 January 1962. At 9lb 11oz he was a far heavier child than Frieda and it was both a longer and much more difficult birth, complicated by the cylinder of gas and air giving out when she most needed it. Writing to Ruth Fainlight,[14] Sylvia explained the way in which her giving birth to a boy had been a different experience for both Ted and herself. She speaks of having nagging pains all day, then of holding Ted's and the midwife's hands and being intoxicated by the gas and air until it ran out. Both of them had been expecting a girl, perhaps hoping that Frieda would be less jealous of a sister. Sylvia found it took her a whole night to recapture her early desire for a son.

Fortunately, Frieda was excited rather than jealous and Nicholas proved a good-natured baby. However, partly because Ted took the brunt of looking after Frieda while Sylvia dealt with their new child, he had less involvement with the new baby than he had had with his first child. Once again he took over the cooking, and coped with a succession of midwives while Sylvia rested. Ted's own comments on the baby in a letter to Bill Merwin were muted: 'Things go quietly here. We acquired a son on Jan 17, a Capricorn of no uncertain hoof. He is solemn, pale, still and has a weird little life. Frieda quite likes him.'[15]

In Ted's letters to other friends he begins to mention how slowly time passed in the countryside in comparison, say, with life in Swiss Cottage where Alvarez lived. At her parents' request, Ted was helping Nicola Tyrer, the sixteen-year-old daughter of a local bank manager, to understand Hopkins' poems and Shakespeare. Sylvia, very conscious of the milk and urine smells of motherhood that surrounded her in the aftermath of the birth of Nicholas, found the well-turned-out, pretty Nicola and her gushing enthusiasm for Ted's work as heard on the BBC a little disturbing, if only because the girl's admiration was so obviously able to alleviate Ted's depression. Her detailed and spiteful descriptions of the Tyrer parents in her journals suggest no great affection for her Devon neighbours.

The winter was a long and cold one but Sylvia's mood, although affected by rain, sleet, the cold east wind and chilblains, did not block her new poetry. It was in this spring that she wrote her verse play *Three Women*, which was to be directed for the BBC by Douglas Cleverdon. And in April 1962 she wrote 'Little Fugue' and began 'Elm', poems already infused with the intensity of the great poems in *Ariel*. Ted, to whom she continued to show all her work, praised the poetry. Nevertheless, he had begun to feel trapped in the myth she was calling upon. Or rather, he heard Sylvia's new true self in the voice of her poems as Caliban's voice when he was 'freed from the Elm', the laughter of Sycorax, or a storm that in his imagination has him huddling under the gabardine hiding place of Trinculo.[16]

Sylvia's preoccupations were invisible to friends, whom she made welcome. These soon included Elizabeth Compton (later Sigmund) and her then husband, the struggling novelist and playwright David Compton. On the radio programme *Poets in Partnership*, broadcast in February 1961, Ted and Sylvia had jokingly complained of composing 'with their writing pads propped on the baby's playpen', and Elizabeth, who was at that time the owner of a large house with three children of her own, had written to offer the Hughes a place of refuge. After about a year, Elizabeth Compton Sigmund received a reply,

> interestingly enough from Ted, saying we too are living in Devon in a big thatched house about twenty miles from you. Will you come and have lunch? ... And we went down with my young son to play with Frieda and the house was to my mind stunning ... I thought it was a wonderful house, a poet's house ... The furnishing was very sparse. We had lunch in the sitting room with a floor of black and white tiles, probably Dutch. And it had a funny sort of rickety table, which Sylvia had painted with white paint and little flowers, and we were sitting in deckchairs. Nicholas was outside in his pram in the little piece of garden at the front, and Sylvia kept running in and out to see he was OK.[17]

Elizabeth Compton Sigmund today is round-faced and smiling, comfortably dressed for the countryside. Although crippled by arthritis, she remains remarkably energetic; she has campaigned vigorously for compensation to be paid to injured farm workers and against the use of organophosphates. She has been accused, however, of inventing many of her memories, even when her written and spoken accounts have been entirely consistent. Janet Malcolm quotes David Compton, her first husband, in an indignant letter to Edward Butscher concerning Elizabeth's hostile remarks about Aurelia Plath, and warning him that his ex-wife's recollections were likely to be coloured by her vivid sense of the dramatic.[18]

There seems no reason, however, to doubt that she was a supportive friend to Sylvia while she lived in Devon and that Sylvia felt her warmth and affection. Elizabeth was born in the North of England into a mill-owner's family. This gave her, she thought, a link with Ted which Sylvia did not understand, even though – unlike Ted – Elizabeth's grandfather had owned two cotton-bleaching mills and the family had been extremely well off for several generations. Ted, who teased her about her Lancashire roots, also found her likeable initially. Although Elizabeth's first contact with Sylvia had been hearing her speak on the radio of her life as a writer, she had no idea what Sylvia wrote or how successfully. On that first meeting, Sylvia was more inclined to talk about her pride in Ted's genius than her own work. Soon after this, however, she and Ted visited Elizabeth and David at their home, Mill House, which had no electricity and was lit only by oil lamps. There, Sylvia saw Elizabeth, with her three children, as a kind of Earth Mother and told her she would always think of her with 'twinkly little lights' all round her. On that occasion Elizabeth recalled saying to Ted, 'I didn't know Sylvia wrote poetry,' because it came up in conversation, and she was told, 'She *is* a poet.' She remembers, 'I felt very small and silly because I could see the difference immediately.'[19]

The Comptons' house was built on a stream – a relic of its use as a mill – crossed by an old bridge. Elizabeth recalled an image of Ted and Sylvia 'standing on the bridge, looking down, and he has his arm round her shoulders and they are looking at the water and talking to each other, and it was such an intimate close thing that you felt it was an enormously important relationship, with so many echoes behind it'.[20]

Elizabeth saw something of Sylvia in the spring of 1962, mainly when Ted was in London or working. Sylvia confessed to Elizabeth how being in Yorkshire had frightened her, while Elizabeth tried to explain the habitual mix of taciturnity and bluntness in Northern speech, as well as something about the class system, which she felt Sylvia was unable to grasp. Elizabeth thought that 'somewhere within Ted there must have been this knowledge that, in the eyes of people like my family, they were inferior.'[21] If there were children from grand houses at Mexborough Grammar, they might well, I suppose, have contrasted their situations in such snobbish terms, but according to Alice Wilson, Ted's first girlfriend, the Hughes family were regarded all through the school as 'an unusual and special family'[22] and several of the teachers, notably Pauline Mayne and John Fisher visited Ted's parents as friends. It was at Cambridge, rather than at school, that Ted became aware of the ubiquity of English snobbishness, and he had already found his own way through it.

When Elizabeth tentatively suggested to Sylvia later in the year that 'somewhere Ted has a very small but perhaps pungent inferiority complex that makes him want to be supported by extra-marital relationships', Sylvia snapped cogently, 'Don't be ridiculous. Ted has had lunch with the Duke of Edinburgh.'

Elizabeth recalled Sylvia's excitement at discovering that she worked for the Liberal Party. This seemed important to Sylvia, not only because she had 'discovered a committed woman', as she cried at the time, but also because some of her terrors remained focused on the threat of nuclear war. Through Elizabeth, Sylvia became friendly with Mark Bonham-Carter, the distinguished Liberal politician, and Elizabeth, very much later, asked him about his impressions of Sylvia: 'Because I didn't know, I wasn't there when they met, but he said, "I can't go back over all that. But she was wonderful – she was brilliant and very witty and I just loved her." And he wasn't a sentimental man, not at all, but he was very upset. [by her death]'[23]

In April, Ted and Sylvia heard of the birth of the Sillitoes' first child, David, and the welcome possibility of a visit from these close friends. The weather changed. It was suddenly spring, and Ted and Sylvia were proud their new house. Sylvia wrote to Ruth Fainlight, that she was 'delighted to hear about the arrival of David' and giving a description of the daffodils 'shivering wildly and very wonderful among the taciturn black twigs'.[24] She and Ted picked a hundred a week, selling some and giving others to friends, without apparently depleting the numbers of flowers waiting to open.

No one who has read *Birthday Letters* will forget the lovely portrait of the whole family picking daffodils. While the daffodils were in full bloom there were visitors: first Aunt Hilda and Ted's cousin Vicky and then, on 4 May 1962, the Sillitoes. It was the occasion on which Sylvia and Ruth became closest, and also for the dedication of Plath's poem 'Elm' to Ruth. The two women had already spoken intimately when Sylvia came to stay with the Sillitoes in London in 1961:

> We talked and we felt very warm towards each other and she went back to Devon the next day ... Ted was in Devon looking after the child ... They couldn't be in London together, and couldn't afford train fares because they were very poor ... Then David was born. And from then on we went abroad. We had lived in Spain all through the fifties. ... We set off from England about six weeks after David's birth ... But we went down to Court Green for a weekend before we left.[25]

Ruth Fainlight remembered 'sitting in a room at Court Green talking to Sylvia, both of us with babies at our breast'. She was unable to remember what they talked about, but observed 'things weren't good between her and Ted. Frieda was running around; Nick was five months old; David five weeks old. So this was the last time I saw Sylvia. But of course we went on writing [to each other]'.[26]

Ruth and Alan helped with the housework and the cooking, and the four genuinely liked each other. Although Ruth had observed tensions between Ted and Sylvia, it was a happy weekend, as Sylvia's letter to Ruth of 12 May makes clear: 'It was heavenly having you and Alan and David here, and like a vacation for me ... We ate our first minuscule radish this week, in a ceremony with butter. If Ted is as eager to pull our stuff up as with this, we shall be living like midgets on infantine vegetables.'[27] A week later, their guests were David and Assia Wevill, the new tenants of 3 Chalcot Square. David Wevill, part of the group around George MacBeth, had already won an Eric Gregory Award and was to go on to win prizes in America. His wife Assia, a beautiful woman with huge eyes and 'the passport of Europe on her face' as Sylvia described her,[28] was a few years older than her husband. Both of them were working in advertising: Assia at the prestigious J. Walter Thompson company, David Wevill for Ogilvy, Mather & Benson alongside the novelist Fay Weldon. In contrast to Sylvia, who described herself that week as 'rather weary,[29] from nights of lost sleep, Assia had a glamour that was rarely found outside films. Everything about her – from the way her hair fell over her face to her husky voice – was seductive.

Assia was born Assia Gutman in Germany to a Jewish physician of Russian origin and a German Protestant mother. Her family had left Germany on the eve of the Second World War for Palestine, then a British colony, where her father was able to practise medicine and where she and her sister, Celia, were brought up. The sisters went to school in a German enclave, only mixing with Jewish children and speaking the Hebrew language after school hours.

In 1945, when she was barely sixteen, Assia already had a remarkable sophistication. Mira Hamermesh, a Polish-born film-maker and a close friend, who had reached the safety of Palestine in 1941, remembers seeing her from a bus in 1945:

> To me she came across as a beautifully-attired teenager ... the most urbanised representative of the fashionably dressed young girl that I would have liked to become ... She was tanned, with brownish hair, beautiful violet-blue eyes. But it was her poise that struck me – I'd never seen anyone so poised, except from what I remembered of

Hollywood films. Only from that world did I know people like her
... She was wearing a choker; an open-shouldered blouse in crisp
white. Everything about her was crisp.[30]

A year later, while travelling to London to take up a British Council
scholarship to study Art at the Slade in London, Mira met Assia again.
They became friends, and although there was a brief separation at the
time of the Israeli War of Independence – when Mira went back to Israel
to fight – the two young women kept in touch. Mira – incidentally a
remarkably pretty woman herself – recognized a very similar vulnerability
to her own beneath the charming surface. 'We were *driftwood*, [my italics]
post-war driftwood. Living in an English country where people don't
ask – it's good manners not to question. So they would never know about
me or her, the real core of our being, what is ticking behind that beautiful,
poised exterior. The truth is we didn't even dare to know it ourselves –
we were vulnerable, desperately vulnerable.'[31]

After the war, the Gutman family had left Palestine for Canada, with
Assia already married for the first time, although that marriage soon ended
in divorce. David Wevill was Assia's third husband. Her second had been
Dr Richard G. Lipsey a LSE Professor of Economics. Assia had not taken
the breakdown of her second marriage calmly, and had exacted a stylish
revenge. Suzette Macedo, who found Assia's stories as 'compelling as
Scheherazade',[32] was much taken with her arranging for a male friend to
send her ex-husband's new partner a rose every day, without any note.
According to Assia, this drove Lipsey so mad with jealousy that he
telephoned the shop to find out where the roses came from.

Suzette's involvement with Assia amounted for some years to an obsession. She had met her with David at a party given by Jean and Malcolm
Hart,[33] recognizing her at once from Sylvia's description of their new
tenant at Chalcot Square: 'And I fell in love with Assia ... her huge
beautiful eyes, the way her hair fell, her husky voice, the way she could
tell a story ... I once said to her: you must be a hundred years old to have
lived the life you have. She had been a hat-check girl for a time, among
other exotic employment.'[34] Assia had met her present husband on board
ship, crossing from Canada to England in 1956, where David, who already
had a degree, was at Cambridge reading English. She was still married to
Lipsey at the time, but David fell in love with her and offered to remain
available if she ever needed him. In October 1958, he began a two-year
teaching stint at the University of Mandalay in Burma. When her marriage

to Lipsey broke down, Assia joined David there in 1959, where she enjoyed learning Balinese dancing and acquiring a cut-glass Kensington accent. Assia was seen as a scarlet woman, according to Suzette Macedo.[35] After David left the University of Mandalay, he and Assia got married.

By 1962, Assia was earning a high salary from advertising and could afford luxuries. She loved expensive clothes and shops, and had her own dressmaker. She introduced her friend Suzette Macedo to Fortnum & Mason's and other similar emporia, and her generosity was overwhelming: 'You couldn't say you liked something, or she would instantly give it to you.'[36] She tried to buy Suzette a little fur hat and muff, which Suzette refused, accepting instead a charming Burmese sculpture.

Over that weekend in May, Ted fell overwhelmingly in love with this beautiful stranger, although friends differ a great deal on the extent of Assia's calculation in the matter. Suzette Macedo insists that, even before their invitation to Court Green, Assia had already whispered of Ted: ' "He's *gorgeous.*" I didn't really believe her. Because she adored David . . . She spoiled David. Buying him little delicacies.'[37] Al Alvarez spoke of Assia as quite simply 'predatory'[38] and said she made a pass at every man she met.

Suzette, who is an extraordinarily good mimic, described Assia's mood as she set off for that weekend in Devon: 'When Assia heard that she and David had been invited to visit the Hughes at Court Green, she said, "Well, shall I wear my warpaint?" ' Suzette, who was, after all, also a friend of Sylvia, was horrified: 'It was a bad time in the marriage . . . Ted must have been sexually frustrated . . . in the last months there had been little sex . . . and Sylvia, who had been breastfeeding, and looking after two children, was a complete *Schlumke*[39] . . . Assia was perfumed and manicured.'[40]

As Suzette tells the story, there was an unmistakable sexual electricity between Ted and Assia all through the weekend. The first afternoon, Ted and David had spent talking about poetry, especially Robert Lowell, since Ted had a record of him reading that they all listened to. Ted had been his usual generous and attentive self. Suzette, who tells stories in compulsive detail, related what Assia told her had happened the following day:

> The next morning Sylvia was going to do a roast, ordered Assia to peel the potatoes and left the room. So Assia began to peel the potatoes and then Ted came into the kitchen. Suddenly she felt the

'spear' of his gaze at her back, and he said to her, 'You know what's happened to us, don't you?' and she said, 'Yes.' Then Sylvia appeared in the doorway, saying, 'What are you talking about?' And Ted said they were talking astrology and Assia reported that he made up some mumbo jumbo ... Sylvia's eyes were sharp and black and she said, 'I'd like you to leave after lunch. I'm exhausted,' and then she drove them to the station to catch a train. Assia said, 'She knew,' I joked, 'What did she know?' And Assia said, 'It's very serious, darling.'[41]

Ted's own analysis of the meeting, in 'Dreamers',[42] suggested an encounter at once calmer and more fated, and includes the fascination Sylvia herself felt for 'the ancestral Black Forest whisper' which was all that remained of Assia's accent. He saw the marvellous, black-ringed grey iris of Assia's almost unnaturally huge eyes as resembling a 'Black Forest wolf', or a 'witch's daughter'. It is a strange poem, and many of Assia's friends have objected to the lines where Ted writes of Assia sitting

> in her soot-wet mascara,
> In flame-orange silks, in gold bracelets,
> Slightly filthy with erotic mystery –

Nevertheless, the poem insists that Assia was as helpless as Ted and Sylvia:

> That moment the dreamer in me
> Fell in love with her, and I knew it.[43]

'The affair began in June; David knew nothing of it until October,' wrote Olwyn in a letter to Anne Stevenson at the time she was writing *Bitter Fame*.[44] Olwyn was, however, in France at the time of this drama. A letter from David Wevill dated 20 January 1989[45] points out that Sylvia didn't 'throw them out' of Court Green, as legend has it, since they were due to leave in the afternoon anyway, and in fact Ted came in the car with them to the station. He also pointed out that Sylvia probably meant exactly what she said about being exhausted, since she could only take a certain amount of company at any one time. He ridiculed the idea, voiced in Stevenson's *Bitter Fame*, that the attraction between Assia and Ted might not have turned into an affair if Sylvia had not behaved so badly.

David's is a sane and loving voice, well aware of Assia as a woman who needed protection. However, the rest of the story unfolded inexorably.

Suzette Macedo, who met up with Assia some time after this weekend, saw Assia pull out of her bag a note in handwriting that Suzette recognized as Ted's. Ted had called on Assia at her place of work, sending up a message to say that a 'Mr Hughes' was there to see her. Alarmed, Assia had sent back a message to say she was in a meeting, so he had left the note, which Assia showed Suzette. It read: 'I have come to see you, despite all marriages.'

Suzette said, 'For God's sake, don't answer it.'

Assia replied, 'Too late. I haven't answered it exactly. I sent a red rose pressed between two sheets of paper.'

Suzette retorted, 'He won't know who that's from.'

Assia shrugged: 'It's up too him.'

Suzette's memory of a rose sent in an envelope does not accord with Hughes' own recollection. In *Capriccio*, a book of poems that were all one way or another concerned with Assia, which was published by Leonard Baskin's Gehenna Press in 1990 in an edition of only fifty copies, one of the most beautiful opens with:

> She sent him a blade of grass, but no word
> Inside it.[46]

NINE

The Single Life

In late May 1962, Ted's father, mother and Uncle Walt arrived for a six-day visit to Court Green, after which Edith wrote to Aurelia Plath that Sylvia was 'a lovely mother',[1] and seemed to notice nothing wrong between the couple. Al Alvarez, calling on his way to Cornwall, also saw little amiss, registering mainly that Sylvia was no longer an appendage to Ted and that Ted seemed content to sit back and play with his daughter Frieda. Yet Sylvia had already written 'Event', a poem recording a serious marital rift, which leaves a couple silent and bleak, lying 'Back to back' in the moonlight. Ted read the poem and was appalled to see an intimate quarrel used as subject matter. Sylvia sent it off for publication in the *Observer* nonetheless.

When Mrs Plath came on 21 June for a visit of several weeks, she found a warm welcome and for a time enjoyed the house, the garden and her grandchildren. The first week of her stay went smoothly enough and any tension that Aurelia observed in Ted she attributed to his suffering from bee stings. Quite recently, Sylvia and Ted had gone along to a meeting of bee-keepers, where Sylvia had been taken with the idea of making their own honey, perhaps remembering her father's expertise. She ordered a hive of Italian hybrid bees for Court Green and sited the hive well away from the house, but Ted was stung six times and was still suffering from the effects when Aurelia arrived.

According to Sylvia, her life was blissful. She had everything she had always wanted: a successful husband, a beautiful house and beautiful children. Aurelia watched the two of them set off together for London to record for the BBC: Ted for *Children's School Hour* and Sylvia for *World of Books*. In their absence, Percy Key, a neighbour who had been suffering from lung cancer, died, and on their return to Devon, Ted and Sylvia went to his funeral. Together, they watched him lowered into a grave in the cemetery next to Court Green. Details of this experience, mingled with a vision of a Normandy beachhead, went into Sylvia's poem 'Berck-Plage'.

Ted, who had often helped Percy in his last illness, was saddened by this death, but his thoughts were elsewhere. Sylvia saw his preoccupation and became suspicious, particularly when he went up to London again, though she knew he had good reason to be at the BBC. Ted was indeed determined to pursue his relationship with Assia Wevill. Some time in late June, he arranged to spend a night with her at a small London hotel near King's Cross railway station. Assia had prepared for their encounter by shopping for a champagne-coloured silk and lace nightdress[2] on a shopping expedition with Suzette Macedo. The ostensible reason for the purchase was that Assia was going into hospital for a 'scrape' – a dilation and curettage of the womb – the common treatment to cure excessive bleeding during menstruation. When Suzette offered to visit her in hospital, however, Assia firmly refused. She had chosen the delicately beautiful nightwear for a first rendezvous that she imagined would be romantic, and already ordered peaches and champagne.

The following Sunday she telephoned Suzette in some agitation and arranged to meet her at Cosmos, a restaurant in Swiss Cottage.[3] There she confessed that the ardour of Ted's lovemaking had taken her by surprise: he had torn the expensive nightgown from her shoulders. Suzette remarked that for Assia sex was always 'sex in the head', but added that she was ashen and seemed to have genuinely found Ted's passion alarming. From time to time she repeated that she had decided never to see him again. She was, in any case, far from committed to abandoning David Wevill. For all the drama of this account – both in Assia's remembered words[4] and Suzette's graphic retelling – it was clear that Assia was nevertheless fascinated by the experience. As Suzette put it: 'Although she sounded quite horrified and frightened, it was as if there was something she needed and wanted, even while she was saying, "I never want to see him again," even as she spoke with such compunction of "darling David and his sweet face on the pillow" '.[5]

When Ted returned to Devon, he found his wife in a rage of hysterical suspicion. He denied her accusations – an evasion that only makes sense if he was still reluctant to break up the marriage. Sylvia did not believe his denials. A few days after this first encounter with Assia, when he was once again away in London, Sylvia made a bonfire of all the papers in his study and watched while they burned. Her mother looked on, appalled by her daughter's distress. Fearing that her presence could only make matters worse, Aurelia retreated from Court Green to stay with Winifred Davies, Sylvia's midwife.

Somehow the marriage survived the quarrel that ensued on Ted's return. Perhaps Ted, in spite of his desire for Assia, drew back from the brink. At any rate, he continued to try to please Sylvia by doing what she wanted. In July, for instance, he went with her, albeit reluctantly, to see Elizabeth Compton Sigmund for her thirty-fourth birthday. Sylvia took an enormous iced birthday cake, wrapped in a coloured shawl, for her friend. Elizabeth remembers her tramping down the path, 'Ted in tow, looking rather disgruntled, I have to say. I don't think he wanted to be there and without being rude he made it clear that he really wished he were somewhere else, which was understandable ... I had a gut feeling that there was something slightly wrong [then], that Ted was not happy ... I thought it was just being with us, but of course it was more than that.'[6]

If Ted hesitated to continue the affair he had begun, it would explain why Assia tried to contact him by telephone. On 9 July, after shopping with her mother in Exeter, Sylvia returned to Court Green, where Ted was looking after the children, and rushed to answer a phone she could hear ringing. The caller, using low tones like a man, asked to speak to Ted. But Sylvia thought she recognized Assia's voice. After Ted had spoken briefly to Assia, Sylvia ripped the telephone line out of its socket. She was sure now of what she had so far only suspected. It was this incident that went into her poem, 'Words heard, by accident, over the phone', and it led Sylvia to ask Ted to leave Court Green. Sheepishly, and uncertain what his plans were, he packed a few things; Sylvia and her mother drove him to the station. In London, he went to stay at Al Alvarez's London flat in Swiss Cottage. Later that evening, while her mother looked after Frieda, Sylvia put Nicholas in their Morris and drove over to see Elizabeth Compton Sigmund in a state of great distress: 'She was absolutely gutted, crying and sobbing and saying, "My milk's dried up. My mother's here watching all this. I can't bear it." She said, "Ted is lying to me – that's what I can't bear – because he's become a *little* man." '[7]

In Elizabeth Compton Sigmund's opinion, Assia's phone call was made in an attempt to destabilize Sylvia, but this hardly fits with the account given by Suzette Macedo of Assia's reaction to hearing that Ted had been ordered out of the house. Assia thought this outcome 'a disaster'. She also told Suzette that Ted was pushing her to leave David but that she had no intention of doing so. Ted's own intentions were far from clear, even to himself.

Once in London, he fell into a black mood. Suzette recalled a night when she and Helder met Assia and David – who was still apparently unaware of what was going on – in the company of Ted and Alvarez, at a pub on the corner of St George's Terrace, where the Merwins had their London flat. They were all supposed to be making their way to a party at the palatial house of the poet Nathaniel Tarn in Hampstead Garden Suburb, although Alvarez did not join them. In the car Ted started to sing a folk song, from which Suzette particularly remembers the lines:

> If it weren't for my mother
> I would hate all women.

The lines are from James Joyce's favourite Irish ballad, which has a peculiarly mournful refrain – 'O the brown ale and the yellow ale' – and was often sung by Ted in his Cambridge days.

Ted and Sylvia had not broken off all contact. Indeed, they travelled together in July to give a reading for Brian Cox's *Critical Quarterly* in Bangor, North Wales, while Aurelia looked after the children. On the way, they stayed overnight with Dan and Helga Huws, both of whom believed that the difficulties between Ted and Sylvia were only temporary. Brian Cox thought it a sign of the two poets' sense of duty that they kept to their commitment:[8] 'Before the reading we took them to Beaumaris in Anglesey for dinner. At first they seemed strained, but as the red wine flowed we all relaxed and the laughter and conviviality of our earlier dinners were restored. They must have separated permanently only a few weeks later.'[9]

The separation, however, continued to be intermittent rather than permanent. Ted always insisted that it had been planned initially to last for only a month. The decision to part upset both of them; in a letter she wrote to Elizabeth Compton Sigmund,[10] Aurelia Plath spoke of Frieda running in to her just before she was due to leave England and saying, 'Daddy and Mummy are outside and they're crying.'[11] When Mrs Plath left Exeter on 4 August, Ted and Sylvia were standing together with their children to wave goodbye. They had already decided on a separation, but were able to put on a show of togetherness for Mrs Prouty, Sylvia's earlier benefactress, who was visiting London with her sister-in-law. At Mrs Prouty's expense, Ted and Sylvia spent a night together at the Connaught, ate an expensive dinner and saw Agatha Christie's play *The Mousetrap*.

On 25 August, John Malcolm Brinnin, the first biographer of Dylan Thomas, visited Ted – who by then was evidently back at Court Green – to sound out the possibility of Ted's accepting a job at the University of Connecticut the following year. Ted, who had shown no signs of tension during Brinnin's brief visit, explained nevertheless, as he walked Brinnin to his car, that there were arrangements he needed to make in his own personal life, which put any such decision out of the question.

In the first days of September 1962, Sylvia drove her station wagon off the road, although without suffering any injury. It may be that she had just realized that she was about to take on the responsibility of looking after two children on her own, just as her mother had done. On 5 September, she was fined £1 for this traffic offence. The accident was trivial, but Ted mentioned it to Alvarez with some gloom. In 'Lady Lazarus', Sylvia writes as if it were as significant as her 1953 attempt at suicide.

For more than a year, Sylvia had been writing to Clarissa Roche, then living in Kent, asking her to visit Court Green. Now her letters took on great urgency. Clarissa made the long journey from Kent to North Tawton, and was welcomed by Sylvia at the station with the cry, 'You have saved my life.' For four days and nights the two women entered into an intimacy quite different from anything they had found together in America, as Sylvia poured out her anger. Clarissa understood that for Sylvia, whose wounds were raw, 'the strong passionate Heathcliff had turned round and now appeared to her as a massive, crude, oafish peasant, who could not protect her from herself nor from the consequences of having grasped at womanhood.'[12] That she was indeed in need of someone's protection was only too clear. Clarissa wondered whether all along Sylvia had needed a Leonard Woolf, or perhaps merely spinsterhood.

According to Elizabeth Compton Sigmund, Sylvia spoke in early September of a plan that she and Ted had to visit Ireland together, which she thought might be 'a possible renewal of their marriage ... [Ireland] was their Mecca, their spiritual centre, and it was dreadfully sad because she had been so excited, and then she came back thin as a beanpole and smoking, and saying, "He just left me there in the middle of the night. Left me there and went off. I had to come back alone." '[13] Elizabeth Compton Sigmund may be reporting Sylvia's appearance and words on her return in mid-September from the Irish trip, since, whatever her secret hopes may have been, the plan was not as it is here described. In fact, she and Ted had already talked by then of a longer separation, which might begin in November. Sylvia decided that what she needed was to take a winter break in Ireland, and Ted was to accompany her to Cleggan, in Connemara on the coast of Galway, to help her find a cottage. A nanny was in place to look after the children in their absence.

Before they set off for Ireland to stay with Richard Murphy in the second week of September, Sylvia was not yet admitting the situation fully to any friends who knew them as a couple. For instance, in a letter to Ruth Fainlight,[14] Sylvia is still talking about going with Ted to Spain, even asking Ruth for practical hints about facilities for babies there. 'Are there paddipads in Spain? Strained baby foods?' She was even able to mock her own string of questions with, 'Is there a God? Where is Franco?'[15] Apart from a bitter comment on Ted's attitude towards Nicholas – 'Ted never touches him, nor has since he was born' – there was no mention of marital problems.

Richard Murphy makes clear that there was no quarrel during their stay in Ireland. However, Sylvia did tell him about Ted's infidelity and her loathing of his deception, while Murphy urged Sylvia not to divorce Ted for an affair that might very well not last.[16] Ted did not discuss Sylvia's faults, but admitted that, after six or seven years that had been marvellously creative, the marriage had suddenly become destructive for him.[17] Murphy, whose own marriage had recently broken up, found signs that Sylvia might have a sexual interest in himself deeply alarming. One morning, after a long night spent with the poet Thomas Kinsella and Murphy over a ouija board, Ted set out alone to visit the American painter Barrie Cook in County Clare and did not return. Murphy wondered whether Sylvia had engineered the situation in order to be alone with him. Far from any such plan, Sylvia saw Ted's departure as an act of cavalier abandonment, and she went home alone to Court Green. There she found letters from both her mother and her old analyst, Ruth Beuscher, urging her to sue for a divorce. From then on, that was the course upon which she seemed to be firmly set.

In Ted's letter to Aurelia Plath in 1975,[18] he insisted that the original arrangement had been for the couple to part for only one month, and that it was Sylvia who had refused absolutely to let him come home in case it prejudiced their divorce. It is far from clear when he himself thought of returning, however; by the time he was moving nomadically from friend to friend in London, he was writing of his separation from Sylvia as 'inevitable' to Gerald,[19] and claiming that for all the qualities that made Sylvia one of the most gifted and capable women he had ever known, she was finally impossible for him to remain married to. There are phrases in this letter, in which he speaks of Sylvia's 'death-ray' quality, which have to be taken into consideration when imagining a possible reconciliation.

Ted said nothing in this letter to Gerald about any overwhelming attraction to Assia, although he did mention how painful it was for Sylvia to have her 'mixed up' in his departure. He well knew that Sylvia envied Assia her appearance, and was aware how much she had been hurt by the discovery of his infidelity, but he encouraged himself with the thought that the separation was beneficial for her, too. His own residual unhappiness, as he reported it to Gerald, centred on his separation from his daughter, Frieda.

By October, Sylvia was presenting to Ted the same front of steely contempt that she presented to her mother in *Letters Home*, rejoicing in the end of their marriage and the freedom that her new life had brought her. She triumphantly waved letters from friends in America at him, stressing that her therapist Dr Beuscher agreed that Ted's behaviour was that of a villain and was urging her to free herself from him. Ted believed that a divorce was what she wanted and although, as he wrote to Aurelia,[20] he realized that he may well have deserved these furious attacks, they made it impossible for him to think there was any chance of reconciliation.[21]

Sylvia's elation came from the extraordinary liberation that her pain had brought to her poems. From the first week of October 1962, she began to transmute her anger into a savage vision of her own power. In 'Stings', she wrote:

> Have a self to recover, a queen.
> Is she dead, is she sleeping?
> Where has she been,
> With her lion-red body, her wings of glass?[22]

On 11 October, in 'The Applicant', she ridiculed a vision of matrimony where a woman is like a doll – 'It can sew, it can cook' – but has no inconvenient inner world.[23] Her own marriage hardly resembled that fantasy, but the feminist movement was not altogether mistaken in taking her up as an icon. For although she may also have wanted to find a lover, it was essentially her free self, in so far as she could make that manifest in her poetry, that she hoped could sustain her. She would have freedom, her children and her writing; and, to anaesthetize her longing for what had been lost, she indulged in ferocious caricature.

With her most celebrated poem, 'Daddy', written on 12 October, she fused the images of Ted and her dead feather, presenting both as Nazi oppressors and tormentors. In Aurelia's account of her marriage, Otto was a fairly tyrannical husband and father even by the conventions of the day. He suppressed his wife's impulse to study and was too focused on his own career to have much to do with his children. In this, nothing could be less like Hughes. Otto was also German born, and proud of it. Was he a supporter of Hitler? Sylvia once told Suzette Macedo[24] that, like many biologists – and, indeed, H.G. Wells and Marie Stopes – Otto was a great believer in eugenics, but it is a long way from that to being a Nazi. Politically, Ted had no such sympathies, and his black cord jackets – worn with grey flannel trousers – were a convenience rather than a political statement.

What makes 'Daddy' live so memorably is Plath's perfect craft: the combination of nursery rhythms – a single bizarre repeated end-rhyme – and the subtle internal echoes within the lines themselves:

> You do not do, you do not do
> Any more, black shoe
> In which I have lived like a foot
> For thirty years, poor and white,
> Barely daring to breathe or Achoo.[25]

Plath takes an intense delight in syllables like Ezra Pound at his most lyrical, as she savours 'the freakish Atlantic/Where it pours bean green over blue'. Nevertheless, the focus of 'Daddy' is crucially on Sylvia's masochism, a common enough element in female sexuality, which feminism is unlikely to eradicate:

> Every woman adores a Fascist,
> The boot in the face, the brute
> Brute heart of a brute like you.[26]

Sylvia's image of Hughes as a vampire substitute for her dead father with a 'Meinkampf look' and 'a love of the rack and the screw' would live in the minds of readers for nearly half a century, and it says a great deal about the honour that Hughes felt for her genius that he sent the poem out into the world.

Plath's own knowledge of the triumphant originality of her new poems lies underneath the jaunty front that she was able to maintain that autumn, even though she was often feverish and had lost twenty pounds in weight. She also had a prescient certainty that what she was writing would bring her the fame she craved.

There have been many objections, notably to Plath's appropriation of the imagery of the death camps, not only in 'Daddy' but in 'Lady Lazarus'. Seamus Heaney, for instance, while admiring 'Daddy' as a brilliant tour de force found the use of another peoples suffering in the camps took away all claim on our sympathy, however miserable Plath's emotional situation.

The balance and common sense of this is undeniable, although it was the same imagery, it should be remembered, that filled every daily newspaper from 11 April 1961, when the trial of Adolf Eichmann began in Jerusalem, until 31 May 1962, when he was hanged. Moreover, the poem is not trying to induce *sympathy*; it is intended to induce *elation*, as indeed is 'Lady Lazarus', which was written between 23 and 29 October 1962. Heaney recognizes as much when he writes that Plath has given herself over 'as a vehicle for possession'. She makes her own suffering and flirtation with death a striptease for which her readers become a ghoulish audience. Yet it is also a conscious performance. Even though Lady Lazarus seems to come, unbidden, from Plath's inner being, it is her skill that maintains the half-rhymes that find their climax in the strong end-rhyme – which picks up both 'Beware' and 'Herr Lucifer' – and makes the last three lines among the most memorable in the English language:

> Out of the ash
> I rise with my red hair
> And I eat men like air.[27]

The emotion is not of grief but *glee*. For BBC Radio, Plath described the speaker in the poem as having the great and terrible gift of being reborn, but the sheer theatricality of the poem, and the throwaway, colloquial tone of many of the crucial lines, work against a sense of transcendence. These are poems which invoke the power to avenge.

In a letter to Ruth Fainlight of 22 October 1962, after a couple of paragraphs about horse riding and the publication of 'Elm' in the *New Yorker*, Sylvia wrote: 'I am very happy about the divorce; it is as if life were being restored to me.' It is the tone of the letter that signals her hurt as she gives an account of what she claimed Ted had been saying to her as they parted: 'A week after I almost died of influenza this summer, Ted took the opportunity of telling me that he had never had the courage to say he didn't want children, that the house in the country (his dream, for which he got me to leave the life in London I loved) was a sort of hoax, and bye-by[e] . . .'[28] People say unforgivable things to one another when they separate; however, Ted's letter to Aurelia Plath[29] confirms that he had indeed not initially wanted children.

Sylvia assured her friend that the writer in her was prospering – and it was in fact the most richly fruitful period of her short life, comparable to Keats' 'marvellous year' – although bitterness and humiliation return later in the letter as she writes: 'You can imagine how I felt about Ted watching us invest everything in this place, he writing glowing letters about it, and quite coolly saying "Plenty of children get along without fathers and are poor etc" and walking out for good.'[30]

As to 'walking out for good', it was still far from clear that Ted had any such intention. Both Ted's brother and mother wrote to Sylvia, assuring her that Ted's idiocy was only temporary. It was Sylvia who continued to insist on a divorce, still urged on by her mother and Ruth Beuscher while Ted protested that it was foolish even to consider such a course of action. Sylvia was implacable. That was why she would not let him come back to Court Green and, above all – as a poem in *Howls and Whispers*[31] made clear – insisted that there should be no sexual resolution. There is no sign in the world of Sylvia's poems of any wish to have Ted back, although Elizabeth Compton Sigmund reports that Sylvia had written in a letter that 'one cannot help crying for lost Edens'. She also recalls the pathos of Sylvia saying, 'When you give someone your whole heart and he doesn't want it, you cannot take it back. It's gone for ever.'[32]

The Merwins were still in Lacan in France, but Dido returned to London late in October to deal with her mother's estate, staying in her mother's large flat in Montague Square in Bloomsbury. Always sympathetic to Ted, she invited him to stay there as well and by early autumn Ted was living in a bare room with little more than a bed and a few boxes. He was by now rather enjoying his experience of the single life, as he wrote to Bill Merwin, who was then in New York, adding that he imagined Sylvia, too, preferred the new situation. Since Sylvia managed to keep up a bright façade in most people's presence – even Alvarez, who had access to the poems that she was writing at this crucial juncture, saw her as self-possessed and even cheerful – it is not surprising that Ted was also deceived into thinking that their separation had been good for her as well as himself, had even thrown her on to her 'better self', as he wrote to Merwin. He was still troubled about the possible loss of Frieda, but was finding it easier to write than he had for some time. Ted returned to Court Green early in October to collect his things, but went straight back to London.

Suzette Macedo, disturbed by what was happening, suggested that Sylvia come and stay in London with herself and Helder. Although she well knew that Suzette was a friend of Assia, Sylvia accepted, leaving the children with Elizabeth Compton Sigmund. To Suzette, too, Sylvia re-emphasized her determination on divorce. On this occasion she went to see the Macedos' GP, Dr Horder. According to Suzette, Helder advised her that she was being too precipitate, but Sylvia insisted that she never wanted to see Ted again: 'She talked as if she completely despised him, saying, "He's become a tailor's dummy to me." '[33] At the same time, she could not resist asking Suzette what Assia was saying about the progress of her relationship with Ted. Suzette told her that she thought Assia did not really want to leave David and that, if Sylvia simply held on, Ted would probably come back to her. Sylvia seemed indifferent to this information at the time. She had no intention of waiting patiently for Ted to come to his senses. Her response to the suggestion was to write a letter to David to tell him Assia was having an affair.

This was some time in late September or early October 1962. Sylvia had bought herself new clothes – a camel suit from Jaeger -and had had her hair cut more fashionably. To Suzette she spoke with excitement of setting up a literary salon, insisting that she was hungry for the literary life and that her relationship with Ted had been a mistake: 'She was high and flirtatious and enchanting but that night, after she went to bed, I could hear her sobbing ... she was sobbing in her sleep. Sobbing in her sleep.'[34] Assia and Ted left for Spain for a fortnight together. Before leaving, Assia phoned Suzette at the hairdresser in her lunch hour because she guessed how upset David would be and wanted Helder to go round to be with him. Helder found that David had punched his fists through the door of his flat and had slashed an Italian handbag Assia loved. 'David was in a terrible state. Helder took him out to walk on Primrose Hill,' Suzette recalls.[35] At the end of her brief two weeks with Ted, Assia returned home to David. Although she probably lied to him and saw Ted when she was pretending to see Suzette, David and Assia patched up their marriage and were back together by Christmas. Suzette was well aware that she was in a sense being used as a messenger by both Sylvia and Assia.

Sylvia knew that her only chance of establishing a life of her own lay in returning to London and finding a larger flat, with domestic help to allow her time to write. So Sylvia once again stayed with the Macedos while she looked for suitable accommodation, and on 4 November, Ted met her to discuss establishing a base.[36] He also went to see one or two flats with her. However, it was on a further visit to the Macedos' GP, Dr Horder in Primrose Hill, that Sylvia happened to notice a nearby house at 23 Fitzroy Road whose blue plaque announced that Yeats had lived there. A board of the agents Morton Smith & Co announced a flat to let and, hardly able to believe her luck, Sylvia went off at once to try to negotiate a five-year lease. It was hard for a woman to take on a lease by herself, even more so when she was a freelance writer. Moreover, there was a rival offer for the flat. It was only with Ted's help that Sylvia was able to put down a year's rent in advance to secure the property. The Macedos lent Sylvia an old bed; she bought cheap, unpainted wooden furniture from John Lewis, and put down rush mats on the floors. Ted drove down to Devon to collect some red corduroy material to make curtains, and by 12 December 1962 Sylvia had moved decisively back to London.

That drive to Devon must have been the occasion that lies behind one of the saddest poems of *Birthday Letters*, 'Robbing Myself', in which Ted returns to Court Green in 'the blue December twilight' to fork up a few potatoes and pick over the stored apples, before standing in the empty house listening to the absence of the life he remembered. He stared at a rickety walnut desk, bought for £6, and a horsehair Victorian chair which had cost only five shillings. Then he filled a sack with potatoes and another with apples before setting off back to London. On the icy roads, it was a journey that took twelve hours.

Ruth Fainlight, with whom Sylvia remained in touch by letter, was still out of the country. She was living in Tangiers with Alan Sillitoe in a house overlooking the straits of Gibraltar. As it happened, Alan had been invited to Moscow, where he was in great favour at the time as a proletarian writer. Ruth and Sylvia concocted a plan, which involved Ruth bringing her nanny Fatima to England, and a car – Ruth learned to drive and got her first driving licence for the purpose – so that she and Sylvia could go down to Court Green and take a holiday there together with their children.

Sylvia's most important contact in London was with Al Alvarez, who had already published several of her poems in the *Observer* and who was sympathetic to the kind of work she was doing. They shared an admiration for Lowell, and she had been impressed by his introduction to the Penguin anthology *New Poetry*, with its demand for poetry beyond the expectations of English gentility.

At first Sylvia probably saw Alvarez mainly as a powerful literary figure who could recognize the originality of her voice and could help her find work. He recommended her to the BBC, who offered her a place on their most distinguished literary panel programme, *The Critics*. She may also have hoped to forge a more intimate relationship with him. She called in on him on several occasions, and read aloud her new poems to him: 'Berck-Plage', 'The Moon in the Yew Tree' and 'Elm' at first, but soon 'Lady Lazarus', written the day after her birthday. She had feared abandonment all her life but now she knew how to use the experience. Alvarez put it memorably: 'She turned anger, implacability and her roused, needle-sharp sense of trouble into a kind of celebration.'[37]

When Ted went back to Yorkshire for a family Christmas in December 1962, he went alone. Assia was with David – indeed, they entertained the Macedos at their Highbury flat on Boxing Day. Ted invited Sylvia to bring the children and join him in Yorkshire, but unsurprisingly she refused, hinting at other arrangements, although indeed she had little enough planned. On Christmas Eve Sylvia invited Alvarez to her new flat, but since he was having dinner that evening with the distinguished writer V.S. Pritchett, he could only drop in for a drink.

Alvarez saw that Sylvia had lost a great deal of weight, and memorably records not only her appearance – with her hair hanging straight to her waist instead of in its usual school-mistressy bun, 'giving her pale face and gaunt figure a curious, desolate, rapt air, like a priestess emptied out by the rites of her cult',[38] but also the disturbing animal odour of her hair. She read him several poems, including 'Death & Co.', and he must have felt her desperation. He knew she would have liked a sexual relationship to develop between them.

In his autobiographical memoir *Where Did It All Go Right?* Alvarez adds a telling detail to his previous accounts of that evening. When he was preparing to leave, she burst into tears and pleaded with him not to go. In the face of such extreme need, he was appalled; the responsibility was immense. He had never found her particularly attractive sexually, and was at that time getting back together with the woman who in 1966 became his present wife. He detached himself as gently as he could.

Sylvia had nowhere to go for Christmas Day, so Suzette asked her and the children to celebrate Christmas with Helder and herself, and at the last moment bought a scrawny goose in Camden Town market. In letters to her mother, Sylvia rather exaggerates the splendour of the feast, but Suzette was a good cook and Sylvia kept up her bright manner, insisting that her old life was returning, now that she was back in London. For Boxing Day, however, Suzette and Helder were going to visit Assia and David in Highbury, with Doris Lessing and her son Peter. That day, Sylvia wrote letters. In one to her mother, she expressed the pleasure she took in Nicholas's sturdiness and Frieda's precocious ability to see the resemblance between falling snow and a picture in a favourite book.[39] Apart from her children Sylvia spent the day alone, although she had been invited out for supper that evening by the mother of one of the children at Frieda's nursery school.

In the New Year, Ted returned to London, and all through January 1963 he saw Sylvia several times a week, sometimes several days in succession. She did not see Alvarez at all that month. Janet Malcolm mentions that Sylvia sent Alvarez a card to suggest a visit to the zoo with her children, so that they could examine the condor and decide whether 'nude verdigris'[40] was an inapposite term, as he had claimed on his Christmas Eve visit. She received no reply. Meanwhile, Ruth Fainlight's elaborate plan to bring her Moroccon nanny to England, so that she and her son David could be with Sylvia and her children in Court Green while Alan Sillitoe was in Russia, was slowly moving forward.

Sylvia was not poverty-stricken, as many have imagined. Ted had given her all the money that they had saved in their joint account. In spite of their habitual frugality, this amounted to only a few hundred pounds, since they had spent most of their funds on refurbishing the house. But Ted had not been squandering their earnings, as Aurelia Plath seemed to believe. He had spent no more than usual in 1962, and after leaving Court Green he borrowed £200 from his aunt Hilda to help him survive. Between the end of September 1962 and early February 1963, Ted was able to give Sylvia a further £900 in cash and cheques. He kept strict accounts, in a notebook he retained.[41]

On 14 January 1963, Ted was a guest at a party to launch *The Bell Jar*. He found Sylvia 'in resilient form'.[42] Yet Sylvia was far from surrounded by the London literary world as she had hoped, and the novel's reception was disappointing. Seeing that the Macedos had a wide acquaintance,

Sylvia asked to be introduced to as many new people as possible. Helder Macedo took her to meet Doris Lessing,[43] but Lessing drew back from the desperation she sensed underneath Sylvia's animation.

Through Macedo, Sylvia came to know Jillian and Gerry Becker, who were to be her closest acquaintances in these last weeks of her life. The Beckers, South African Jewish friends of the Macedos, were sympathetic and hospitable, often taking her out to eat with them in restaurants. Clarissa Roche visited Sylvia in her flat in Fitzroy Road in January, and found the snow piled up in a drift against the street door. Sylvia was in a dressing gown when she let her in and looked drained and weary; she was suffering from flu. 'Outwardly she seemed to have things under control. There were no heaps of dirty dishes, no piles of unwashed linen. The children were clean and dressed.'[44] When Clarissa left to go back to Kent, Sylvia promised to return to bed.

It was England's worst winter for 150 years. Frozen pipes made hot water rare, unless flats had central heating. The discomfort of Ted's living accommodation at 110 Cleveland Street, W1, did not trouble him, however, and he found the unexpected wintry weather exhilarating. He adapted easily to the harsh conditions, writing to his brother Gerald as if freedom and the single life were the main gains for himself in parting from Sylvia. He also brooded about how much Sylvia must have been hurt to find the woman whose appearance she most envied involved in Ted's departure but he consoled himself with the thought that the break-up had been good for her too. He was still uncertain how Assia intended their relationship to develop, but he was not unduly distressed by her hesitation.

Ted worried much more about the children, particularly Frieda. He knew that she missed him horribly and he was afraid of losing touch with her altogether, describing her as his 'little pal' to Gerald, and finding separation from her much the most painful part of his own situation. By January 21 1963, Ted was writing to Merwin of his travels round London using Bill's car. In London it was freezing, with people dying of hypothermia and the electricity supply failing under the demands of inadequate single-bar heaters. Ted was nevertheless enjoying his peripatetic life, as he wrote to Bill Merwin with exuberance: 'W11 tonight, W8 tomorrow night, and so on ... However, the Ford starts all right. I have had a new back axle put in. If you're being bombarded by requests to pay parking fines, the address is above. That's the second request.'[45] In a postscript to that letter, he casually sends Assia's greetings to Dido, which suggests that he was once again seeing Assia on a regular basis. David Ross, who lent Ted and Assia his flat early in the relationship, is in no doubt that the affair continued throughout 1962 and into the following year. Ross liked Assia and was impressed by her good looks: 'If you went into the Lamb [a pub in Conduit Street] with Assia, you had no trouble getting a drink – people just fell away from the bar to let you through.'[46] No one reading Dido Merwin's memoir in *Bitter Fame* would expect much sympathy for Sylvia from her. Assia and Dido had more in common; both had been married three times and had no children.

A neighbour living three doors away from Sylvia – a fellow American, Joel Finler – remembers that stand-pipes had to be set up in the streets to ensure a flow of water for cooking and washing.[47] It must have been a nightmare to look after children in such conditions. Sylvia had no telephone and no possibility of installing a line; all phone calls had to be made using coins in a freezing callbox, usually after waiting in a queue.

On Monday, 4 February, Sylvia phoned Gerry Becker from a phone box to explain that her car needed repair; he came round to organize its collection by a garage. In these weeks she relied very heavily on the generosity of the Beckers, who did all they could to help her. She particularly depended on Gerry's good humour. The elation engendered by her poetry was beginning to fail her – although she wrote another twelve poems of genius in Fitzroy Road – and Dr Horder could recognize the onset of a serious depression, for which he prescribed drugs that would take more than a few days to have any effect.

In the last six months of her life, the imagery in Plath's poetry had become effortless: a night sky becomes carbon paper through which the stars, like punctuation, let in points of light; a flock of choughs are like 'bits of burnt paper'. Waking on a winter morning, she can 'taste the tin of the sky' or note 'The wet dawn inks ... doing their blue dissolve'. She can write tenderly. When she describes the 'mouth of a child opening like a cat's' or balloons 'Guileless and clear' that live around the house after Christmas, she is instantly touching. At the same time the lioness of the last stanza of 'Purdah', which carries an allusion to Clytemnestra, a murderous wife, cannot but remind us that *Ariel*, which was both the name of Sylvia's horse and Prospero's spirit, was also the lioness of God.

'The Inscription' is the only poem in *Birthday Letters* that engages with meeting Sylvia in the flesh after their separation and memorably recalls the cold Soho flat where he lives alone, surrounded by the unpacked boxes of his belongings:

Cargo-dumped empty lightness.
Packing-case emptiness, lightness.[48]

He remembers her asking for some assurance, some word he tried to find for her, and in doing so uncovers the most moving, and personally revealing, lines in the whole sequence:

'Do what you like with me. I'm your parcel.
I have only our address on me.'[49]

If she had not suddenly seen the Shakespeare that she had once destroyed, now apparently miraculously restored, he might have said as much at the time. Instead, picking the book up, as if it were a sign of hope, Sylvia found it inscribed by Assia. And as the book shuts, the poem moves on, and the moment is past.

At no point in this whole story had Sylvia competed with Assia, or tried to engineer Ted's return. Her pride had been too committed to the public image of herself rejecting him, which her poems reinforced. Some time in the last week of her life, however, Sylvia saw Ted and broke down in tears, confessing that a divorce was the last thing she wanted. The collapse of her hard-won façade of proud independence roused all his old tenderness. This must have been the 'most important meeting of her life', which she mentioned to Suzette in her last weekend alive, saying, 'It's all falling into place. Everything's going to be all right.'[50]

But what did Ted intend to do? Ted explained to Aurelia in 1975 that Sylvia was seeing 'other friends' that weekend and that by Monday it was too late to save her. The Beckers were those friends. In the letter at Emory, it is notable that Ted has typed over the word 'Thursday', which might once have read 'Tuesday'. Memory is fallible. The account that Jillian Becker gave to Anne Stevenson does not quite square with Ted's, and though Ted also saw Sylvia earlier in the week the last time he saw her was probably Friday.

On Thursday, 7 February, Sylvia telephoned to implore help from Jillian; the Beckers at once offered to collect Sylvia and the children and take them into their comfortable, centrally heated flat at Mountfort Crescent. Jillian also drove back to the flat to collect necessary baby equipment, which Sylvia had forgotten to bring along, and, more surprisingly, a cocktail outfit, curlers and some cosmetics that she had requested.

Sylvia spent most of Friday in bed, apart from a long time in the bathroom, then set off in the evening for a 'very important appointment'. Ted remembered seeing her at her flat early on Friday evening but not in her evening clothes, and saying that she was about to leave for the weekend. She returned, however, to the Beckers in her ordinary street clothes, although her hair looked freshly curled and she seemed happy, as if something had been settled. If that was the occasion on which she recognized for the first time that Ted was prepared to come back to her, it makes sense.

The allegation that Ted knew that Assia was pregnant and told Sylvia of it at that meeting has to be treated with great suspicion. However, these were the days before the pill. An accident cannot be ruled out. What is peculiarly unlikely is that Ted told Sylvia of any such situation while he was trying to comfort her in her unexpected collapse. It was news that Sylvia would have found horribly painful, and it is inconceivable that she would have returned from receiving it with the radiance Suzette Macedo describes.

There has been speculation about why Sylvia returned by taxi from this encounter, but it seems most likely, in that appalling weather, that her car had simply failed to start. She spent Saturday in the Beckers' flat, although according to Macedo, it was on Saturday that Sylvia went out without saying where she was going; Suzette had to go round to the Beckers' and soothe Frieda by taking her to the London Zoo nearby while Jillian looked after Nicholas. A student of Gerry's had arranged to babysit at the Beckers' on Saturday evening, while Jillian and Gerry were dining out. On Sunday, Gerry took the children to the zoo with the wife of Douglas Clevedon, the BBC producer; after eating lunch, Sylvia slept. When she woke, she said she felt so much better that she wanted to return to her own flat, adding that Dr Horder had found her a nanny who was due to arrive the following morning. The Beckers pressed her to stay, but at length Gerry drove her and the children home to Fitzroy Road. She wept all the way in the car without giving any reason.

A biographer has to admit that Sylvia's tears in the car with Gerry on her return to the flat remain unexplained, as does her decision that night to kill herself. Later that evening, Dr Thomas from the flat below, from whom she bought a stamp, bears witness to her agitation. There is always a risk, as antidepressant drugs kick in, that all the barriers to foolish action are removed. Her anxiety would have had some rational basis. Even if Ted had intimated that he very much wanted to be reunited with her,

Sylvia might still have wondered whether any happy end was possible for them. Was Ted willing to stop seeing Assia altogether? Could she believe him even if he promised as much? Sylvia may have decided that she could not bear the uncertainty, and that only death offered any guarantee of release from pain. Her preoccupation with death, running through all her last poems, must have been another factor. For whatever mix of reasons, soon after talking to Dr Thomas, Sylvia went in and, having put out milk and bread for her children, sealed their bedroom door lightly to protect them and turned on the gas.

Al Alvarez has pointed to all the signs that this attempt at suicide was intended to fail, to be a dicing with death such as she envisaged surviving in 'Lady Lazarus'. We cannot know. Certainly her note leaving Dr Horder's telephone number suggests such a possibility. But Sylvia, who had guarded against injuring her children by sealing the door of their room, had not realized that the gas would knock out her downstairs neighbour, Dr Thomas, as well. The nanny booked to start work on Monday morning, failed to get a reply either to the bell of Plath's flat or that of Dr Thomas below, and, perhaps smelling gas, she telephoned the police. Once in the flat, the police discovered Sylvia's body, two crying children and also Dr Horder's telephone number. She was dead, however, long before he arrived. Her attempt was tragically successful. Sylvia Plath died at thirty at the height of her powers and the waste is intolerable.

Lucas Myers has always been of the opinion that Ted would probably have been back with Sylvia within a week if she had not killed herself. Inevitably, the possibility of Hughes' return throws a new, sad light on his relationship with Assia Wevill.

TEN

The Inheritance

L ooking down at Sylvia's white, dead face on Monday, 11 February 1963, Ted was overwhelmed with grief. He had loved Sylvia for the six years of their intense marriage, and he understood both her genius and her vulnerability. Now her body lay in a coffin in an undertaker's in Mornington Crescent. He went there to look at it with Alvarez, whom he knew to be sympathetic to Sylvia.

On Friday, 15 February, there was an inquest in the dingy coroner's court in Camden Town. The Australian nanny gave evidence in tears. Sylvia was not yet famous enough for her death to arouse press interest, but that weekend the *Observer* printed her photograph with one of her last poems and Alvarez's tribute. Although the notice in the *Observer* only reported that Plath had died suddenly, Alvarez published four of her poems alongside it, including 'Edge':

> The woman is perfected.
> Her dead
> Body wears the smile of accomplishment,[1]

The poem suggested that Sylvia had taken her own life. Alvarez spoke of her final work as 'a totally new breakthrough in modern verse and established her, I think, as the most gifted woman poet of her generation'.[2]

It was Dr Horder who confirmed her death. When he needed to contact Ted as next of kin he rang the Macedos, who had introduced Sylvia to him, to ask for Ted's telephone number or address. Suzette didn't have Ted's number and had to phone Assia to get it. When Ted turned up later at the Macedos', he was totally devastated. Suzette remembers him leaning against a piece of furniture and saying to Helder: 'Helder, you must know it was either her or me.'[3]

Assia was still living with David in their Highbury flat near Islington in North London. When Suzette asked her what her plans now were, she was only firm on one point: she had no intention of taking over the children. Otherwise, she was as bewildered as Ted, perhaps more so. Mira Hamermesh remembers that Assia never questioned the role that her behaviour had played in Sylvia's death, although her response to hearing the news – as Macedo remembers it – was to view Sylvia's suicide as an act of aggression against herself. From now on, her life was linked to Ted's by Sylvia's death.

Hughes, who for several months had had to meet the mask of contempt that Sylvia wore in his presence, had seen only in the few days before her death how badly she had been damaged by their separation. A letter from Hughes to Aurelia Plath, written in March 1963 and deposited by her in the Lilly Library to be held unseen until his death, reveals the pain he felt at the thought of Sylvia's vulnerability and his own guilt. In the same letter, he repeated that he had intended to reconcile himself to Plath, and describes his affair with Assia as 'madness', a word he uses in other letters – to Lucas Myers, for instance, and his brother Gerald. He ends his letter to Aurelia by declaring that if there were an eternity, he 'would be damned in it'.[4]

Ted's immediate task was to accompany the body to Heptonstall where he had decided Sylvia should be buried. His own family still lived in Yorkshire, and there were members of his mother's family in the cemetery there, so it was like taking Sylvia home. He felt a great repugnance for Devon, where his marriage had broken down, and had no wish to return to Court Green.

After the funeral in Yorkshire, Ted returned to Fitzroy Road, and Aunt Hilda remained in the flat for a further month to help look after the children. Some of Ted's friends were too far away to offer him immediate support. The Sillitoes were still in Morocco; Ruth Fainlight, in the midst of planning her return to England, only read of Sylvia's death when Alan brought home a copy of the *Observer*. Sometime in February, Assia invited a number of people, including Lucas Myers, to come round and help cheer Ted up. Records were played but it was a far cry from the noisy party with bongo drums described by Plath's downstairs neighbour, Dr Thomas, who later wrote about the apparent callousness of such a gathering in a memoir.[5] Olwyn, who had not gone home for the funeral, spent two or three days in Fitzroy Road, the only occasion on which she visited the flat and was present on the occasion. At this time she had no intention of leaving Paris. Her decision to return to England permanently was not taken for a further six months.

Soon after Ted came back from Yorkshire, his friend David Ross remembers visiting Fitzroy Road with a girl named Sue. Ted had Sylvia's last poems in typescript on the table and read some aloud to David: 'And I was absolutely startled with those poems – they are extraordinary, sent shivers up and down my spine that night . . .' He had no memory of Ted talking about Sylvia herself: 'So far as I remember, we were both so startled by these poems . . . I'd always felt that Sylvia wasn't a particularly good writer, from what I'd read, but those poems were stunning, stunning. To me, and I'm sure to Ted as well.'[6] All this suggests that the last poems were new to Ted. Certainly David Ross had the impression that Ted was not familiar with the typescript. He had seen all that Sylvia wrote 'up to the *Ariel* poems of October 1962, which was when we separated'.[7] Even though he continued to see her after she came to London, she did not show him more than a few carefully selected poems. What she wrote exposed too much, both of her need and of her hatred. From October 1962 through to February 1963, she had avoided Ted's questions about what she planned to do with the poems she was writing.

Sylvia left behind a carbon typescript, with its title page altered from *Daddy* to *Ariel*, containing about thirty-five poems, beginning with 'Morning Song' and ending with the bee poems (without 'Stings'); and a further twelve poems, including 'Totem' and 'The Munich Mannequins', which she had already shown him. Since Sylvia had died intestate and when still married to him, Ted – who continued to be her legal husband – inherited the copyright of all Sylvia's manuscripts and the responsibility of deciding what happened to them. According to David Ross, Ted was even then determined to publish them.[8]

After Alvarez had deplored in the *Observer* in 1971 that *Ariel* was not published for two and a half years after Sylvia's death, Ted, in an article written for the same paper, admitted wryly that he had not been a particularly 'brisk executor'. However, the poems presented him with complications that were absolutely baffling – 'Everything she and her family feared at that time has since come to pass, and more' – and added that neither of her publishers, either in the States or in England, wanted to publish the manuscript when he finally roused himself to send them copies of it.[9]

Ted's unqualified admiration for the sheer quality of the poetry is unmistakable and he felt a binding duty towards the poems. They held Plath's essential spirit, which had to be given to the world, even though the image of himself so purveyed was of a jailer, a torturer, or a Nazi, none of which was in the least apposite. He was not the only man in London to commit adultery and, although his infidelity had caused pain, he had never behaved with cruelty towards Sylvia. The violent anger in these poems was exactly what he had encouraged her to make use of, as he wrote in *Birthday Letters*:

'Get that shoulder under your stanzas
And we'll be away.'[10]

Ted had worked at Sylvia's side to help her set her innermost spirit free; he saw himself as someone who could help her tell the story that might release her from her obsession with her father. Even after her death, he still believed that her poetry was in a sense holy, the visible sign of an attempted psychic rebirth.

Alvarez remembers hesitation nevertheless:

I can remember very clearly walking with Ted and Olwyn, after Sylvia died, and I'd been saying: 'You've got to publish these poems, they're wonderful,' and they obviously had a lot of worries about that because they were so personal. And they said, 'No, all sorts of people are going to be hurt,' and so on and so forth . . . and then I remember walking along [on another occasion] and they said they *were* going to be published and they said, 'Don't worry, we've decided to let "Daddy" go in.'[11]

When Assia told Suzette Macedo in March 1963 that she had decided to leave David and join Ted at Fitzroy Road, Suzette was astonished and wondered how she could bear to think of living in the flat where Sylvia had killed herself. Aunt Hilda, moreover, was still in residence and had responded to Assia's wish to move in with the Yorkshire expression, 'Over my dead body,' according to Macedo. Assia ignored this. Her decision, in Suzette's account, was altogether matter of fact: the lease had been paid for and she had no intention of leaving London to live at Court Green. She insisted on having a nanny from an agency to look after the children when Aunt Hilda returned to Yorkshire. There were many voices ready to blame Assia for what had happened. Alvarez, who admits he never liked her, thought Ted had made no move to bring the situation about: 'I think Ted was probably slightly passive. I think women went for him rather than he pursued them.'[12]

Ted continued to see Alvarez in those early days after Sylvia's death: 'They [Ted and Assia] used to drop in a lot ... and I can remember them sitting on either side of the stove in my studio. These two black figures, hissing at one another.'[13] His present wife, Anne, also remembers Assia from the same period, and spoke of Assia's obsession with Sylvia. She remembers going to visit Assia in Fitzroy Road[14] when Assia had flu, listening to her talk about Sylvia and feeling, 'This was a woman who was really breaking down.' She commented on the mini-climate of bleakness Ted and Assia carried around with them: '... this heavy, heavy atmosphere between them. It wasn't as though, "We are two grieving people together." It was far more, unconsciously, each *blaming* the other. *Not* unconsciously. Blaming each other.'[15] Assia saw herself as an older sister to Anne, offering to find her a job modelling, for instance – Anne evidently had very good legs – and suggesting that she should use belladonna to make her eyes look larger. Anne, however, found something sinister in Assia's very un-English emphasis on glamour. But she was honest enough to add that Assia 'made me feel a little *provincial* ... She was very patronising.'[16]

Meanwhile, since Ted had decided that he could not bear to live at Court Green, it looked as though the best idea was to sell it. He asked Elizabeth Compton Sigmund if she would like to live there, and show people round who were interested in buying it. She accepted, although she feared it would be too pervaded with memories of Sylvia's life to be bearable. Nevertheless, she soon settled in.

Elizabeth told me of a visit she made some time in March to the flat in Fitzroy Road, where she discovered Assia was also living. Aunt Hilda had left, and there was now a nanny from an agency, looking after the children. Elizabeth's account of this episode has been repeated to several biographers, and was developed at length by herself in the *Guardian*,[17] where she suggested that knowledge of Assia's pregnancy had been a factor in Sylvia's decision to take her own life. There is, it must be said, no independent evidence for this. Suzette Macedo, who was very close to Assia at this period and knew of her earlier abortions,[18] categorically denied the story, even as she had described how Assia hated the thought of having a child, since she thought a foetus would be like 'a taproot growing inside her'.[19] Elizabeth described her visit to me with her usual vivacity: 'Ted came into the sitting room and said, "I've got to put a kettle on." He went into the kitchen – where *she'd* killed herself – and put the kettle on and got a hot-water bottle and said Assia had gone to bed because she'd had this operation.' Elizabeth seems to have *assumed* that this operation was an abortion; but, if that were so, it seems unlikely that medical advice would have included using a hot-water bottle, which would increase the danger of haemorrhage. What lingers in the memory is her depiction of Ted as distraught with guilt: 'He leant back against the window and he said, "It doesn't fall to many men to murder a genius." And I said, "Ted, you haven't murdered her," and he said, "I hear the wolves howling in the park and it's very apt." '[20] These words of self-accusation, whilst melodramatic, sound natural enough from a husband still in the shock of his wife's suicide, and spoken to a woman whom he knew had been a helpful friend; nor is the remorse in them discreditable. Their transmission over the years, however, has been damaging. The image of wolves howling from Regent's Park zoo went into one of the very few poems that Ted wrote in 1963. This is evidence that can be used equally well to support Elizabeth's version, or suggest an unconscious source for her memory. In Elizabeth's account of what must surely be the same episode, given to Janet Malcom,[21] there is no mention of any hot-water bottle needed for Assia or of the 'little operation'. In all her reports, however, Ted hands over a copy of *The Bell Jar*, whose first publication, written under the pseudonym Victoria Lucas, was dedicated to Elizabeth.

Olwyn, on her way to Paris, stopped off in London to have a huge Chinese meal with Ted; she brought him some gaiety, which he was finding difficult to maintain. He and Assia were often sombre when alone together. Ruth Fainlight remembers them even in company as two unhappy people, sitting silently in a shared wretchedness in the weeks after Sylvia's death.

By July 1963, Ted was in Yorkshire, needing, as he explained to Gerald,[22] help from Hilda with Frieda and Nicholas. The landscape drew him too, and the prospect of owning Lumb Bank, a magnificent manor house in Heptonstall. He not only loved the idea of living there, but also thought that Gerald might be induced to come back from Australia to join him. It would be a return to his childhood paradise plan to make money out of farming cows: 'Buy new-dropped calves, suckle them for a week and sell them at a profit of $4 a head.' Gerald might contribute his capital, and would be allowed to do what he wanted with it, living free in the house. The only snag was the position: it was barely 200 yards from The Beacon, the Hughes' parental home.[23]

If Court Green was haunted by memories of Sylvia, living in Yorkshire brought conflict with his parents. They found Assia's appearance, style of clothes and drawling, Knightsbridge voice exotic and alien. In their eyes, she was a woman without morals, who had entrapped their son and driven their daughter-in-law to suicide. They knew she had been married three times before taking up with Ted and that she was still married to another man. In Heptonstall, such behaviour was unthinkable. There had already been several explosions in Ted's family about Assia's presence in Yorkshire.

To Lucas Myers also, on 28 August 1963, Ted described a huge place in Yorkshire that he was considering buying, with the idea of setting up a friendly community where such hostility would not impinge. Ted suggested that Myers could live there rent-free with his wife Cynthia. He reassured Myers that he intended to get a woman in to do the housework. Even so, the plan very likely did not appeal to Assia, who visited Lumb Bank at Ted's suggestion but found its position in a hollow rather gloomy.

Ted knew he had to be strong enough to withstand parental criticism of Assia if he were to survive. He saw his parents as old and tired and more in need of looking after than listening to. However, he longed to see his brother again. But Gerald was not attracted to the idea of returning to England, and still less to living in Yorkshire so close to his parents, so Ted's plan to buy Lumb Bank foundered.

Some time in 1963, Ted went down to Court Green with Assia to collect a few things that he thought he might need for their flat. Elizabeth, who was still living in the house, had prepared lunch for him, and naturally fed Assia too although she had not been expecting her; she detected some rudeness in Assia's response to her cooking. After lunch, Assia asked Ted if Elizabeth would show her round the house. Elizabeth did so, nevertheless, until she reached Sylvia's workroom, when she was overcome by a sense of treachery. Meanwhile, Ted was in the playroom trying to roll up a carpet. Elizabeth reports him weeping while he did so as memories of buying Court Green with Sylvia, and their early joint struggles to make the house habitable, came flooding back. 'I just sat and helped him tie things up and Assia came down and said, "Do you think Ted and I can be happy together?" And I said, "You can't be serious – look at him." '[24] Elizabeth's description of Ted's grief is vivid, but in later encounters, Assia is remembered by Elizabeth as distant to the point of arrogance, and it is quite hard to imagine her exposing intimate anxieties so unguardedly to a woman she was meeting for the first time. Moreover, Assia had already spent a weekend in Court Green the previous year, so it is far from clear why she would need to be shown round by anyone.

It was Assia who found and read Sylvia's journal of the last months of her life, according to Suzette Macedo, and was overwhelmed by the spite and malice directed towards herself there. This may have been a factor in Ted's decision to destroy the journal. Olwyn, too, saw Sylvia's diaries and still remembers parts of them, as she mentioned in a recent letter to Lucas Myers,[25] correcting a few factual details in his moving memoir of Hughes, *Crow Steered, Bergs Appeared*, published in 2001.

To Gerald, Ted confided that the confusion about where he was living – and, although he doesn't mention it, with whom – was making it almost impossible to write: 'All I've been interested in is simplifying my existence so that I can write, and all I've ever done is involve myself with other people so that now I can't move without terrible consequences of all kinds on all sides.'[26] Ted had begun to change his mind, as early as June 1963 about the wisdom of selling Court Green. A possible purchaser had pulled out at the last minute and he realized it was unlikely that he could sell it for a good price in his present state of mind. He told himself that it might prove a pleasant country retreat for Frieda and Nicholas in the future. Not that he wanted to continue living in London – he had already determined to sublet Fitzroy Road, which could be done at a profit – but he was rattled by Assia's indecisive behaviour: 'Things have gone from illusion to illusion, perpetual uncertainties and conflicting obligations. A nightmare in retrospect.'[27]

Assia was indeed uncertain that her decision to move in with Ted had been the right one. On the night that John F. Kennedy was assassinated – 23 November 1963 – Anne Adams (later Alvarez) remembers being with Assia, together with Anna Bramble, a flatmate of Assia's who often kept her company at Fitzroy Road when Ted was not there. On this occasion, however, all three women were at David Wevill's flat.[28] This confirms Suzette's bewildered contention that Assia, for all the decisiveness with which she had moved into Fitzroy Road, was continually changing her mind about the wisdom of it.

Ted's letters to Gerald chart for the first time the other circumstances that locked together to make happiness for himself and Assia almost impossible, even when she had fully committed herself to him. Among his obligations, his mother's health was soon to loom large. Always prone to heart problems, she developed severe asthma in the winter of 1963.

She had suffered from arthritis for some time – it was why she had sent her sister Hilda to London rather than coming to look after the children herself – but that winter Ted wrote to Gerald that their mother would probably die, left with no one but his father to look after her in Yorkshire. His father never cared what he ate, his mother had no strength to cook, and they were both living on tea and buttered teacakes. In London there was no space to look after them, even if Ted could have afforded the necessary additional help. It looked as if the only solution was a return to Court Green.

So Ted moved back to Court Green in 1964 – while Assia remained in London – about nine months after Elizabeth Compton Sigmund had originally moved in, and his parents came South to join him. Elizabeth found another house in the village with the help of a friend, and Olwyn gave up her own vibrant life in Paris to come back and care for the children until things sorted themselves out. Elizabeth, whose account of Olwyn is often hostile, saw that Olwyn was affectionate with the children and knew that her return to help her brother out was particularly gallant and generous, since Olwyn had never been drawn towards motherhood herself.

Elizabeth took the children for walks, and sometimes visited Court Green as often as three times a day. Her son James became a great friend of Frieda, but Olwyn did not see the need for so many visits and said so, according to a letter from Ted to Gerald. For her part Elizabeth perceived Olwyn's naturally assured manner as bossy and felt that Olwyn talked to her 'as if I was a stupid idiot, a housewife with no brain'.[29]

Olwyn's relations with Assia were altogether easier at first than her relations with Sylvia had been. She admired Assia's cool sophistication, and Assia recognized an adventurous spirit whose experience of life had been as unconventional as her own. At one time the two of them considered setting up a literary agency for foreign rights in partnership with Suzette Macedo.[30] Even so, Olwyn's closeness to Ted sometimes left Assia feeling like an intruder, particularly when they talked about astrology in a knowing way, as if they had evolved a secret language.[31]

Olwyn was then a very handsome young woman in her early thirties, and no Dorothy Wordsworth. She wanted to see her brother happy; her ferocity in defending him in later years was a sign of that passionate loyalty, but Ted was far from the only man in her life. And Olwyn and Ted did not always see eye to eye. Ted was affectionately exasperated by the 'drifting fog' in which Olwyn had lived her life for the last fifteen years, and attributed it in a letter to Gerald to her smoking fifty cigarettes a day. He bet her £50 she wouldn't be able to stop.[32]

By 10 May 1964, Ted still felt it was impossible to get any serious work done, except for what he calls 'potboiling'; however, the reviews he wrote in 1963–4, for instance for the *Listener*, hardly deserved that description. Take his account of J. Thomas Shaw's magnificent edition of *Letters of Pushkin*, for example. He picks up the pride with which Pushkin emphasized his African descent, and guessed correctly at the childhood loneliness that lay beneath that boldness; he sympathized with a man who, like himself, had been forced to live and to support a family by his pen alone; and he adds, interestingly, that before marriage Pushkin's life was bearable, for all the hostility of the tsar and the court: 'He was happy enough as long as he was allowed to debauch.'

Pushkin's letters do not quite bear out Ted's conviction that Pushkin was a changed man after his marriage and it may be that Hughes' insight was autobiographical; certainly it is worth setting against his own wistfulness, in a much earlier letter to Lucas Myers, in which he advises him to live as uninhibited a life as possible now that so many of his friends had married.

Ted proved himself a most effective advocate of other poets' work, first in a broadcast about the poetry of Keith Douglas, the Second World War poet who had died at the age of twenty-four, and then in an introduction to a volume of Douglas's poems for Faber & Faber. A review of *Louis Macneice and Astrology*, alongside Lethbridge's *Ghost and Divining Rod*, allowed Hughes to defend astrology against its main enemies: common sense, popular science and puritanical Christianity. Perhaps most significantly, he wrote a review for the *New York Review of Books* about the novels of Isaac Bashevis Singer, and the specifically Hasidic superstitions and visions of pre-war Jewish Poland.

This was a time when Hughes initiated some of the most important pioneering ventures into European literature, which helped to open up English poetry after the stultifying insularity of the 1950s. Ted first broached the idea of a magazine of modern poetry in translation at a party given in London on New Year's Eve 1963. Daniel Weissbort was at once excited by the thought. Among others sympathetic to such an enterprise were Al Avarez, George Steiner, Professor Henry Gifford and Professor Max Hayward. It was an idea whose time had come. English intellectuals had begun to look outside their own island, especially to Eastern Europe, and *Modern Poetry in Translation* played a substantial part in introducing some of the most important of these poets on to the English scene. From Poland, Tadseusz Roszevich and Zbigniew Herbert; from Czechoslovakia, Miroslav Holub, and, from what was then Yugoslavia, Vasko Popa, who had evolved a language that enabled men to speak both politically and intimately. Even before Nadezhda Mandelstam's *Hope Against Hope* captured the imagination of the Western world, there was a quality of excitement in the central assumption, shared by Akhmatova, Bulgakov and others, that poetry was a spiritual strength, just as a belief in God might be, and that it was in some ways related to that belief.

At the time of starting the magazine, Daniel Weissbort had just left his father's firm and was a graduate student at the London School of Economics under the late Professor Leonard Shapiro – a distinguished historian and a translator from Russian. Daniel was learning Russian and reading poetry in the new Russian magazines that came into being in the brief period of the 'Thaw'. The poets he read were, as he expressed it, able to confront the 'truly intimidating reality of our time'.[33]

By 14 July 1964, Ted was writing to his brother from Court Green about scything the meadows and not making much headway against the flowers and the weeds. Throughout 1964 Ted lived partly in Court Green and partly in London. Ted confessed to Gerald how vulnerable he felt to all the women who shared in looking after his children. The trap was one that any single mother would recognize: if he didn't keep an eye on the children himself, they would be neglected, just as 'the wolf eats the ass with many owners'.[34] He acknowledged himself an easy prey to female blackmail: 'I've had a great taste of womankind in the last two years – evidently I'm a sucker of some sort. And the minute I cease to be a sucker – *clang*, the two kids are around my neck again, and I'm putting in twelve hours a day nursing.'[35]

The pressure of his financial situation meant that he had to take on more reviewing than he would otherwise have chosen, but this was miraculously alleviated when the University of Vienna, funded by the Abraham Woursel Foundation, wrote to award him £1500 of American money for five years to pursue his artistic talent as he thought best. He had begun to write *Eat Crow*, a play made over from his story 'Difficulties of a Bridegroom', and now he was able to work on it intensively, completing it in June 1964.

This was the year that Ted met Henry Williamson, who had written

Tarka the Otter, one of the first books to delight Ted in his Mexborough childhood. Ted took great pleasure in Williamson's amazing anecdotes about birds and animals, even though he saw clearly enough how Williamson's dream of Hitlerism had messed up his life.

Some time in May 1964, Assia found herself pregnant. As she was once again living with David Wevill, it was natural that there should be some speculation about the parentage of the child she was carrying. It is usually thought that, by this time, David Wevill was little more than a supportive friend to Assia, but Wevill himself rebutted this view of their relationship in a letter to Anne Stevenson,[36] claiming that they were much more than friends for 'two or three years' after she began her affair with Ted. Lucas Myers, a reliable witness who stayed with the Wevills in 1964 while Assia was pregnant, realized that David was in an excruciating position. He points out,[37] however, that Assia showed great tenderness towards her husband. On one occasion she asked Myers, 'Do you think you can love two people at the same time?'[38] That Assia continued with the pregnancy represented a huge emotional commitment. She knew that to have Ted's child would lock her into a relationship that she could no longer easily escape. It may be that she was listening to her biological clock. She was already in her mid-thirties, which in those days would have been considered old for a first pregnancy.

Alexandra Tatiana Eloise Wevill, usually known as Shura, was born on 3 March 1965. Ted always behaved as if Shura was his child, although David Wevill, who remained loyally in love with his wife, gave her his name. Suzette Macedo's first sight of Assia's baby was on a visit made while Assia was still staying with David Wevill. She imagined that the child was David's until Assia whispered to her behind her hand that the child was Ted's.[39] No uncertainty of parentage is suggested in a letter from Assia on 13 March 1965, thanking Lucas Myers for the gift of a charm flute to ease the pains of labour – 'which worked', she wrote, underlining the words several times.[40] Assia describes nine hours of labour and the birth of a daughter, 'miraculously unwrinkled, with black hair – very long – and North Sea blue eyes. She's fair as sweet briar.'[41] She mentions that the child had both the moon and the sun in Pisces with Libra rising, details which suggest that Ted was somewhere close at hand, although Assia remained in David's London flat. Another letter to Myers, written from J. Walter Thompson, gives a piquant sense of her linguistic exuberance: 'It has been raining in England for 11 weeks. Feels like a bog of soda water.'[42] She was still in daily touch with David, who had mentioned wanting to go to Paris for a week, but 'he forgot about it by today.'[43] In a letter to Myers, Assia hinted that Ted was equally indecisive about the long-term nature of the affair: 'Matters with Ted are precisely at the point they were when you left.'[44] Although Ted did not often speak of Sylvia, her poems and his memories of her were much in his mind. He was editing *Ariel* – which came out in March 1965 – while writing a note about her poetry for the Poetry Book Society.

Suzette had been refusing to continue her friendship with Assia because she found all the twists and turns of her relationship with Ted too emotionally upsetting. The last that she saw of Assia was when they said goodbye in Fitzjohn's Avenue, close to Suzette's flat: 'She said, "Let's part friends," and she kissed me. She was very generous. She said: "Maybe it'll be all right." And then she went to Court Green.'[45] Olwyn was still there, but was both exhausted by the burdensome situation and made restless by it. Assia had not wanted to live at Court Green but nevertheless, by 1965 there she was, along with Ted's crippled mother, his two children by Sylvia, and her own child, Shura. It was an exhausting web of responsibilities for a woman used to living with some panache in a metropolitan society. Ruth Fainlight, on a visit, remembers that Assia seemed overwhelmed by what had to be done. Nor was it a harmonious situation. It fell to Ted to try to keep everyone happy, a responsibility that took its toll on even his easygoing nature.

On 25 January 1966, his father was up in the North of England trying, not very effectively, to sell his newsagent's shop. Edith's health continued to fluctuate throughout the year, and letters to Gerald describe her severe depression, which Ted felt only a visit from Gerald could alleviate. This last was so important to Ted that he offered to pay half his brother's fare if he would return for Christmas.

His parents' attitude to Assia also fluctuated. On 25 September 1966, Ted was writing optimistically that his mother had begun to accept Assia and that this was making life easier, but the strain of maintaining this improvement was making work impossible. Just as Edith seemed to be recovering from a bout of illness, she heard that Olwyn, who always felt great affection for her mother, was nonetheless so fed up with life at Court Green that she had decided to move back to London. This produced a relapse that sent his mother back into hospital. Assia's own health, too, suffered and she had begun to take vitamin B tablets for her nerves. Ted began to dream of a house in Ireland with Assia and the children, as he wrote to Gerald, warning him the while not to mention any such plan in letters home in case his mother began to worry about it.

There were occasional breaks – a week in London, a trip to the Edinburgh Festival and the planned vacation in Ireland, which had come to fruition in April 1966. There Ted found a great valuable 'room of silence' to work in, looking out on a hillside and the Atlantic. With Assia and the children at his side, his letters sound almost happy again. By 25 November 1966, however, Ted was writing to Gerald of a crisis. His mother had had pneumonia; water had been drained from her lungs and she was continuing to have heart problems. Ted hoped his mother's diet of onions and orange juice might be helping a little and for a time believed once again that she was coming round to accepting Assia. Unfortunately, the delicate but workable relationship between Ted's father and Assia had more or less broken down in the meanwhile.

By February 1967, Court Green had become an inferno. His father was engaged in a cold war with Assia, which there seemed to be no repairing. Ted could neither bear to stay in the situation, nor see how to extricate himself. 'I just retire to my hut and write about my cows, but it seems phenomenally difficult to get anything done,' he wrote to Lucas Myers. 'I think the simple presence of parents has some sort of magical effect of forcing passivity on you.'[46] He had no complaints about Assia, who was gallantly putting things into shape, however frustrated by the presence of Ted's parents. 'The framework remains intact.'[47]

Ted was by now finishing off the work that went into *Wodwo*, a book that includes stories as well as poems. Some of the poems have the character of those in *Lupercal*: 'Thistles', for instance, with their spikes 'a revengeful burst/Of resurrection' from the dead body of a Viking, buried underground; 'Fern', which has a resemblance to 'Snowdrop' in its unfurling; or the marvellously casual accuracy in 'Gnat-Psalm' of gnats 'Scribbling on the air'. There are poems about memories of the First World War, such as 'Out', which take off from his father's experience. There are surprises, however. In 'Ghost Crabs', what chills us as much as the creatures that spill out of the sea is the sinister last line, 'They are God's only toys.' There are people in the poems, observed with the kind of purity Hughes uses to look at animals. An intriguing portrait of a Yorkshire miner, for instance, in 'Her Husband':

Comes home dull with coal-dust deliberately
To grime the sink and foul towels and let her

157

Learn with scrubbing brush and scrubbing board
The stubborn character of money.[48]

The miner's wife may offer him fried, woody chips in revenge, but there is no likelihood of justice for the women of this chauvinist society:

Their brief
Goes straight up to heaven and nothing more is heard of it.[49]

In 'Full Moon and Little Frieda', an alertness to space and sky is there from the first line – 'A cool small evening shrunk to a dog bark and the clank of a bucket' – but it is the child's excitement at her ability to find the word for her experience that gives the poem its tenderness:

'Moon' you cry suddenly, 'Moon! Moon!'[50]

The Wodwo itself is a creature from *Gawain and the Green Knight*, a medieval poem whose thudding, alliterate power Hughes had already learned to use in earlier books but now, in the title poem, renounces for another kind of verse altogether: unpunctuated, open, a series of questions moving on in a stream of dazed wonder:

Do these weeds
know me and name me to each other have they
seen me before, do I fit in their world?[51]

The poem's innocent, baffled voice reflects Hughes' sense of the true situation of any living creature in a recalcitrant world, although some of the recent changes in his own life were surprisingly for the better: Olwyn was working now as his literary agent, and proving very good at it. She managed to raise his fee from a flat £1000 to £390-odd a week for his work with Peter Brook on a translation of *Seneca's Oedipus*.

However, his mother continued to be seriously ill. Having been given a sedative by her GP, she lay in one position for thirty-six hours and developed 'horrendous bedsores'. His father, too, though relatively spry, now caught flu and once again could not 'stand the sight of Assia so never speaks to her'.[52]

Peter Redgrove, although he cannot be specific about which year, recalls a visit to Court Green when Assia was in a state of tension and Mrs Hughes was dying. Assia was setting up an antique shop in the stables at Court Green . . . and Mrs Hughes was very ill and sitting up in bed. Assia either refused to take a tray of food to her, or Mrs Hughes refused to take a tray from her – or I've invented all that – but I do remember taking the tray myself. And Hughes sat down by the bed and said to his mother, 'What are you going to do when you're dead?'[53]

In Redgrove's observation, Mrs Hughes was a triumphant matriarch, while Ted's father, dressed in his farmer's tweeds, said very little and remained quite separate from all the quarrelling.

In 1967 Ted was co-director – and he and Assia made a glamorous couple – at the first International Poetry Festival in London. The excitement of the readings themselves far surpassed any expectation of the organizers. There were long queues for return tickets. Every auditorium was packed with listeners, hungry to be in the presence of greatness. Much has been written about the 1960s: the political innocence of flower power, the indulgence in drugs and sex that went alongside a hatred of war. The sudden and widespread love of poetry read aloud, which lasted for about a decade, has not been much analysed. No doubt the series of *Penguin Poets in Translation*, which familiarized English readers with the names of foreign writers, plus the fact that many of the poets were not only great performers but were perceived as heroic dissidents, played a part in the romance of the occasion. Maybe everyone wanted to see the ageing Auden in the flesh, or listen to the young and scandalous Allen Ginsberg. Or it may be that it was a rare moment in literary time, when it was possible to bring together a generation that included Ungaretti from Italy and Neruda from Chile. Ted had written many of the letters of invitation himself and many of the programme notes for the Festival. Some of his appreciation is unexpected. Drafts for a piece on Allen Ginsberg,[54] for instance, praise his pursuit of spiritual experience and his rejection of the materialism of Western civilization.

Ruth Fainlight remembers how Ted and Assia came to stay with them for a week, introducing them to Yehudah Amichai, the great Israeli poet, whose work Assia had translated. Having Amichai for a friend may have been part of Assia's awakening interest in her own Jewishness. Yehuda's parents, like Assia's, had fled from Germany to Israel in the 1930s. Like any Jew, secular or not, Amichai argued with God. Ironic, moving, eminently sane, his poems are among the most memorable of the last century.

Although the Sillitoes were the hosts on this occasion, Fainlight reported: 'I shall never forget there was an amazing Middle European generosity when the Amichais arrived, bearing gifts . . . Assia was at Ted's side then as the consort and looked very happy . . . perhaps she was already unhappy in Court Green.'[55] Elizabeth Sigmund certainly believes so. Meeting Assia on a North Tawton street, she saw that she looked much stouter than she had, and that there was a tinge of grey in her hair. Elizabeth's eldest daughter also reported that she had been in the village chemist buying henna while Ted was there, and that he had said, 'You should use Seawitch – that's what Assia uses.'[56] Elizabeth intended me to condemn Ted's casual revelation, but the effect was to remind me painfully how an awareness of such village gossip would reinforce Assia's sense of isolation.

Ted had returned to his identification with Beethoven from his college days; he asked Lucas to get hold of a plaster mask of the composer. For some reason he had found it difficult to get one in London, although they were often on sale in Paris. 'Either a life or a death mask,' he requested, 'preferably both.'[57]

By the end of 1967 Ted had decided that the only way to engineer some peace for himself was for Assia to move back to London. He would then care for Frieda, Nicholas and his parents at Court Green, while two local women did the housework. With a hut in the garden as a retreat, he was at last able to work on completing his extraordinary poem *Crow*.

Some time in 1967, Leonard Baskin invited Ted to write some poems to go alongside engravings that he had made of crows. Ted decided that the voice of a crow should be unmusical and 'super-ugly', and he called up memories of Eskimo and Red Indian stories in which the crow usually figures as a trickster. A trickster is a 'demon of phallic energy, bearing the spirit of the sperm, is repetitive and indestructible. No matter what fatal mistakes he makes, and what tragic flaws he indulges, he refuses to let sufferings or death detain him.'[58] Soon Hughes was pleased to find that *Crow* had begun to 'sing his own songs, which are something quite new for me'.[59]

Since Sylvia's death, Hughes had been searching for a way to make sense of the damage that human beings inflict on one another in a cruelly indifferent universe. Under the influence of Baskin, and Central European poets such as János Pilinszky and Vasko Popa, who understood the brutality of experience under totalitarian regimes, Hughes grappled with a darkness that few English poets of the time felt any necessity to allow into their poetry. His vision is comparable only to Beckett's in its bleakness.

ELEVEN

Assia

While Ted was once again at work, however, Assia was going under in London. She was living on the first floor of Oakover Manor on the north side of Clapham Common. Much was on her side: she had gone back to a good job at J. Walter Thompson, she adored her child and she could afford domestic help. But she was lonely. Fay Weldon, the novelist, who still worked at Ogilvy, Benson & Mather, remembers that Assia had lost her exuberance and stopped expecting people to be interested in her. She no longer saw her old friend Suzette Macedo. When she had lunch at The Lamb in Conduit Street, frequented by other copywriters, she attracted much less attention.

At first, Ted came up to London frequently. He could afford to do so, since his financial situation, already alleviated by the grant of £1500 a year from the University of Vienna, had been further eased, unexpectedly, by royalties from *Ariel*, for which Ted had written a punctilious introduction. Although the order of poems was not precisely as Plath had left it, and now included her bleak, last poems – notably 'Edge' – which seemed to point inexorably to her suicide, Plath's greatest work was at large in the world. Ted's reasons for changing the order are set out in an interview that he gave to the *Paris Review* in 1995, and he argues cogently that in his experience Plath often altered the order of her manuscript.

Sylvia, all her life, had made sure that her work was constantly sent out and under consideration by publishers, yet, after a few rejections from literary editors, she made no effort to promote these poems, which she knew 'would make her name'.[1] It was Ted who helped *Ariel* to gain public recognition, feeling it a duty to Sylvia's memory and also because he understood the greatness of her poems. He could not have anticipated the rapture with which they were received. Sylvia had enjoyed only moderate success in her lifetime; her worldwide fame was entirely posthumous. In the two years since 17 February 1963, when Alvarez had run the first four of her late poems in the *Observer*, the *London Magazine* had run seven others and the *Atlantic Monthly* a further two. In August 1963, the *New Yorker* ran another seven. Most of these were poems that had been rejected by the same magazines before her death. It was as if her reputation had been growing silently underground. By the time *Ariel* was published as a book, there was an eager audience waiting. And Ted had come to realize that Plath's manuscripts themselves were extremely valuable, as he wrote to his brother Gerald with some astonishment.[2]

Ted and Assia worked together on the translation of the poems of Yehuda Amichai, some of which Assia had already translated on her own. They brought out the first English translations of Amichai's poems from Cape Goliard in London in 1968. Although she tried hard not to nag or fall into the anxieties that Ted had so disliked in Sylvia, Assia knew that Ted was not always working in his garden study, and guessed that he was not always alone. In a letter to Peter Redgrove early in 1968, Ted writes after a hasty meeting in Exeter that his 'entanglements grow two heads whenever I lop one'.[3] Among these entanglements by now was Brenda Hedden.

Brenda and her husband Trevor had first met Ted in late 1964, soon after the Heddens moved to Devon. Trevor, who had been married before, decided in his late thirties that he would train as a mature student of English Literature at a teacher training college in Exeter. The Heddens were introduced to the Hughes family by Elizabeth Compton Sigmund and they became friendly with Ted and Olwyn, sharing meals, discussions and sometimes playing poker. The Heddens were asked to look after Frieda and Nicholas when Olwyn wanted to get away occasionally. When the Hughes parents came to Devon and were alone at Court Green, the Heddens also provided the practical support they needed.

Ted's letters[4] from Ireland to the Heddens – from the winter of 1995 to April 1996 – show that he knew them well enough to entrust the responsibilities of Court Green to their care; and he expressed thanks 'ten million, million times for all the help'.[5]

On 27 April 1967, Ted wrote to Gerald about a quarrel that Assia had had with Brenda, after she and her husband had visited Court Green to play poker. Brenda Hedden points out that Assia did not play cards; and that while Assia was at Court Green, social relations with the Heddens were on a different basis. Both Brenda and Trevor found Assia aloof, and neither developed a close enough relationship to quarrel with her. Assia certainly knew the Heddens, however, and described Brenda to her sister Celia as 'an ex-social worker, with the looks of an emaciated Marilyn Monroe'.[6]

The puzzle, then, is why Ted mentions to Gerald that his father, who liked the young couple and was on particularly poor terms with Assia at the time, complained at losing his companions at the card table. Brenda believes that Ted, when writing to Gerald, wanted to provide a reason for the continuing friction between Assia and William.

Assia herself was already in the grip of a profound depression. There is a letter to her sister dated 11 March 1967 in which she pleaded for Celia to come over to England and be with her. She attributed her misery, in rather general terms, to the strain of the years since Sylvia's death and what she described as the contempt of Ted's friends. Even at Court Green, she explained, she saw little of Ted, who often lunched with his father while Assia took her lunch with Shura. Celia was married with three young children, so she could not go to her sister's help, and Assia was prevented from going to join Celia by her fear that Ted would find another woman in her absence.

It was after Assia had left for London in 1968 that Ted's relationship with Brenda Hedden became a love affair, although Ted made clear to her that 'Assia and Shura would always remain part of his life'.[7] Brenda continued to believe that her own future lay with Trevor and their children, even though Trevor had encouraged her to believe they could enjoy an open marriage. As Brenda needed a period of reflection, the couple agreed that Brenda could move to Welcombe with their children in the late autumn of 1968.

'Ted would come over and see me there . . . and Trevor also came, with a girlfriend, a very nice girl who offered to babysit if I wanted to go out. Ted always came alone.'[8]

However, Brenda was not the only woman in whom Ted had become interested. Ted's friend Michael Dyton, an antiques dealer, had introduced him to Jack Orchard and his family, and Ted was seeing one of his daughters, Carol, who had trained as a nurse. Brenda knew as much; but Ted had been candid about his need for more than one woman and believed Ted's assurances that she herself was a significant figure in his emotional life. Letters written to Brenda after August 1969 repeatedly express how happy he was when with her, and certainly suggest a man genuinely in love.

That year, 1968–9, was a confusing time for Ted, as he admitted in a rueful letter to Peter Redgrove in 1970, in which he reflected that, for all the emotional rollercoaster of the preceding two years, he had deliberately refused to make any use of this experience in his poetry as if it would be immoral to 'cash in his life for poems'.[9] It may be that he still disapproved of Sylvia for having done just that, and did not want to fall into the same trap. At this point he was not even keeping a diary of his moods and experiences. Whenever he put his thoughts on paper, as he complained in a letter to Gerald they were likely to be discovered, ripped up, stolen or sold. He does not name the people who were overlooking his every written word so jealously, and Brenda points out that Ted's work place in the garden, built for him by his father, was habitually locked, as was his study.

She readily confirmed her awareness of being only one of the women in his life. He was quite open about it to her: 'Ted was a man who needed several women . . . other men do, don't they? He isn't unique.'[10] Ted also spoke to Brenda of not wanting to be in any one woman's power again. When I wondered whether he was remembering his years with Sylvia, Brenda agreed, but added: 'He also had a very strong mother and very powerful elder sister.'[11] Ted's letters to Gerald of this period suggest that *any* woman who had the care of his children was in a position to exert blackmail.

Assia had returned to a London buzzing with the celebrity of Sylvia Plath, which after the 1965 publication of *Ariel* began to take on some of the characteristics of a cult. Hughes had been afraid of the effects that publication of Sylvia's last poems would have on his children and on his own reputation, but the first to suffer from Sylvia's fame was Assia. Both *Time* and *Life* featured *Ariel* prominently, and celebrated with a fanfare of excitement the 'strange and terrible' poems written by a beautiful young American on her last sick slide towards death.

Alvarez guessed that Assia, who would have liked to consider herself a poet, had always been envious of Sylvia's talent; she had often in his hearing mocked Sylvia's poems. The feminist movement had no part in this – indeed, Fay Weldon pointed out that both Sylvia and Assia would have been less likely to kill themselves if the feminist movement had been strong in those years, since feminism would have helped them to realize that they could cope on their own[12] and there would have been a network of support to question whether any man was worth such a sacrifice.

Most women who read Plath's poems in 1965 recognized her unhappiness and were astonished at the triumph she managed to conjure up from her situation. Assia was convinced that anyone who knew her part in the story must blame her for Sylvia's death. Nor was she imagining this hostility; several of her remaining friends agree that people sometimes turned their backs on her when she came into a room.

Ruth Fainlight and Alan Sillitoe had let their Clapham house and were living in Regent's Park, in the home of the film director Mira Hamermesh. Mira was a close friend of Assia so Ruth saw a great deal of Assia that year: 'She was terribly unhappy. ... She was fatter than she had been – a beautiful middle-aged woman. And she knew it. And she felt humiliated by it ... At the same time, she was like a nineteenth-century Russian heroine: she was formed in that mould physically, and she'd read all the books at an impressionable age.'[13]

Hughes was spending most of his days working. He was writing an important series of radio talks, *Poetry in the Making*, and an essay introducing the poetry of Emily Dickinson. He also served, with great responsibility, on the Literature Panel of the Arts Council. Between 1966 and 1968 the literary agent Giles Gordon was on the same panel and was impressed by the quality of attention Hughes brought to the task. Unlike many fellow panel members, Hughes was never voluble, but Gordon was struck by the emphasis he always placed on the greatest generosity being extended towards young poets.

Fay Weldon, who had known Assia well in the period before Sylvia's death and who recalled stories of her staying at Giles Gordon's[14] flat in Belsize Park with David Wevill, got to know her most intimately in the period after Assia had returned to London. She remembers having tea with her at a café in Charing Cross and watching her suddenly go completely white: 'And she pointed to someone who was standing at the door and said, "It's Sylvia." And I turned and it wasn't. She said, "I see her everywhere. She haunts me." '[15] Fay thought that Assia left Court Green not only because she felt that Ted's mother and father hated her, but even more because she came to feel that Ted himself blamed her for Sylvia's death: 'Ted would say "You are the dark force. You are the dark destructive force that destroyed Sylvia." '[16]

This is partly suggested by Ted's own poem 'Dreamers',[17] in which he describes Assia's orange silks and gold bracelets and her 'filthy', 'erotic' quality. Whenever he remembered Sylvia with grief, he projected his own remorse on to the figure of Assia, since she had been the source of his overpowering desire. If he expressed such feelings to her, it could hardly fail to hurt.

Fay Weldon thought that by 1968 Assia would have liked to start her life again without Ted, but could not imagine life without a man: 'She would say, "I must try to start my life without him." She even went to a dating agency ... Much more humiliating in those days than it would be now.'[18] In those days, indeed, to be alone as a woman represented a profound failure, and men were reluctant to take on any woman who already had a child. So it was that Assia's life continued to centre on Ted's phone calls, while he was spending most of the time in his garden hut, working on *Crow*, and sometimes refusing to answer the telephone.

By the time Assia was living in Clapham she had become, as Fay Weldon put it, 'stolid with misery'. When Fay met Ted in Assia's flat in Clapham Common, she observed that the drama that had once been so much part of Assia's personality had completely disappeared: 'I think she became very doleful in his presence.' Fay also observed that by now Ted was 'incredibly dismissive of her ... It was as if she was second-rate. He behaved as if she was second eleven.'[19]

To borrow a phrase from Congreve's *Way of the World* (1700), Assia had begun to 'dwindle into a wife'. Many other areas of Ted's life had begun to excite him, notably the theatre, where he continued to work extremely well with Peter Brook, who was already one of the world's most original and imaginative directors. On 15 March 1968, writing to Gerald, Ted mentions his sense of being on the brink of making 'a lot of cash', partly through having Brook direct his version of *Seneca's Oedipus* and because a great deal of work in the theatre was beginning to come his way. Hughes had at first used an existing translation of David Turner, but this he soon made over into a powerful language of his own, marked by stylized repetitions and a deliberate avoidance of syntactic connections, recalling the title poem of *Wodwo*, or even the lyric daze of Whitman-influenced American poets such as Charles Olson and his Black Mountain followers.

Olwyn continued to act as Ted's agent when he started working with Brook on a film of *King Lear* six months later.

Olwyn often stayed with Ted at Court Green. She had taken over the task of promoting Ted's work, which Sylvia had once seen as peculiarly her own domain. Although she had once liked and admired Assia, Olwyn now saw her as a drag on Ted's spirits. Elizabeth remembers meeting Olwyn in the street some time in 1968, after Assia's departure, and announcing that she had refused to allow Assia to speak to Ted on the telephone the night before.

In her desperation at failing to reach Ted, Assia may have threatened to kill herself. She certainly made such a threat many times to Mira Hamermesh, one of Assia's most loyal supporters, who tried to tease her out of repeating it. Assia's rhetorical style worked against her whenever she needed people to believe she was seriously at risk.

Ted's own personal freedom had very much increased, since by 20 October 1968, his mother and father had returned to Yorkshire, although his mother soon had to go into hospital and was suffering from pain in her knee. This would have made it easier for him to bring Assia back to live at Court Green, had he wanted to do so – or had she wanted to give up her job and have another try – but if there were any discussions about that possibility, they came to nothing. There were still storms on the domestic front, Ted wrote to Gerald, and they were likely to be arguments with Assia.

Ted had some of his closest friends to stay with him at Court Green, including Leonard Baskin and Peter Redgrove. And he was developing under the influence of the poets of Central and Eastern Europe, among whom he could now count Amichai, who represented the generation of Jews who left Germany for Palestine in the 1930s. He was also now deeply involved in the magazine he had set up with his old Cambridge friend, Daniel Weissbort: *Modern Poetry in Translation*.

For her part, Assia was working on translations from Hebrew independently from Ted, notably on a play by Eda Megged, the wife of the Israeli cultural attaché in London. Assia had only become interested in her own Jewishness in the last years of her life, partly through Ted – who was fascinated by Cabbala – and partly through the rich poetry of Amichai, which had given another dimension – colloquial, ironic, witty – to her own childhood knowledge of Hebrew.

Eda Megged became a close friend of Assia's in the autumn of 1968, often meeting her for lunch at Dickins & Jones, a department store in Regent Street. Eda was a writer herself, and wanted Assia's help in translating her own play from the Hebrew. The subject of the play – the despair of an abandoned woman alone with her child, and at the final curtain contemplating suicide – depressed Assia and, although she admired the work, she at first drew back from working on it. Once Assia agreed to take the play on, she and Eda met at least once a week, as Eda has explained in her moving memoir.[20]

To Eda, Assia seemed a woman of classical Renaissance beauty; since she had never known Assia when she was younger, she was less struck by the thickening of her body, which so many of her friends observed sadly. Assia often entertained Eda Megged in her Clapham flat, in a dark room with late-Victorian furnishings and some Burmese art on the walls. There were also a few drawings on her own in brown ink, sketches of women for the most part, which Eda found admirable. Assia served tea and biscuits and explained that she lived alone with her four-year-old daughter and very rarely went out in the evenings.

Eda remembers hearing the child crying in her sleep. 'I had never heard such bitter, heartrending crying as Shura's . . . It was a weeping with no immediate cause, crying in her sleep, the wailing of nightmares. And even when Assia picked her up and cuddled her, the child would go on whimpering and sobbing.'[21] Eda described Assia's child as having 'a long, bird-like face that seemed never to have been exposed to the sun'. She saw a resemblance to Ted in the child, but remembered Assia saying quickly that Ted had very little interest in his daughter. Eda noticed, however, that Ted was always gentle and considerate when she saw him at Assia's flat, and in a footnote she quoted an unnamed friend who corrects Assia's description of Ted's indifference to the child: 'She said that? When I saw T. and Shura together in Devon, he was very loving. He, I and Shura went to the coast together for a day – he was very attentive to her, imaginatively entering her child's world.'[22] Once when Eda had to return to catch the Tube to her flat in North London, Assia came to walk her to the station. 'We took a short cut across the broad, woody common. When I suggested it wasn't such a good idea for her to cut across the common alone on her way back, she waved her hand derisively and said, "I don't care any more." '[23]

Assia spent Christmas 1968 with Ruth Fainlight and Alan Sillitoe, since Ted had gone up to Yorkshire: 'I invited her and Shura to Mira's flat in Hanover Gate Mansions. . . . I think it was Mira . . . said that Assia said she would have killed herself over that holiday period if she had been alone . . . you know . . . I did it as a mitzvah[24] because she was lonely and needed it.' When asked what Assia spoke of, she said: 'Shura. Money. Loneliness.'[25]

Early in March 1969, Ted took Assia with him on a tour of German universities. He liked working on trains and has described how some of his best work that year was done accompanied by Assia and Shura, as they travelled from town to town. It was Assia's first visit to post-war Germany and she might well have found this traumatic. However, Martin Baker, a friend who had undertaken to phone her on the day of her return to London, received a postcard from Heidelberg gently mocking Teutonic ways. Partly because he then concluded that the trip had exorcised some of Assia's demons, he did not call as he had promised.

Assia was already forty. To friends, including Eda as well as Mira Hamermesh, Assia often spoke of losing all will to live. She was good at her work but no longer took much satisfaction in it. Perhaps that was why she was working on the translation of Eda's play, because the task helped to keep her going. She gave the manuscript of the play to a typist on 23 March 1969.

Ted and Assia still made expeditions to look for possible alternative houses. On 22 March, when Eda Megged met her at her office to go through the final version of Eda's play, Assia seemed withdrawn. 'The day was a particularly cold one ... and Assia, tall and graceful, with an astounding Renaissance beauty, struck me on this occasion as heavy and awkward in her movements ... she was dressed all in grey: a straight woollen skirt, a grey sweater, black stockings and black wedgie shoes.'[26] Her misery was palpable. Her GP had recognized the onset of a serious depression, and had prescribed pills. Eda suggested that therapy might help, but the example of Sylvia Plath had put Assia off such treatment, which was not then thought appropriate in any case for the sane and troubled. She spoke instead of the trip she was about to take to look at a house that might be suitable for Ted and herself, 'perched on a high cliff and looking out over the ocean ... I could see she was staking everything on that house, and focused on it all her hopes about her future life with Ted.'[27]

After that trip to Tyneside, where Ted and Assia discovered a splendid house outside Newcastle that delighted both of them, Assia returned to her Clapham flat, while Ted went off to Manchester to give a poetry reading. Ted wrote his last poem for *Crow* – 'A Horrible Religious Error' – on the train coming back from Manchester afterwards. It is one of the most blackly ambiguous. At the end of the lyric, just as the man's and woman's knees have buckled and they are ready to whisper, 'Your will is our peace' in mistaken allegiance to the serpent, Crow picks up the creature by the nape of its neck, then kills and eats it.

The attraction of Tyneside – at first sight a bewildering choice for Assia of a place to live – presumably lay in its distance both from Ted's parents – now back at The Beacon – and from Ted's commitments in Devon. After the reading in Manchester, Ted returned to Court Green to relieve Olwyn, who was looking after the children. As Assia took the train back to London that afternoon, she must have reflected on the distance that she would be moving away from her own work and her few friends. She must have wondered too about the large house, in which she might often be left alone with her young daughter. When she spoke to Ted on the telephone that afternoon, he failed to give her the reassurance she needed. Later, he came to attribute this failure to his own exhaustion and other distractions. After the conversation, Assia sent her German au pair out to shop, and deliberately began setting her possessions in order. Then she put a mattress and pillows next to the gas stove. She gave her daughter a drink which contained sleeping pills, then drank whisky and sleeping pills herself, before lying down with Shura in her arms and turning on the gas.

On hearing the news of Assia's death, Ted was numbed. It was a torpor he compared to a lobotomy when his much-loved mother died only a few weeks later. Assia's funeral took place on 31 March 1969. Gathered in a small chapel, which was also a crematorium, were about twenty or thirty friends, among them Fay Weldon, who remembers with horror the two coffins, the smaller of them containing the body of Shura. She saw Ted, informally dressed in an open-necked shirt, but they did not speak to one another. A few days later, Ted Hughes wrote courteously to Eda Megged to say that Assia's translation of her play was waiting for her at the offices of J. Walter Thompson.

There is a letter in the Emory archive from Olwyn to W.S. Merwin, confirming the horrifying news of Assia's death. Olwyn believed that Assia had killed herself because she felt her looks were going and because she no longer believed that Ted really wanted to set up a home with her. Olwyn made no attempt to explain why Assia killed her child as well as herself.[28] Fay Weldon believes that it was because she was so closely attached to Shura that she could not imagine the child living on without her. Ruth Fainlight saw a similar maternal intensity: 'She was the archetypal young mother doing everything for her child. If Shura hadn't died, it would have been a real problem for Shura because there was such an oppressive concentration of Assia on her.'[29]

In the May of the year of Assia's death, Ted wrote to his brother suggesting that he had come to think that it was he himself who was the true depressive, and that people who lived with him caught the darkness from him, without having similar resources to deal with it. He thought this was particularly true of Assia. In the same month he wrote to Assia's sister, saying that his life was now completely empty, and he blamed himself for not handling his last telephone conversation with Assia more sensitively. Many of their quarrels, he thought, sprang from Assia's habit of testing the strength of his love; she had threatened to kill herself so often before. Assia, who had been thinking of suicide for about two years, had made many wills. She had also secretly stolen several pages of Sylvia's manuscripts and sent them to her sister Celia to provide for Shura's future financial security. After the child's death, Celia returned these to Ted, feeling she no longer had any right to them.

In 'Fanaticism', a poem of Hughes' in *Capriccio*,[30] he writes of Assia saying:

> 'After forty I'll end it', you said laughing
> (You were serious) as you folded your future
> Into your empty clothes. Which Oxfam took.

In several of the poems in *Capriccio*, Ted attributed Assia's misery to her childhood terrors. As he wrote of her then, she was haunted by 'ancestors become demons', by the smell of burning, by her Black Forest childhood and her sense of being an alien in England. He noted sadly how many languages she spoke, and the perfection of her English, and yet how readily people sniffed out what he calls the 'lick of the tar brush', meaning her Jewish and foreign origins. He does not write as if he imagined Assia could have had any difficulty in finding another lover. His affair with Brenda Hedden is treated as an irrelevance. He could only bear to see Assia's death – rather like Sylvia's – as destined from childhood on, as if she had always been 'waiting for the knock on the door'[31].

In a letter to Assia's sister, Celia, quoted by Eilat Negev[32], Ted spoke sorrowfully of Assia as his 'true wife'. Although meant warmly and loyally, this description of Assia unintentionally suggests a possible reason for Ted looking outside their relationship for romance, even though he would never have abandoned her. In his north of England childhood, he would often have heard wives referred to as 'Mother'. At a verbal stroke, men would be claiming the indulgence of a child and be licensed to look elsewhere for their erotic pleasures. At the same time, it was a culture where marital bonds were strong, and Ted had always chafed at the inherent tensions.

Assia did not slip away from the world unlamented and forgotten, as she had feared in her depression. Jill Neville, the Australian novelist, who had worked at the same advertising agency as Assia, was late in hearing the news and was dislocated by it. Writing to Ted,[33] she spoke of Assia as a goddess. And when Yehuda Amichai heard the news of her death, he wrote:

> Half an hour ago . . .
> My crying stopped . . .
> I can't understand your death in London
> In the mist.[34]

TWELVE

Surviving

After his mother's death, in a Yorkshire hospital in May 1969, Ted retreated for a while to Lumb Bank, which he had bought impulsively on the day of her funeral. Later that autumn, he asked Brenda Hedden and her children to share his life there. The Heddens had agreed on a separation in 1968. Frieda and Nicholas already knew Brenda from time spent together in Devon, especially at Welcombe in the summer of 1969, when she had taught them to surf.

Ted had not yet fully allowed himself to feel the pain of either his mother's death or Assia's, as he confessed to his brother Gerald in a letter.[1] He was able to share his feeling of 'numbness and suspended bereavement'[2] with Brenda.

In his mother's absence Ted found that the Yorkshire branches of his family had become part of an alien world. He was well aware how he was regarded by those who knew his story, and saw him living with yet another young woman while she was still married to someone else. He and Brenda entertained Ted's Uncle Walt[3] at Lumb Bank but, however festive the dinner that Brenda prepared, Ted knew how his family felt about his situation. As he remarked defiantly to Gerald, he was beginning to think that the instincts he had had so strongly at eighteen were proving absolutely right.[4]

In 1969 Hughes' most important work was the introduction to Anne Pennington's translation of the *Selected Poems of Vasko Popa*. Hughes looked on Popa, along with Amichai, Zbigniev, Herbert and Miroslav Holub, as poets who wrote with the consciousness of a whole people behind them. They were all men who had come back as it were from the dead with a first-hand experience of the twentieth century in all its brutality, giving them an unerring sense of what really counted. For these poets, the wish to go on existing was not, as in Beckett's vision, *absurd*; on the contrary, the wish to continue living was in accord with the whole universe. Hughes longed to count himself among them. He was a survivor, as they were, although his own tragedies had been domestic. Such poets were not, in Hughes' words, 'the spoiled brats of civilization, disappointed of impossible and unreal expectations . . . They have got back to the simple animal courage of accepting the odds.' He adds, tellingly: 'I think it was Milosz, the Polish poet, who when he lay in a doorway and watched the bullets lifting the cobbles out of the street beside him realized that most poetry is not equipped for life in a world where people actually do die. But some is.'[5]

In a letter of 1970 to Peter Redgrove, one of the few close friends to whom he tried to describe his feelings in the aftermath of the loss of both Assia and his mother, he explained that he felt as if life had swallowed him whole, and was at present chewing him up and digesting him: 'until what gets shat out in the clear air and sunlight and universal peace is no longer qualified to speak of what has passed'.[6] He was not yet able to take control of his life, and he knew as much. Lumb Bank itself had come to feel oppressive. Although he had eyed it as a possible home for nearly a decade, he could not settle there. Both Olwyn and Aunt Hilda had told Brenda at different times that she should remove herself from Ted's life but Ted was reluctant to dismiss her. Some of the battles had a hilarious side, as Ted described them to Peter Redgrove, but he might have found it easier to see the humour if he had not lived through such a dark year. Ted understood that his situation was tangled up with something deep inside himself, which he had been forced to confront since the deaths of Assia and his mother. He told Redgrove that he could spend the rest of his life trying to understand and come to terms with what had happened to him.

Ted continued to believe in the healing power of poetry but, rather than using his own inner pain as material, he used myths as a means of exploring the stories by which all men live. It may be that he found the tone more easily since his success in writing children's stories such as 'The Iron Man' initially made up a bedtime story for his children. Its fiery climax owes something perhaps to Hughes' awareness of the martyrdom of Bishop Farrar about whom he had already written a poem. For an imaginative child, the attraction of the Iron Man himself lies in the creature's stoicism and lack of self-pity, characteristics that the children readily identified in their own father. Whatever else had preoccupied him during the day, by the evening he was ready to read to them before they went to sleep.

Ted and Brenda left Yorkshire in January 1970, after Ted had persuaded Brenda that his own feelings did not accord with those among his family, who had asked her to leave. They lived first in a large farmhouse in North Devon, which Ted rented, but Ted was living with Brenda at Court Green again by June 1970. He continued his relationship with Carol Orchard, however. Brenda offered an insight into the difficulty Ted clearly felt in deciding where to be and whom to be with. She writes: 'He would not let go of his "entanglements", and those who were materially inaccessible exerted the greatest power over him. Ted warned me that his "domestic life" was entry into his own inner conflicts and struggles – the women who shared his fantasy life fared better.'[7] Seamus and Maria Heaney visited Ted in early July and gave Ted and Brenda a rubric to protect Court Green. Penelope Shuttle, the poet, now Peter Redgrove's wife, remembered Ted's dark mood when she visited Ted at Court Green while Brenda was living there, and the four of them going out for dinner at a hotel that Ted insisted was haunted. Indeed, Peter Redgrove had a hallucinatory experience of his own there.[8]

It was Carol Orchard whom Hughes married in August 1970. Brenda Hedden recalls a period of considerable confusion. Ted sent an urgent note to her from London, seeking help as well as forgiveness, dated 21 August 1970, and returned the next day to Court Green.

> He assured me that nothing had changed between us, and insisted on pursuing plans already in place. I resolved within a few weeks, however, to act outside the terms of Ted's continuing 'entanglement' and by mid-September 1970 I had successfully obtained both inter-esting work and a house in Sussex.[9]

There Brenda moved, with her two pre-school age children. In the following months Ted continued, both in letters and on visits to Sussex, to express his urgent wish to keep Brenda as part of his life. His last attempt to retrieve the relationship in some form was in 1971.

However, Hughes did not mention this aspect of his life to his friends. He wrote to Peter Redgrove, inviting him to meet his new wife and assuring him emphatically that she was *not* the young woman he had introduced to him earlier that year. Carol was tall, beautiful and years younger than Ted. As Hughes explained to Redgrove, she was not par-ticularly interested in literature but had perfect taste and judgement in what she did read. Unlike Sylvia and Assia, Carol was at ease in the countryside and had no ambition for a glamorous London life. What she loved in Ted was not his success but his person. She had only one exotic strand to her ancestry and Hughes enjoyed emphasizing it, telling Redgrove that her family name had West Country gypsy origins. He may well have liked to think of her sharing some of the superstitious beliefs that might have gone along with such an inheritance, but he knew that she did not. What he was absolutely sure about was that her wholesome common sense was exceedingly good for him. Ted assured Gerald that Carol was an even greater blessing than he had dreamed she would be, as she set about making over Court Green for what would be its third time.

When an intruder set fire to part of Lumb Bank in 1971, about a year after Hughes' wedding, there was less damage than might have been feared since Ted had moved his books down to Court Green the week before. Yet carpets and bedroom floors were destroyed and a ton of papers went up in the flames, including manuscripts and journals that he had not had the courage to jettison.

There was speculation in Yorkshire that Brenda might have been involved. Two detectives from the Sussex Constabulary visited Brenda, and thorough investigations ensued, which included interviewing a series of witnesses. Travelling to the West Riding of Yorkshire from Brighton would have involved a 750–800-mile return journey and the police were fully satisfied of Brenda's innocence. Later, Ted's solicitors wrote on his behalf confirming that Ted himself did not associate Brenda in any way with the incident. She was understandably concerned to hear that a letter from Ted in Emory conjectures that she might have been involved, and was pleased to set the record straight.

In October 1970, Ted Hughes published *Crow*, which he dedicated to the memory of Assia and Shura. In this form, *Crow, From the Life and Songs of the Crow* represents about the first two thirds that Hughes had planned for the epic poem:

> Hughes' intention ... was to bring Crow at last to a river he must cross. But his way is barred by a huge foul ogress, who demands to be carried on his shoulders. On the way, her weight increases to the point where he cannot move. Then she asks him a riddle which he must answer before her weight will decrease to allow him to stagger a few more steps. This happens seven times. The first question was, 'Who paid most? Him or her?'[10]

Crow can be read as myth and legend: a quest myth, which is no doubt how Hughes presented the story to himself in order to release into his writing some of the pain that he otherwise felt with such unbearable intensity. Yet what remains memorable, especially to anyone listening to the poems read aloud by Hughes, is the way that the great evil joke at the heart of the universe is sexuality. The whole of God's creation founders in the laughter at that joke.

In Hughes' version of the creation myth, God is a baffled figure, outplayed at every turn by the trickster Crow. Take 'A Childish Prank', which opens with a man and woman lying without souls while God wonders what to do with them. Crow laughs, and bites the worm in two:

> He stuffed the head half headfirst into woman
> And it crept in deeper and up
> To peer out through her eyes
> Calling its tail-half to join up quickly, quickly
> Because O it was painful.[11]

In response, man is dragged across towards the woman as if entirely passive to the needs of the cut worm, which is at once the Son of God, the phallus and the Snake in the Garden of Eden. If sex is the ultimate joke on which the universe turns, the one insurmountable, unfunny truth is the ineluctable power of Death. Take 'Examination at the Womb-Door', one of the most memorable lyrics in the whole powerful sequence. The interrogator is not identified.

> Who owns these scrawny little feet? *Death.*
> Who owns this bristly scorched-looking face? *Death.*
> Who owns these still-working lungs? *Death.*[12]

As the questions pile up, from the first vision of a newborn creature at birth, Hughes rises to confront his terrifying knowledge. Death owns 'the whole rainy, stony earth' and 'all of space' and is stronger than hope and love.

> But who is stronger than death?
> *Me, evidently.*
> Pass, Crow.[13]

178

This poem has in it the whole Central European obsession with the arbitrary nature of survival. Some of the poems are far stranger; for instance 'Revenge Fable', in which a man attempts to destroy his mother. When she dies, his own head 'fell off like a leaf'. In 'Lovesong', two hungry lovers in their passion wake up in the morning to find themselves wearing each other's face.

Ted dedicated *Crow* to the memory of Assia and Shura, and some of the poems intended for that sequence – which he did not find the heart to continue after Assia's death in 1969 – found their final home in *Cave Birds*.

Now happy in his new marriage to Carol, Hughes travelled with her as part of a group of English poets, including Denis Enright, Peter Porter and Dannie Abse, who were visiting Israel for the first time. Dannie observed that Hughes got on to the plane with a tiger's foot in his pocket, which evidently gave the security guards on the Israeli airline El Al some problems. As Dannie remembered, Hughes had enormous authority even then, although he was several years younger than the other poets apart from Porter:

> When we were squabbling about who'd read first, and who'd read last, he said, 'You will read first. You will read second. You will read fourth,' and they all accepted it. So he had an authoritative presence even then, and obviously even earlier before I knew him ... In Israel he read *Crow*, and I always remember wondering how he felt when *Crow* was being read and people were laughing in the audience. So I asked him – and he was delighted [at the laughter]. There are people obviously who can see the comic aspect of *Crow* – I must say I don't – and I was worried they were laughing at the wrong time, and felt myself, as a Jew, responsible for their laughter. He was very pro-Israel and I remember him saying to me that he wouldn't give one yard, one inch, back to the Arabs.[14]

Ted was moved and impressed by Israel and its people, and particularly overwhelmed by Jerusalem. He found the rock – where Abraham was to sacrifice Isaac – the most electrical place on earth. (It is of course inside the Aqsa Mosque, which sits on the old foundations of the ancient Jewish temple.) It was only a few years since Israel had, to the amazement of the world, defeated Egypt after Nasser blocked their access to the Suez Canal. Many liberal Westerners, who in those days still remembered the valiant but doomed courage of the Jewish fighters in the Warsaw ghetto in the Second World War, feared the young state would go under in 1967. For the most part they were sympathetic to the ill-armed Jews surrounded by so many enemies. In the final outcome, the Israelis defeated the attacking Arab states in the Six Day War.

Abse had cause to remember Hughes' strength and rapid responses with gratitude. On one occasion, they were going round a corner in a typically overfilled Israeli taxi, when the door sprang open. Only Hughes' quick arm saved Dannie from falling out on to the road. Dannie thought that Ted and Carol were on their honeymoon, which bespeaks their closeness on that trip, and he mentioned his great admiration for Carol's skill at bargaining in the Jerusalem bazaars when he was buying a present for his wife Joan.

In 1971, Ted packed Assia and Shura's belongings into crates and shipped them to her sister Celia in Canada. The ship sank and her sister feared that every last trace of Assia had been lost. After some months, as if miraculously, the crates resurfaced and were recovered.

The unstoppable rise of Sylvia Plath's reputation received a new and decisive spiral upwards in 1971 with the first of two articles by Al Alvarez in the *Observer*. These were trails for his forthcoming book, *The Savage God: A Study of Suicide*, which gave an account of Plath's last year, leading up to her taking her own life in February 1963. The effect on Hughes of reading Alvarez's account was devastating. Frieda and Nicholas, then aged eleven and nine, had been sent away to boarding school. Unable to bear the thought of their reading of their mother's desolation in Alvarez's cool prose or hearing of it from some knowing school friend, he brought them home to tell them the story himself. There had never before seemed a right moment for him to explain that their mother had taken her own life. Nor was it easy for him then. It took him the whole of the weekend to reach the point where he felt he could explain that their mother had killed herself. Frieda took the news very calmly, saying she had always guessed as much.

The furious letter that Hughes wrote to Alvarez to demand that the second section of his piece be pulled from the newspaper was, surprisingly, effective: the *Observer* and Alvarez capitulated, although the chapter appeared nevertheless in Alvarez's best-selling book.[15] As far as Hughes' demonization was concerned, however, the damage had begun. It would follow him almost to the end of his life.

That year was essentially the beginning of the feminist movement.

Germaine Greer had already published *The Female Eunuch*, and in the United States Betty Friedan and others had begun to make their mark, alerting women to their foolishness in allowing themselves to be exploited by their husbands, and urging them to higher self-esteem. None of this had much relevance to Plath and Hughes, but the suicide of Sylvia Plath gave the movement an incontestable female genius who had suffered and died. From this time on, Hughes was to become the target of feminist hatred.

For Hughes' part, he found it humiliating to have his late wife's last days exhumed, as Alvarez had done in his memoir, for classroom discussion.[16] He could not imagine how someone who had once been his friend could have persuaded himself it was necessary. The force of the letter needs little further comment:

> You tell yourself maybe it is all literary history, she belongs to the public, she gave herself to the public etc. You know that is rubbish. She didn't give her family, and she didn't hand over the inner life of her children ... can't you see they won't be able to get it out of their minds? They won't be able to escape it, because you've programmed their acquaintance, the general public.[17]

Ted feared that Frieda and Nicholas would have to cope with an even more dangerous situation than had Sylvia, with her father's early death. He also feared that their image of her was going to decide their lives: 'You have robbed them of any natural way of dealing with her death.'[18]

In this cogently argued letter to Alvarez, many pages long, Hughes also expresses some of the feelings he had not hitherto voiced about what he felt was the 'treachery' of Sylvia's writings. He mentions the effect on their children, and perhaps also on Sylvia's mother, but he must have felt too that, in creating great triumphant poetry that pilloried him unjustly, she had betrayed their marriage as much in her own way as his adultery had in his. For Alvarez, he had nothing but contempt, regarding the article as indefensible journalism, masquerading as material that students could use to obtain good grades and better jobs.

As a postscript, he accused Alvarez of knowing him and Sylvia far less well than he pretended, particularly objecting to the suggestion that there was some sort of artistic jealousy between himself and Sylvia. It is a very telling letter: 'It is infuriating for me to see my private experience and feeling reinvented for me, in that crude, bland, unanswerable way, and interpreted and published as official history.'[19]

Alvarez had not realized that Hughes had concealed the facts of Sylvia's death from his children, and felt there was no way that they would not have found out in any case. Both men skirted the most explosive fact that the children would have to discover: namely that it was a separation between Ted and Sylvia that had precipitated their mother's despair. Alvarez's reply was dignified and equally cogent. For ten years, he wrote, he had done his best to promote Ted's and Sylvia's poetry because he believed they were the most gifted poets of their generation: 'Sylvia knew this and knew I understood in some way what she was trying to do. That, presumably, is why she came to me with her poems after the separation.'[20] Alvarez believed that his article was carefully and tactfully written, a suggestion that Ted rebutted easily: 'I see only care of a very narrow, technical sort – care to get the tone right and keep it right, and I can believe that was difficult, and depressing too.' Crucially, Hughes speaks of Sylvia's death as 'the sickness of my life as it must be also of her mother's and as it will be of Frieda's and Nick's'.[21]

Hughes knew that the effect of Alvarez's article – and soon his book – would be open 'to the mob, with official notices, the most sacred part of mine and my children's life'.[22] All the forces that Hughes identifies in the same letter – women's lib, the insanity of United States' society, the schizophrenia of modern man, and so on – would shortly focus their attention on him. He was right to fear them. Hughes was a naturally private man, even a shy one in his earlier days, and he felt such public animosity keenly. His instinct was to be proved right: the silence and forgetfulness that he had hoped would allow him some space to make a life with his new wife were never to be his. There were paradoxical elements in his situation. At a time when young people, freed from unwanted pregnancies by the pill, enjoyed a culture of free love that earlier generations could barely imagine, Ted was beginning to pay for his affair with Assia more grossly than any other man of his time. From now on, all he could hope for was a series of holidays from the attention of the English media.

The creation of *Orghast*, with his friend, the director Peter Brook, was one such holiday. This was a play based on a language of noises invented by Ted, which loosely told the story of Prometheus. Brook thought the play could be made comprehensible to primitive peoples across Africa if his actors learned the correct skills. And the trip with Brook to the Shiraz Festival in Persia, which lasted from May to September 1970, was another such opportunity. Surprisingly, for all the splendour of the Shah's palace and the warmth of the Persian welcome, Ted reported[23] that he found the food filthy and was worried about possible food poisoning.

He was engaged in writing an introduction to his selection of Shakespeare's verse, setting out some of the forces at work in Shakespeare's inner world, which he was later to develop into the 'tragic equation' of *Shakespeare and the Goddess of Complete Being*. Even in its earlier form, the preoccupations that he identified in Shakespeare had a resonance in his own life: the hatred of puritanism, for instance; the passionate interest in occult neoplatonism; the Rosicrucian mysteries, and the worship of a female goddess.

There were other important new ventures. Hughes' letters to Gerald had for many years been filled with entrepreneurial plans of one kind and another, some fanciful. In January 1971, Ted proposed that Olwyn set up the Rainbow Press, which published limited editions of some of Hughes' poems not included in *Crow*, and a book of poems by Hughes, Alan Sillitoe and Ruth Fainlight. In April 1971, Ted also arranged for the publication of Plath's *Crossing the Water*, and in September the same year her *Winter Trees*. These limited editions, in very beautiful bindings on expensive paper, were ways of publishing Plath's poems quietly without drawing the attention of a readership he now felt to be hostile. It was a scheme that was successful financially, and presumably that is why it came to be perceived as yet another way of exploiting Plath's literary inheritance.

His marriage continued to be happy. Nevertheless, in 1971 Ted fell into a depression that led him to wonder whether he had wasted his entire life. In his depression, Lumb Bank became so horrible to him that he wanted to sell it, and he even found it difficult to live at Court Green. He wrote to Gerald: 'From the age of about 16–17 my life has been quite false, and since Ma's death and Assia's this false arrangement has been falling to pieces with great drama. Finally I think I've reached the end of it – where I can begin again . . .'[24] Unfortunately, the key to this letter is in a sentence that is scratched out so vehemently as to be illegible. It was at the age he speaks of that Ted had committed himself wholeheartedly to literature and he may well have become disillusioned about a dedication that left him so vulnerable to the world's assaults. Fortunately, Carol was a steadying presence, and he knew he must not inflict his past on her any more than was inevitable.

The glare of media attention, which soon fell on Hughes again, was precipitated by his allowing *The Bell Jar* to be published in the United States. He had always been reluctant to permit this, because the book contained a portrait of Sylvia's mother that was bound to be hurtful to Aurelia Plath. However, Hughes' hand was forced when Fran McCullough, an editor at Harper & Row, discovered that US copyright law only gave protection for seven years to a book published abroad by an American citizen. Plath's rising celebrity made *The Bell Jar* a hot property, and it seemed inevitable that some publisher would issue a pirate edition in the United States if Hughes took no action. Once this was pointed out to him, Hughes agreed that it was only common sense to secure future royalties for himself and his growing children.

He cannot have expected the huge income that accrued, but by now any Plath publication was assured of a wide readership. This queer, slangy novel, as Plath had described it, missed its due the first time round in its UK edition. This time, *The Bell Jar* was in the top ten bestsellers in the States for several months, and earned sums in excess of £50,000 – an astronomical fortune, in the days when a university head of department would earn no more than £3000 a year – even though there was no certainty that the success would continue, and Hughes himself regarded it as a one-off windfall. However, the price that windfall was to be high. Plath's reputation was now such that Hughes' private tragedy was about to become public property on a grand scale.

When Sylvia's mother asked him to release the copyright of Sylvia's letters to her, he felt he could hardly refuse Aurelia the chance to correct the hurtful image of herself as a monstrous mother in *The Bell Jar* by showing Sylvia, whose letters revealed her as a loving and appreciative daughter. Yet Hughes guessed shrewdly that these letters, published as *Letters Home*, were bound to be damaging. His motive for releasing their copyright has often been misunderstood, and not only by his enemies. Janet Malcolm quoted a letter of his to Aurelia about *The Bell Jar*, written early in 1970, which suggested that he needed money to buy another house; it also suggested that on this basis a deal was struck for the publication of *The Bell Jar*, followed by the release of *Letters Home*. A photocopy of a letter to Janet Malcolm in the archive at Emory[25] shows that this was not so. That year – 1970 – preceded the 'detonation' of Sylvia's success. When Aurelia had made clear her initial reluctance to publishing *The Bell Jar* in America, Hughes dropped *both* the idea of its US publication *and* the plan to buy the house. It was only when the US copyright situation was clarified to Aurelia, as it had been to Ted, and she had accepted the fact that the book was bound to appear in the States anyway, that Sylvia's novel was published. It is a cogent explanation of how *Letters Home* came to be published, in what Hughes describes as the 'general calamity'[26] of *The Bell Jar*'s success.

The decision to send Frieda and Nicholas away to school had been a wrench for Ted, since they were so altogether the centre of his life; but it left him with far more time to think and work. While Carol plunged herself into refurbishing Court Green, Hughes now began to take pleasure in the acquisition of unusual objects for his home: animal skins, the skulls of animals, especially badgers, and the claws of eagles, for instance, some of which he asked Gerald to send him from Australia. He wrote to thank Gerald particularly for a python skin. These trophies seemed to excite him as much as anything else in his life on a farm where he now owned a sizeable acreage of land. Hughes thought of the money from *The Bell Jar* as 'the kids' money' and was always looking for safe places, such as land, to invest it. The idea was to build up a good herd of beef-producing cows.[27] Carol's knowledge of and interest in farming helped Hughes to solve many of his problems in retreating from the world, although he did not cut himself off from London entirely.

Hughes' life, however, continued to be eaten away by the interest surrounding Sylvia. As her poems began to receive widening critical appraisal, Hughes discovered that the critics who disapproved of them could involve him as painfully as Alvarez's praise. David Holbrook, whose Leavisite training made Plath an obvious target for moral condemnation, particularly challenged the popularity that her poems now enjoyed. In response to a letter from Hughes, he wrote on 24 January 1973:

> You ask me to feel concern for your children (and I do). I begin there with Sylvia Plath. The poem 'Edge' is very beautiful and it seduces us into feeling that it would be perfect to fold one's children back into one's body and destroy them and oneself. People love this poem, and fail to see to what they have given assent ... I talked to a group of psychotherapists in London. They related how often they were fighting to enable a patient to go on living – when some cultural work was pushing them over the edge. Sylvia Plath's poetry especially, they said, tended to do this.[28]

Holbrook was not condemning Plath and, when describing the 'cracked structure of the self', he wrote: 'In the face of such agony, how could anyone not feel a deep respect and poignant compassion for the predicament and for the brave record of the suffering.'[29]

Between 1973 and 1974 Ted was mildly ill and decided for some weeks that he had throat cancer. Indeed, he went so far as to make his will. Fortunately, a throat specialist was able to diagnose nothing more serious than a viral infection of the tonsils. At the same time, he suddenly found himself with unexpected financial commitments, which looked like eating up some of the huge windfall gains from *The Bell Jar*. He wanted to find £11,000 to help Olwyn buy a new house, £12,000 or more for refurbishing Lumb Bank, and there was US tax of £5000 to pay for 1972 – after Sylvia's novel had succeeded in the States – plus £4000 UK supertax. It was rather more than he had previously spent in his entire life.

One reason for his depression in 1974 was his final realization that there was no chance of his brother Gerald ever coming back to live in England. Ted's love for Gerald was probably one of the most enduring and sustaining forces in his life. He had bought Moortown, a farm of ninety-five acres near Winkleigh, about five miles from Court Green, with the hope that Gerald might return to England to run it. In the meantime Carol's father, Jack Orchard, an enormously capable figure whom Peter Redgrove characterized as an 'earth father', was in control of its day-to-day administration. Ted believed that Gerald was unhappy in Australia but, whether he was or not, he did not give up his job in the aircraft firm where he worked to take up the offer. The discovery that he could never look forward again to more than occasional visits from his brother knocked Ted out, as he put it, even though he received a Gold Medal for poetry in 1974. Olwyn believed that the chief reason for his depression during these years was astrological.

THIRTEEN

The Accused

Although Ted Hughes had been invited for many years to read at the most prestigious venues in America, he very rarely accepted. The novelist Susan Fromberg Schaeffer and her husband Neil Schaeffer, both Professors in the English Department at Brooklyn College, had become friends with Hughes while on vacation in England. They tried on several occasions to persuade him to take up an academic post in New York, which was his for the asking and would not involve him in a heavy teaching load. Ted always refused politely. He had never wanted to be part of an academic institution, and his earlier distrust of American suburban values had deepened. With the growth of Plath's reputation, he had a new reluctance to visit the States. Feminists who had once blamed Sylvia's suicide on his desertion were now beginning to accuse him of cruelty during their marriage, using Sylvia's own poems such as 'The Jailer', and particularly 'Daddy' to suggest torture and black magic.

Ted's unease about his likely reception in the States was realistic enough. Plath was becoming 'a true cult figure', as Marjorie Perloff reported[1] in the *Iowa Review*: 'At this writing, the Savile Bookshop[2] has a huge window display where copies of *The Colossus*, *The Bell Jar* and *Ariel* encircle a very large photograph [of Sylvia] which rests against A. Alvarez' *The Savage God: A study of suicide*, that ultimate tribute to Sylvia Plath, our Extremist Poet par excellence.'

Plath certainly brought out extreme reactions. Her gigantic celebrity, alongside accusations of domestic abuse and Nazi proclivities, led to passionate threats of violent revenge, in Robin Morgan's poem, 'The Arraignment'. In the first stanza of this poem,[3] Morgan writes:

How can
I accuse
Ted Hughes
of what the entire British and American
literary and critical establishment
has been at great lengths to deny
without ever saying it in so many words, of course,
the murder of Sylvia Plath.[4]

The rest of the poem attacks Hughes for making money out of his dead wife's work, and ends with a threat to dismember Hughes and stuff his penis in his mouth. The indignation, though heartfelt, was a dangerous hyperbole: even Hughes' angriest critics did not believe that he had *murdered* Sylvia.[5]

In the circumstances, keeping away from the American literary scene must have looked like common sense, although Hughes' habitual quiet dignity when reading his poems could have done something to dispel the caricature. In any case, just as his instinct in the face of the wildest accusations was to remain silent, his instinct in the face of physical threat was to refuse confrontation. When Hughes did make a brief visit to the United States in 1972, Carol did not accompany him, but he called to see Lucas Myers, who was now living with his wife Agi in the Catskills. Ted left a note – since Myers was out when he dropped in – congratulating him on remaining married for so long and advising him not to be too much involved in acquiring land and property.[6]

Since that was exactly what Hughes and Carol were engaged in at that time, it seems an odd piece of advice. Hughes was far less reclusively rural, however, than legend suggests. He enjoyed the part he played in the labour of farming – which fed into some of the finest poems of this decade – but he was not pinned to Moortown. Jack Orchard's management and Carol's own involvement made it possible for him to travel up to London frequently for meetings – for instance as one of the judges of the Gregory Awards for Young Poets, or to make decisions connected to Rainbow Press. He enjoyed meeting many of the poets he admired who were published in *Modern Poetry in Translation*, or poets from the Poetry International Festivals of the previous decade, on their arrival in London. At first these visitors were entertained in restaurants, but after February 1972, when Olwyn moved to her North London house in Chetwynd Road, Tufnell Park, she organized hospitality there. To begin with,

Hughes stayed with Olwyn, then rented a small flat in Kentish Town.

However, he always returned to Court Green at weekends. Carol rarely travelled up from Devon for literary dinners in London, although she was a wonderful hostess at Court Green to those of Hughes' friends who were invited there. Since Olwyn was then my agent, I was present at some of the London dinners, which often went on into the small hours of the morning.

In England, Hughes' reputation remained as high as ever. When the Cambridge Poetry Festival committee[7] received his acceptance to read there in April 1975, there was boundless excitement, even though the distinguished poets who were already reading at the Festival included the Czech Miroslav Holub, the Pole Zbigniew Herbert, and Robert Creeley and John Ashbery from the United States. When Hughes gave a reading in the Union Chamber, it was impossible to get a seat; people listened to him read the poems from *Crow* in an impassioned stillness. Alone among the poets, Hughes refused to allow television cameras to record his performance. Perhaps some atavistic superstition lay behind his dislike of the cameras; or he may have remembered that the last time he read for television was on the weekend of Assia's suicide. It was an unintentional stroke of public relations' genius, however, since those who were present felt all the more privileged to be there. Afterwards, at a party in my Cambridge house, he sat quietly among the press of people eager to meet him. As always, there were many young women attracted to his side.

It was through me that year that Ted Hughes met the Russian poet Yevgeny Yevtushenko and his wife Jan. Yevtushenko had come to see me, unexpectedly, a year earlier in Cambridge, after he had mentioned my translations of the great Russian poet Marina Tsvetaeva to George Steiner, at a dinner in Churchill College and been told that I lived in the city. Arriving late in the evening, Yevtushenko urged me – since I was writing a biography of Tsvetaeva – to visit Russia with my husband, where he would look after us. (He generously made good his promise in the autumn of 1974.) It so happened that my birthday on 24 October 1975 fell during a week in which I had arranged to teach at the Arvon Foundation, at Totleigh Barton in Devon, so I invited Yevgeny and Jan to join us.

The Arvon Foundation was originally the idea of two poets – John Moat and John Fairfax – who set it up in 1968. Moat and Fairfax tutored the first Arvon course – at the Beaford Centre in Devon for a group of school children – and invited Ted to be a guest reader. The format of these courses has remained remarkably stable over the thirty-plus years that the Foundation has been in existence. The shopping is done for the whole group by the resident centre directors, but the cooking and washing up are shared out on a rota basis, to include both those who have come to learn and those who have come to teach. It gives the whole group a feeling of unity, enhanced by shared dormitories and shared pre-occupations. Ted, who was excited by the atmosphere and by the whole idea of writers living side by side, sharing chores as they dedicated themselves to literary work, threw his considerable weight behind the scheme.

Totleigh Barton, an isolated farmhouse surrounded by several acres of land, was initially purchased by Moat and his wife Antoinette in 1972, and then leased to the Arvon Foundation. Its success was soon evident in the number of writers applying for places on the courses. Ted had the inspired idea of solving the problem of what to do with Lumb Bank by setting up a second writers' centre there. In the summer of 1972, six months before David Pease was appointed as the National Director of the Arvon Foundation, Ted and Carol worked with him to adapt Lumb Bank for the purpose.[8]

The Arvon Foundation and its two centres became one of the most important ways in which Hughes encouraged aspiring writers. On a promotional leaflet, designed to attract support for Arvon in 1986, Ted was asked whether he thought an Arvon course could discover new talent. He replied: 'What these courses do is reveal that a large proportion of people have some talent, given the right conditions for it to show itself ... We often hear that talent will always find a way; it is not true. The few who emerge as artists have often been helped by the most unlikely strokes of luck in the way of human contacts.'[9]

Yevtushenko came the more willingly to Devon in October 1975 because he knew Ted Hughes had also promised to be there. He and his wife Jan had some difficulty finding the farmhouse at Totleigh Barton; while we waited their arrival, all sitting at a long trestle table, we drank some of the wine we had brought for the occasion. Yevtushenko's arrival was greeted by a mixture of excitement and awe, since he was then at the height of his reputation.

My fellow tutor, was my friend Emma Tennant. Emma is the daughter of Baron Glenconnor by his second marriage. She is tall, striking, witty, animated and – at least in appearance – boundlessly confident. She was brought up in a nineteenth-century Gothic castle in Scotland, and at seventeen was duly presented at court as a debutante. Three times married – first to the son of Henry Yorke (Henry Greene, the celebrated novelist) then to Alexander Cockburn, a well-known left-wing journalist, and (briefly) to Christopher Booker, an editor of the satirical magazine *Private Eye* – Emma already had a life of reckless ebullience behind her. In her early twenties she had published a novel rather in the manner of Evelyn Waugh under a pseudonym, and was rapidly coming to be known in her thirties as the highly original author of several science-fiction and Gothic novels, notably *Hotel de Dream*. She had also launched the literary newspaper *Bananas*, which included work by Angela Carter and J.G. Ballard, among other writers both distinguished and unknown.[10] As Tennant admits in *Burnt Diaries* (published in 1999), her acceptance of the invitation to teach a group of aspirant writers had been undertaken with the hope of seeing something more of Ted Hughes, whom she had already contacted as a possible contributor to *Bananas*. Emma reports in *Burnt Diaries* that Ted made his sexual interest in her evident, and she took his offer to make a writing table for her, as he once had for Sylvia, as a sign of his readiness to recognize something of Sylvia in her lively cleverness.

The following day my husband, who had arrived from Cambridge for my birthday, and I were driven with Emma to The George, a pub in the nearby village of Hatherleigh. Yevtushenko talked with his usual flamboyance, while Ted watched and listened. Later, we moved on to Court Green, and Yevtushenko returned to London.

For both my husband and myself the most exciting event of the day was our first meeting with Ted's close friend Leonard Baskin, who was staying at Court Green. Baskin was altogether more suspicious of Yevtushenko than I was, and I remember Ted questioning me closely – after Yevtushenko had left – about how friendship with a representative of the Soviet regime could be reconciled with knowledge of what was being done to Jewish refuseniks in Russia. Yevtushenko had been as pressing to Ted in his invitation to visit Russia as he had been to me, although his motives were very different.[11] Hughes' presence in the Soviet Union would have represented a huge personal coup for Yevtushenko, and Hughes was aware of this. He and Philip Larkin were the only contemporary English poets thought worthy of translation into Russian at that time. Any journey that Hughes made to Russia would be a political statement, and it was one he was unwilling to make at a time when so many of his friends in the satellite countries of the Russian Empire were silenced and ignored. Nevertheless, he found Yevtushenko an exuberant companion and they continued to meet in London. The long evenings that they spent together were high points for Ted in a period otherwise consumed by ongoing problems in handling the Plath estate.

Some of these were of his own making, although his reasons for releasing to Aurelia Plath the copyright he held in all Sylvia's writings, so that she could pursue her plan of publishing *Letters Home*, were entirely decent. For a time the thought of releasing the material seemed to offer Ted some form of psychological release, even though he knew that six or seven years of his life would become public as a result and that he was bound to become an even more dubious figure in romantic legend. In April 1974, Fran McCullough, the Plath editor at Harper & Row, appeared altogether sympathetic to him, and wrote amusing letters about the difficulties she was having with the sick and grieving Aurelia, 'who would just sit and cry all day and tell me stories about Otto (all quite hair-raising)'.[12] McCullough wrote as if Sylvia's letters would only make an interesting book if she succeeded in persuading Aurelia to accept its reduction to a manageable length, and her tone, as she wrote about cutting and pasting and bullying, was misleadingly jolly. Notably, her letters to Ted include a request that he, Frieda and Nicholas sign a document saying that none of them would sue about Sylvia's derogatory remarks.

It was only when Hughes saw the work in galley form in January 1975 that he realized what he had done in agreeing to let Aurelia publish the book. For Sylvia's letters to her mother, written after her separation from Ted, were filled not only with entirely understandable hurt and rage but also with wildly inaccurate accusations, which could only fuel the hatred felt for Hughes in America. And Aurelia had pointed up her daughter's miserable situation with commentary of her own. Dismally, he began to understand that he was now to face a far worse pillorying than anything he had undergone so far.

It was Olwyn who made the first cool and factual protest about the contents of the book, insisting that McCullough acknowledge the fact that Ted had generously made over the copyright of the letters and that she also state that Aurelia had made a selection from them. In January 1975, Hughes wrote a remarkable letter to Aurelia Plath,[13] wondering whether Aurelia really *believed* all that Sylvia had written. Sylvia's assertion that she had been abandoned without money, for instance, was not true, and her claim that Ted had spent most of what they had saved could be disproved by examining his cheque stubs and statements from the period, which he had preserved.[14]

Hughes challenged much of Aurelia's interpolated comment. Aurelia had suggested that Sylvia burned the typescript of a completed novel that took the story of their relationship from their first meeting at St Botolph's to the marital break-up. Hughes did not believe that a second novel could have been completed in the time at her disposal between their separation and her death.[15] He throws considerable doubt on the existence of a complete manuscript. 'Did you see it?' he writes quietly, wondering in which months it was feasible for her to have written such a novel about the breakdown of their marriage, simultaneously with her great outburst of poetry.

Hughes reminded Aurelia that one of the reasons he had given permission for her to publish these letters was to correct Sylvia's unjust picture of her as a destructive mother, so there were some ironies in her now using Sylvia's letters to blacken Hughes, who found the portrait that emerged of himself, not only in the letters but even more in Aurelia's commentary, extremely damaging. Certainly many of the letters, written at a time of great rage, present a false picture of the marriage. Most observers would agree with Hughes' description of himself as being 'easygoing' in his demands on Sylvia, while she found life unmanageable unless she had four hours every morning in which to work.

Hughes knew that Sylvia's most angry letters were going to be read in a kind of open court, where he would not be represented, and he particularly objected to being depicted as a husband for whom everything had been sacrificed. For the first time, in this letter, we hear how the impulse to have children had been Sylvia's alone and how, in spite of his reluctance to give up their projected life as wanderers, those children had come to be the centre of his own. It was inaccurate, he said, for Aurelia to speak of Sylvia renouncing a subservient role, since she had never had one.

Hughes admitted that it had probably been his mistake to move to Devon. The decision came from his fixed conviction that writing was work as much as studying to become a dentist, and could not be sustained on a part-time basis while taking a job to pay the mortgage. At no point in this lengthy letter does he deny the justice of Sylvia's rage against him on discovering his affair with Assia. At the same time he defended the Hughes family, particularly his mother, who had written begging Sylvia to be patient and trying to calm her – reminding her (possibly rather tactlessly) that she still had everything, even if Ted was absent. Both his mother and Gerald had written to Sylvia as if what Ted calls his 'idiocy' was only temporary.[16] There is also a long rebuttal of any wish on his part for a divorce, and an understanding that future biographers would go through his papers looking for the truth of these matters.

According to McCullough, Aurelia took on board these first comments with equanimity, but by the end of January Hughes himself had revised his stance considerably.[17] He could see the effect that the book was bound to have on his future life and on those close to him. Accordingly he wrote and suggested far more serious revisions, one of which would have involved ending *Letters Home* before his marriage to Plath began to break up. It would still be a sizeable volume and, Hughes suggested, it would still contain the most brilliant parts, certainly satisfying Aurelia's original requirement: to offer another version of her daughter's attitude towards her.

McCullough was horrified at the suggestion of this compromise, which would have involved removing letters that refer to his and Sylvia's life together in Court Green. Hughes wanted to take out any mention of Court Green, however innocuous, which might establish his home as Plath's monument, reducing his life there with Carol to a curatorship: 'Her ghost is too strong here as it is – and I've enough experience of its effects on people near me,' he wrote.

It must have rather surprised Hughes that Aurelia did not comply, but that was in fact the case. In March 1975, she reminded Ted that he had always known there would be references to him in the book, and that she had already cut out a great many personal details. When she finally felt the necessity of consulting lawyers, they advised her that Hughes had been given ample opportunity to see the manuscript, that cuts had already been made according to his suggestions and that his last demands were unreasonable, given that he was a public figure and that the details of his career and marriage to Sylvia Plath were widely known. Nevertheless, Aurelia agreed to remove references to Court Green and a few further cuts were made. Publication in England was left to Ted, who delayed it. The names of Olwyn and Ted were taken out of the acknowledgements in *Letters Home*.

This transatlantic drama was being played out against a life of peace and fruitfulness, of which by far the best record appears in Ted's poetry of the mid-1970s, giving as affecting an account of English farming life as he had once given of the wild life on the moors: equally unsentimental, even violent, but with all the lyricism of his early poetry. The poems in both *Season Songs* and *Moortown Diary* came out of the happiness he felt at having a farm of his own, which was managed by Jack Orchard with enormous benignity.

The majority of the poems in *Season Songs* were written between 1973 and 1974, although some had been conceived earlier as 'Autumn Songs for Children's Voices' while he was writing *Crow* in 1968. Introducing these poems on the radio, he spoke of wanting to remain 'within the hearing of children'. The contents of *Moortown Diary* and *Season Songs* overlap; indeed, the poem 'Sheep' is in both collections. It is a poem marked with compassion as Hughes watches a sheep, grieving for her sick lamb:

> Its stubby
> White wool pyramid head, on a tottery neck,
> Had sad and defeated eyes, pinched, pathetic,
> Too small,[18]

In the second section of the poem, Hughes takes on the bewildered voice of a ewe, terrified by the buzzing noise of the saw that shears off her wool. It is an act of empathy equal to his taking on the voice of a hawk, and equally striking. In the third part, Hughes becomes no more than an observer as lambs try to find their mothers among these now-shorn strangers. The realities of farming are not pretty, and Hughes does not attempt to make them so, well aware of how very much farmed creatures want to live, as he notes in 'A March Calf'. The poem that most people remember, however, is 'February 17th', Hughes' overwhelming account of a sheep unable to give birth and his own struggle to save the mother's life by hooking out the body of the dead lamb.

When Jack Orchard was diagnosed with cancer of the bronchus, which soon developed secondaries, Hughes realized that his whole relationship to the countryside was endangered. When Jack died, in February 1976, Hughes felt as if a linchpin of his stability had been taken away. It was not only that he loved the man and that Carol was stunned with grief; he was uncertain if he could cope with a farm and cattle alone. When Peter Redgrove heard of Orchard's death, he was concerned to hear that Hughes was on the verge of giving up the farm. He was afraid that such a decision would leave Hughes without an anchor and perhaps, too, without a physical outlet for his vast energies. Hughes' effortless relation to landscape makes it easy for him to use an old trope movingly, but in 'The Day He Died', a poem in memory of Jack Orchard, the lines that follow are not so much a pathetic fallacy as a literal record of his inner state:

> The bright fields looked dazed.
> Their expression is changed.
> They have been somewhere awful
> And come back without him.[19]

In March 1976, however, Hughes set off with his own father, whom he hoped Gerald might look after for a time, towards Australia, and the Adelaide Literary Festival.

FOURTEEN

Australia

Melbourne in Southern Australia is far removed from the landscape that Gerald had described in his letters, or from that of
Lawrence's *Kangaroo*, for that matter, which is set largely on
the Eastern Australian seaboard. Yet the fragipani trees were exotic, the
scent of their flowers was everywhere, and it was very hot. For all the
country's seeming modernity, there were snakes in the suburban under-
growth and red-backed spiders in the bathrooms, whose dangers to the
unwary Australians still like to describe with relish. All that Hughes
saw of the vast uncultivated land[1] was the primeval scrub between the
bungalows, but he was aware that the light was different in Australia,
casting a 'weird disastrous darkness; over everything'.[2] Ted stayed with
Gerald and his sister-in-law long enough to see his father safely into their
hands, and flew on to Adelaide alone.

Adelaide is a pretty town, with red-brick Victorian churches and an
English feel to it, suggesting that it might well be rather dull outside
the Festival season. During the Festival, however – one of the largest
multicultural festivals anywhere – the theatres are alive with the best plays
from all over the world; playwrights, companies of dancers, musicians
and opera singers attend one another's performances and are lavishly
entertained. Many of the smaller events take place in open tents.

Hughes' reading at Adelaide proved to be a hideous occasion, during
which placards were held up accusing him of Sylvia's murder, and women
in the audience hurled angry abuse at him. It was an unusually scandalous
event, which Michael Boddy, then in Australia, remembers reading about
in the newspapers with horror. The transcript shows that Ted continued
to give his reading, although his comments between poems are uncharacteristically stilted. At his side, confronting the hostile crowd, was Jill

Barber, the beautiful Australian-born press co-ordinator of the Tenth Adelaide Writers Week. She was in her late twenties, with high cheekbones, sparkling eyes and an athletic build. Ted found her presence an unexpected tonic and, in spite of the hostility he had encountered there, began to enjoy his remaining time in Australia. On his last day, he visited a farm seventy miles outside Adelaide, and marvelled at the kookaburra and the lyre-bird, whose cries evoked in his mind the calls of lizards or prehistoric animals.

Although Jill had a well-established career in public relations behind her in Australia, she had literary ambitions of her own and was already committed to a life in London; she had bought a flat in Fulham that was in some need of refurbishment. While Hughes' father remained in Australia with Gerald, Jill and Ted returned to England separately, though already lovers.[3] Hughes' fellow writers, including Ian Hamilton, were neither shocked nor censorious. By 24 September 1976, Ted and Jill were often seen together at London literary events, as Jill casually reported to her mother:

> I have just been down in Whitstable nibbling oysters . . . My big news is that I went to a poetry reading at the Festival Hall by Yevtushenko and Ian McKellen. Ted took me and his sister Olwyn to the special dinner afterwards given by Yevtushenko, Yevgeny (nickname, pron: Zhenia). We got tipsy, first time drinking vodka shots, toasting went on until 5.30 a.m. YY was born on 15 July, my birthday (of course some years earlier). He calls me his 'Australian sister'. Last time I saw him was a couple of years ago when I promoted his volume of poetry *Stolen Apples* for W.H. Allen (a Fleet Street publisher). . . . He asked Ted to bring me to Georgia. Of course, Ted agreed.[4]

Ted admitted to Lucas Myers that he was having a year of considerable folly – 'oldstyle',[5] which he attributed both to having spent the preceding four years working on the farm and then to his decision to let the farm go. Nor was he ready to return to a quiet rural life even when back in England. While Jill waited for her flat's extensive repairs, she and Hughes lived together on weekdays in friends' houses.[6] She was seemingly unaffected by the myth of Hughes as a Heathcliff figure, and Ted was observably relaxed in her presence. As Jill explained both by letter[7] and in conversation, she 'fortunately never felt jealous around Ted and other women, a blessing. I just did not feel that way, one of the reasons we were so happy together, and his love for me was of the kind that made me feel secure and not threatened. I was young, strong, independent and confident.' Jill's confidence was unshaken by the discovery that Emma Tennant was by now also passionately involved with him. Emma had fallen in love not only with Hughes' physical presence – she memorably describes in *Burnt Diaries* his face resembling an Easter Island carving – but also with the very legends that pursued him, which Jill must also have known about but found less absorbing than the affectionate physical reality. Of his relationship to Jill, Emma at first knew nothing.

From a reading of Hughes' letters at Emory, it is soon evident that Ted wrote very differently to the many and various friends with whom he sustained a correspondence. With those who believed as he did in astrology or other forms of magic, he wrote with one part of himself; to others he wrote with a matter-of-fact shrewdness that was equally part of his complex character. So it is unsurprising that Jill and Emma met very different sides of his personality.

In *Burnt Diaries*, Emma described the shock she experienced when meeting the 'bouncy Australian girl', clearly Jill, whom Emma in the book identifies as 'Sally', at a party: 'She is clinging on to his arm. Her complexion is bright and rosy, her hair is curly and brown. To make matters even clearer, she goes up on the tips of her toes . . . and kisses him on the side of the neck . . . The surprise – or so it seems, the sheer boldness – of such a move on arriving in the room causes Ted to laugh. Then he looks back at me. His smile is lupine, taunting.'[8] Equally shattering was the whisper of another guest, revealing that Jill had been with Hughes for the whole year in which Emma imagined that her only rival was Hughes' wife. As he had written to Myers, Hughes was indeed having a year of considerable folly. He told Emma that women who grew close to him always died, although this was clearly not something that had been much stressed in his relationship with Jill, who was altogether convinced that Ted wanted to marry her, except that he was afraid of the effect on his son, Nicholas.[9]

On several occasions, Ted warned Emma not to take their love too seriously but, for all the gaps in their relationship, Hughes encouraged her to dream of running away to Scotland to live with him. And in some ways Hughes gave her a great deal. Emma was just finding her own style and was writing *The Bad Sister*, a wild, free novel that might never have been written without Hughes to arouse her imagination. Hughes, too, sensed something he wanted that was not simply sexual. He read Yeats' poem to her about the Windy Gap somewhere in the Highlands where an old woman promised that his future life would be better than his past. There is a letter' in Ted's unmistakable spiky, black hand,[10] written to 'Lovely Emma', which speaks of that 'Windy Gap' and how he never found it.

Carol was still grieving for her father. She continued to live quietly at Court Green, where Ted spent all his weekends even though he was living quite openly with Jill during the week. Writing to her mother on 29 September 1976,[11] Jill describes the wedding of Abbie Morley, a friend who had rented her a flat in King Edwards Mansions, while Jill's flat in the same block was being renovated:

> '[Abbie] married Charles Little, the Australian actor I represented [in Sydney 1968] on 18 September in Wargrave, Berkshire. Her father, Robert Morley, gave her away. Ted escorted me to the wedding ... We now just have to wait for the surveyor ... In the meantime, Ted and I happily gypsied all over London to friends who seemed to be only too happy to have us stay. Finally, through a poetry reading in Earls Court, he met Liliana Gardini, the Italian translator, who let us a huge flat in Trebovir Road, Earls Court.[12]

In the event, the surveyor from Jill's mortgage brokers agreed that her own flat was suitable for conversion and Jill was given a council grant to bring the property up to her requirements, although it was a year before she was able to move in. She had been given an international photo and features agency by Amnon Bartur, her business partner, who was then moving to New York. As she wrote to her mother, 'I have never felt freer and more creative in a working relationship.' Nevertheless, she was even more eager to edit the literary magazine *Mars* with her friend Kristina Dusseldorp.

Jill was indignant at the portrait given of her in *Burnt Diaries* as someone whose main occupation in life was selling pieces of jewellery. She raged at the acerbic description of Kristina's flat on the King's Road to which Emma was invited to dinner:[13]

> This is the flat to which Emma was invited to dinner ... Large rooms, ample furniture, decorating style shabby-chic. Lots of first edition books and no empty Riesling bottles, etc. We did not serve Riesling, usually Sancerre with fish and good chateaux reds, and of course the

best Australian wines. I had introduced Ted to Australian wine (as you know, he was quite the connoisseur). I served a lot of vegetables. I had spent the previous summer as a chef on a boat in the South of France and had worked my way through the Elizabeth David cookbook. Ted, Olwyn, Liliana, Emma and myself enjoyed the meal. Emma was quiet, resplendent in aqua, the only detail she seems to remember [*correctly*]. The reason for the dinner was to discuss distribution of *Mars*, created and published by [an] Australian, Kristina Dusseldorp . . .

Emma was invited to Kristina's flat on King's Road, which was the center of the creation of *Mars*. There was no burnt fish (Ted an expert at the delicate preparation of fish) and never any chance of Emma seeing me draped in a sheet exposing body, or bed. (Too well-bred, dahling) . . .

Emma was like a teenager after dinner at Liliana's. On 14 February [1977] she pushed under the door a crude home-made valentine. I think it was a nymph and Pan frolicking across a woodcut mounted on blue cardboard. (This she must have art-directed herself). I admired her nerve. She made it plain she was besotted, what woman wasn't (and plenty of men). I knew she may have got her hands on him but put no mind to it . . .

Ted and I enjoyed working with Kristina to create the best literary magazine we could . . . It was not a tinpot operation, it cost a lot of money. She published the best, both *avant garde* and mainstream writers, photographers and artists. No doubt she paid Emma well for distribution with *Bananas* . . .

Ted was kind to Emma and to *Bananas*, giving her material for it, no payment, Olwyn too . . .

We worked hard. I was syndicating material to Japan, Europe and US. Ted became productive and he set up reading tours both in UK and US so that we could be together on the road.[14]

Jill does not comment on the importance of *Bananas* in the literary scene of the 1970s. Although always threatened by financial collapse, *Bananas* enjoyed a wide readership and had a distinctive voice. Emma saw a different part of Ted's being, one that was still obsessed with Sylvia, as indeed Emma was herself. In *Burnt Diaries*, one of the most remarkable of Ted's utterances is about his continuing spiritual loyalty to his first wife. Staring up at a flock of geese, Emma remembers him explaining the sexual fidelity of the greylag geese, which remain faithful to their first mate for life, according to Konrad Lorenz. Tennant reported that Ted added casually: 'They are faithful to their first mate . . . I may be.'[15]

Meanwhile, Hughes was working on his introduction to the poems of the Hungarian János Pilinszky. During his visit to London there was an evening at Olwyn's house where I met Pilinszky for the first time. He had a face of extraordinarily delicate beauty; his skin was almost translucent as if his spirit illuminated it from inside. Hughes explained genially, 'Nous sommes tous en français.' Hughes could handle the language well enough, although he did not have Olwyn's Parisian accent, and – as always – his presence filled the room even though Pilinszky did most of the talking.

Pilinszky was an important poet to Ted because he was a survivor of horrors. His own suffering lay in what he had been forced to witness. Wartime Hungary had been in alliance with Germany. In 1944 Pilinszky was conscripted for military service, just in time to be scooped up by the retreating German armies, and he had to spend the last year of the war in a series of prison camps. What he saw there scarred his mind with images of men waiting to be shot or being beaten to death and thrown on a refuse heap. The poems that Pilinszky wrote about this experience were torn from him. As he said, 'I would like to write as if I had remained silent.'

In his introduction to the translation he made of Pilinszky's poems, Hughes wrote of the silence of artistic integrity 'after Auschwitz' as a real thing in the face of the mass of human evidence from the camps, or similar situations that called into question the meaning of words like 'truth' and 'reality'. Hughes pointed out that Pilinszky's poems grew from a religious awareness of a God altogether different from that of Christianity: '[a] God of absences and negative attributes, quite comfortless. A God in whose creation the camps and modern physics are equally at home. But this God has the one Almightiness that matters: He is the Truth.'[16] It is this metaphysical blackness as much as the luminosity of Pilinszky's language that Hughes so admired. His own experience of surviving two suicides confirmed Pilinszky's vision.

Hughes' public vilification continued with the publication of Edward Butscher's account of Sylvia's life in *Method and Madness*.[17] Several of Hughes' friends urged him to defend himself. In October 1976, after reading Butscher's book, Peter Redgrove wrote with genuine concern:

We wanted to say again that the only way to handle this that we can see is for you to write your own story. It would take you to pieces to do so, but that is what poets are for, to be taken to pieces. This will have occurred to you ... there will be many such books as Butscher's unless you act, and the effect of them will gradually become permanent. On the contrary, to tell your story would be a noble action, however harrowing or even shameful you might consider the truth to be.[18]

It was advice that Ted did not take. Instead he wrote the symbolic poem *Gaudete*, published in 1977, which was far less well received than *Crow*; in part – as his friend Susan Fromberg Schaeffer noted in a letter to Hughes that received no reply – because of a certain discomfort at seeing parallels to Hughes' own life in the adventures of the Reverend Lumb.

Gaudete is a puzzling book. It began life as a projected film script, was conceived in 1962 and was sent to a Swedish film director in 1964. Nothing came of that venture, however, and in 1971 Ted had a series of dreams connected with the myth behind *Crow*, which led him to begin rewriting the story. The changeling Nicholas Lumb has been cut out of an oak tree while the vicar himself is about some necessary business in the underworld. As Hughes explained in a programme note for an acting version of *Gaudete* performed in 1977: 'This changeling proceeds to interpret the job of ministering the Gospel of Love in his own log-like way. He organises the women of his parish into a coven, a love society. And the purpose of this society, evidently, is to produce the Messiah. So all the women have to be brought under Lumb's power and made pregnant by him, since he is to be the father of the Messiah.'[19] Ekbert Faas described the poem as Hughes' 'most *personal* book to date' (my italics) and sees in its protagonists – both Reverend Lumb and his double – self-caricatures, like Dostoevsky's anti-hero in *Notes from Underground*. In conversation with Faas, Hughes himself was insistent that his opinion of the behaviour of both Lumb and his doppelgänger is as much withheld as it would be in a drama. Nevertheless, the story has disturbing resonances, and Faas's position is understandable. The Reverend Lumb's effort to revitalize the Great Mother sounds like something Hughes himself might have approved. When the underworld allows the husbands of the parish to know what the changeling has been doing, they murder him. The original Lumb then appears in the West of Ireland and composes psalms of an ambiguous but seductive lyricism.

Whatever reason Hughes had for choosing this story inside his failing marriage to Sylvia Plath in 1962, it was Faas's knowledge of the two suicides in Hughes' life that led him to read the poem as 'personal'. Both Keith Sagar and Ann Skea offer interpretations of the poem, which see spiritual resurrection rather than misogyny as the source. Michael Schmidt – the poet, critic and publisher – described the book as 'appalling'. Yet a Yorkshire poet of another generation, Simon Armitage, wrote an admiring letter of praise to Hughes about *Gaudete*, as if he intuited something of what Hughes had in mind.

The epigraphs, from Heraclitus and *Parzival*, suggest a man at war with himself, in the ruins of whatever disaster has emptied the streets. As the changeling goes invisibly about his sexual business among the wives and daughters of the parish, all, as Faas declares, are 'deluded, drugged and betrayed'. Janet, who has found herself pregnant by Lumb, hangs herself; Felicity is led into a scene of ritual sacrifice and is mounted sexually by Lumb, with his housekeeper Maud abetting him, before being ritually butchered. Maud, who is in several respects the most frightening figure in the poem, goes off in the aftermath of the sacrifice and curls up like a foetus around Lumb's knife to kill herself. These are frightening and frightened dreams, all the more since the loveliness of the world continues lyrically alongside the horror:

> The chair topples, deciding a pigeon
> To clap up through the window gap.
> An opportunistic jay
> Scrambles up the air and vanishes.[20]

A young girl kills herself after her sister Jennifer explains that Lumb now loves her instead. Felicity is floating on a lake where Lumb is fishing, while the naked changeling clutches the stern of the boat. The doubles confront one another – 'One grinning and the other appalled' – and the hand of one is torn off and hurled away, but there is no resolution of their conflict. It is only when the changeling has been done to death by the husbands of the parish that the true Reverend Lumb is allowed to reappear, and his songs of praise have an almost biblical rebirth of wonder:

> The lark sizzles in my ear
> Like a fuse –[21]

Sometimes the speaker seems to be Hughes himself:

I turned
I bowed
In the morgue I kissed
Your temple's refrigerated glazed
As rained-on graveyard marble, my
Lips queasy, heart non-existent[22]

It is as if Hughes has allowed the whole underworld of his dreaming mind to throw up everything that he did not want to remember. But *Gaudete* may well have been a necessary rite of passage, since his poetry thereafter seems to spring from a 'world of light rather than blood'.[23]

Gaudete was not, however, well received on either side of the Atlantic. In America the effects of Hughes' failing reputation had already made themselves felt. Harper & Row, the publisher that had benefited most from the success of *Letters Home*, had already turned down Hughes' *Cave Birds*,[24] and his marvellous translations of János Pilinszky. And when *Gaudete* appeared, it was greeted savagely.

On 3 March 1978, Fran McCullough wrote to Hughes, enclosing a fistful of reviews about *Gaudete* and advising him that he would do well not to read them. She admitted that the book was not really selling. Quite soon afterwards, she was telling him with enthusiasm that Sylvia Plath's *Johnny Panic and The Bible of Dreams* had sold more than 18,000 copies.[25]

Some time in 1976, when my husband and I were visiting Court Green, Leonard Baskin and his second wife Lisa were also staying there. While he was drawing a cover for what was to be my book of selected poems, *Some Unease and Angels*, Baskin quizzed me persistently as to my knowledge of what Ted was up to in London, and how much Olwyn was involved in it. We quarrelled absurdly. What astonished me was that Baskin, who was so close to Ted, knew nothing of Jill Barber. It was clear that if he had known of the affair he would have profoundly disapproved.

When Henry Williamson died that year, Ted gave a memorable tribute to the man whose work had been a seminal influence on his own childhood. He had liked Williamson for his knowledge of wildlife and his wonderful fund of anecdotes, in spite of Williamson's damaging admiration of Hitler, whom he had once imagined would restore an England of great country estates.

Some time in 1978, when Jill was thirty-four, there were a couple of weeks in which she wondered whether she might be pregnant. She described Ted's horror at the prospect.[26] It was a false alarm, as it turned out, but Jill recognized in that moment how much she herself did want both children and a normal married life. Their love affair began to cool on both sides, although it did not end until Jill moved to the West Village in New York in 1980.[27]

Hughes had already written to Gerald[28] in 1977 that he felt his life had gone off its own track, although he was no longer certain what that track might be. He felt that something was denying him access to his full energy, almost as if he was being stifled by a whole wrong way of living.

FIFTEEN

Responsibility

To the women concerned, and to many bystanders, Ted's London jaunts may have seemed the most significant part of his life in the 1970s. Yet, quite apart from his poetry, Hughes had other pressing concerns and family responsibilities that he made no attempt to neglect. High on the list of these was his father, who did not, as Ted confessed he had hoped,[1] stay on for long in Australia with Gerald. Four months later he was back in England and, although Olwyn put him up for a time at Chetwynd Road, by 23 August 1976, William was once again in Ted's care.

Hughes had watched his father adjust more easily than expected to Edith's death, and guessed that he had grown accustomed to the thought of losing her even before she died. But William no longer wanted to live in Yorkshire and his inability to cope on his own troubled his son. He found a small house for him in North Tawton, since he thought that to have him permanently at Court Green would be a serious burden on Carol. As his father sat about in a chair all day, with very little interest even in his food, Hughes began to wonder if he would not be happier in a local nursing home[2] where he would be looked after kindly and which, for a time at least, could be funded out of his father's savings.

At first this proved a successful move, but by 2 May 1977, Hughes was reporting to his brother[3] that his father had taken to shouting at the night staff, and behaving in other embarrassing ways such as spitting on the carpet, or walking outside when he wanted to urinate. Ted visited his father regularly, even though he realized that by then William hardly recognized him. As he wrote sadly, 'I took him [Dad] out for a drink the other night and after sundry comments, he suddenly said, "Do you ever see Ted these days?" '[4]

Ted continued to take his father on excursions, sometimes to the sea, although once – after a pleasant day out – Ted gave his father too much to eat and he was ill on his return to the nursing home. His care there cost £80 a week, which ate up his father's savings fairly rapidly, and Ted wrote to Gerald to suggest that, if and when it came to that, he might bear a third of the cost. For the rest of the decade, his father went on sitting about, watching TV, sleeping and smiling.

And Ted continued to work on what mattered to him most. In 1979 he wrote *Remains of Elmet*, poems in response to Fay Godwin's photographs of the landscape of Hughes' childhood. She was at this time suffering from cancer, and the sharpness of her black and white images suggest a bleakness that an innocent hiker, passing through the same area on a sunny day, might well miss. The poems reflect that bleakness. The valley is haunted by those who served the oppressive looms and comforted themselves with biblical texts, and by conscripts who once marched away to die in the First World War. Hughes' own childhood memories of loaches in jam jars and Mount Zion chapel also figure, but with little sign of the merriment he experienced while growing up. The poems are starkly beautiful, particularly the haunting lyric for Emily Brontë.

For all his refusal to talk about Plath in public, Hughes continued to brood about her painfully. By 1979 he had turned some of his memories into poems: 'You Hated Spain' and 'The Earthenware Head.'[5] In their different ways, both suggest the difficulties of living with Plath, but perhaps it is the first, with its suggestion that Plath had made a mistake in crying wolf when she was only mildly ill, that is the most significant, since it is suffused with Hughes' bitter regret for his failure to realize her danger at the last. Critics have found the poem self-exculpatory, but the tone is closer to bewilderment. And alongside these memories, his own inexorable social success seemed almost Faustian. The critics may have disliked *Gaudete*, but some time in March 1979 Ted had to buy a suit because he had been invited to lunch with the Queen.

His father was not the only member of his family in need of his emotional support. By the end of the decade Olwyn, too, required help. In the early 1970s she had been living with Keith Gordon, a young man who helped with promotion and sales for both *Modern Poetry in Translation* and the Rainbow Press. By 1978 her companion was Richard, an Irishman whom she went on to marry. He was much the same build as Ted, and very good-looking. Olwyn and he got on enormously well, and took holidays – for instance to Turkey in 1977 – which they enjoyed 'happily and hilariously'[6] together. Olwyn encouraged Richard's studies at the Open University and Hughes could see that they were very much in love. He was happy for her, even though, as he wrote to Gerald, he knew that Richard could be aggressive.

Nevertheless, by the early spring of 1980 quarrels between Richard and Olwyn had reached the point where Olwyn decided that a break with him was essential. With the thought of moving to Cambridge, she came to stay with me for a few days in my house in Park Parade. While there, she had a series of alarming phone calls from Richard. The police were called but were deceived by Richard's charm into going away again. Soon afterwards Olwyn bought a house in Lensfield Road, Cambridge, and moved there in March 1980.[7] Ted held on to the basement of Chetwynd Road as a flat, and they sold the main house for £65,000. They had only paid £23,000 for it so both Ted and Olwyn were delighted.

Olwyn's decision to move to Cambridge proved to be a mistake, however, and Lensfield Road – though grander than any house Olwyn had owned in London – was hard to make congenial. Cambridge was not a city in which Olwyn was likely to find the kind of life she enjoyed; nor did it resolve her relationship with Richard. He continued to threaten her with such persistence that Ted had to come up to Cambridge for a few days to give Olwyn some kind of protection. She was uncharacteristically frightened. While Ted was at Lensfield Road, Richard did appear, very drunk, and the three of them, 'had a long night of it, at the end of which he [Richard] gashed his wrists'.[8]

Despite this drama, by 16 May of the same year Olwyn and Richard were back together, first taking a holiday in Tunisia; by July they were living together at Lensfield Road. All this made nonsense of the move out of London. Ted reflected ruefully that when a couple breaks up it is a good idea not to comment, since they usually get back together again and turn on the third party as a traitor. Richard and Olwyn were not getting on any more peacefully, however.

Hughes could only back away from this situation, although he remained deeply involved with the rest of his family. On 20 May 1980, he wrote to Gerald from his father's bedside in Exeter Hospital about his disappointment at failing to interest Gerald in taking a fishing trip to Alaska. He was pleased, however, that Gerald went on drawing and encouraged him to go back to painting, even as he brooded over his father's decline.

His father's health had begun to fail ever since he had a fall and broke his hip, perhaps because he had some sort of stroke under the anaesthetic.

Ted went to the hospital to sit with his father every third day, although sometimes they barely exchanged a word. By 27 January 1981,[9] Ted recogized that his father was fading. He wrote to Gerald saying that if he wanted to come and pay his last respects, it would have to be that year, and warned him that he should not expect much in the way of response. Indeed, by 1 February, Ted had the impression that his father was likely to die at any moment. 'I go every other day now and each time his face seems even more changed – just a tiny ancient bird and obviously not happy.'[10]

There were family pleasures to balance Ted's distress at his father's failing health. Ted and Nick were forging a close relationship over his son's passion for fishing. It turned out that they shared a similar sense of humour too and so, when they travelled to Iceland together in 1979, both found something hilarious in their pursuit of fish where there seemed to be none. 'It was a memorable trip, even though we only caught one big fish.'[11] Hughes found Nick 'really marvellous, very merry and high-spirited throughout'.[12] In 1980 they travelled together to Alaska, a landscape that Hughes found intoxicating and which probably set Nicholas on course for his life's work. Nicholas had already gained As in all his subjects at A Level, and had secured a place at Oxford to read Zoology, but his trips with his father confirmed his wish to devote his life to research on aquatic life.

Throughout 1980, in the aftermath of these explorations, Hughes worked on *River*, a book of poems that not only celebrate his experience in Alaska but also record his growing awareness of an ineluctable force, animating all the living creatures on the planet. It is the most magical of the books of his later period. In *River*, which was not published until 1983, we enter a world of calmness and light, as if while writing these poems Hughes was able to leave behind whatever Furies were pursuing him. Here water has many forms, capable at one moment of splintering the brilliance of sunlight, seemingly unassailable in the next. In the title poem:

> It is a god, and inviolable.
> Immortal. And will wash itself of all deaths.[13]

In 'Low Water', the river becomes a beautiful, lazy woman who 'lolls on her deep couch', stretching in ecstasy. It is not without danger. Ophelia, in the poem of the same name, slips into the 'afterworld' with a 'finger to her lips'. And a woman hurrying to meet her lover with snow in her hair falls into a river suddenly become a 'gutter of death'. That last is one of the 'Japanese River Tales'. Hughes, always fascinated by Kabuki theatre, may have been inspired by seeing a Japanese troupe who visited London in 1981, to perform their traditional stories.

At the core of *River* are the poems about salmon forcing themselves upriver to spawn. In 'October Salmon' Hughes watches an exhausted young salmon resting in a pool of water before throwing himself upstream:

> What a change! from that covenant of polar light
> To this shroud in a gutter.[14]

Bears are waiting to pick the fish out of the water with their talons. And yet the salmon continue to struggle to reach the place where they can release their sperm and eggs. It is an awesome vision both of creative force and natural waste.

The most mysterious poem in this book, 'The Gulkana', centres on a huge river in Alaska where salmon move 'like ... somnambulists' to a consummation that must mean death for most of them. The fisherman's neck prickles with fear, and at the same time an almost erotic awe:

> The voice of the river moved in me.
> It was lovesickness.[15]

William Hughes died in early February 1981 at five-twenty in the afternoon. Ted and Carol had been to the funeral of a Farrar relative in Yorkshire and were having tea with Aunt Hilda when they heard the news. On their return to Devon, Ted and Carol visited Exeter to view William's body, lying in a funeral parlour and looking 'like a noble old Spaniard'.[16] It was 11 February. With his usual passionate interest in calendar dates, Ted noted sombrely that it was eighteen years to the day since he had seen Sylvia's dead body.

His father was buried in Yorkshire, and Ted, Carol, Olwyn and Frieda travelled to Heptonstall for the funeral. Ted went to see the body in the chapel of rest, which Olwyn did not want to do. After the service, they carried the coffin into the graveyard where Edith had been buried, and lowered it in next to her. Carol, Frieda, Olwyn and Hilda each threw a freesia into the open grave; Ted threw in 'a handful of wet, horrible Heptonstall soil'.[17]

Hughes spent a great deal of 1981 'in the coils of the Plath journals', as he put it in a letter to Keith Sagar.[18] In 1981, Plath's *Collected Poems* appeared, edited and introduced by Hughes. The book sold outstandingly well in both the UK and the USA. *Crossing the Water* and *Winter Trees*, already published in the early 1970s, had sold at least 60,000 copies each, but it was the *Collected Poems* that established Plath's astounding range and accomplishment. In 1982, the book went on to win the Pulitzer Prize for poetry.

Hughes was also choosing Sylvia Plath's prose, and writing the introduction to *Johnny Panic and the Bible of Dreams*. Although Hughes had seen the huge success of *The Bell Jar*, he remained convinced that Plath's genius lay mainly in poetry. It was a division made more strictly in those days; now writers attempt both genres more freely. In her short life some of Plath's best prose is to be found in her journals, but *Johnny Panic* had a quality that fitted in with the Gothic interests of the times.

Hughes' charitable work to encourage poetry continued, and in November – alongside Seamus Heaney, Philip Larkin and Charles Causley – he was a judge for the *Observer*/Arvon Foundation Poetry Competition; this was an idea of his to help raise money for Arvon. Ted's reputation was enough to involve London Weekend Television, as well as the *Observer*. The number of entrants was high: over 35,000, each paying £1.50 per entry. Although it was punishing work for the judges, it saved the Arvon Foundation's collapsing finances and tapped into the national passion for writing poems, which was far greater than anyone had guessed. Hughes wrote to Keith Sagar afterwards. 'That's the last judging I shall ever do. Ever. Ever. Ever. Ever. Ever.'[19] Andrew Motion, who won that first national prize, remembers how kind Hughes was nonetheless, and his own shyness in meeting him. Motion went on to become Poet Laureate in succession to Hughes.

Among the distinguished poets on the judging panel, Seamus Heaney was closest to Hughes in spirit. Seven years younger, with a First Class degree in English from Queen's College Belfast, Heaney had found recognition easily. He had been part of a writers' workshop, under the guidance of Philip Hobsbaum, that included Derek Mahon and Michael Longley. Ted Hughes was among his earliest influences, as was already evident in *Death of a Naturalist* (published in 1965), and particularly in poems that followed the publication of P.V. Glob's *The Bog People*, a book describing a series of bodies over two thousand years old, found in the bogs of Denmark. This material enabled Heaney to address the issues in Northern Ireland through a study of these victims of tribal sacrifice and punishment.

Ted, who had always loved Ireland and Irish poetry, found in Seamus a man of his own size, with a warm and engaging personality. They had been close friends for years and often stayed in one another's homes. Hughes came to recognize in Heaney the voice of the greatest Irish poet since Yeats. The correspondence between them at the Special Collections Department[20] at Emory University is not available to scholars but it must contain – whatever else – some of the most important exchanges about poetry in the twentieth century. Hughes and Heaney went on to collaborate on *The Rattlebag* (1982) and *The School Bag* (1997).

In April 1981, Ted Hughes heard that John Fisher, his old grammar school teacher, had died from cancer of the lung. This had gone undiagnosed for some time: a piece of medical neglect that Ted found inexcusable but which Fisher bore with Yorkshire stoicism. Ted was indignant at his resignation, and was unhappy when he thought about all the things that Fisher had always wanted to do in his retirement but had never got round to: 'I think he died mainly of boredom – the depression of boredom, under the sulphur towers of that power station in Mexborough. And his wife can register only relief – very strange. They simply didn't know what to do with their lives.'[21]

Ted's depression at returning to Mexborough went far beyond his dislike of the polluted air. It recalled the time in Lumb Bank when he had reflected on his impatience with the prevailing ethos of the area, rather as Lawrence had felt when he contrasted the industrial Midlands with the hill towns of northern Italy. Like William Blake long before them, Hughes had always recognized the dangers of stifling human desire. In 1969, thinking about the teaching that he and his brother had received in their childhood, Hughes had fulminated against the pleasure-denying ordinances of his upbringing, with their seeming unawareness that there was a natural and God-given imperative to live your life richly. Now he was simply saddened to see what had happened to a teacher to whom he had owed so much.

He was determined that his children should be allowed to find their own way, even though he did not entirely approve of Frieda's first romantic attachment to a young man with a dangerously fast motorbike. Quite soon after her seemingly happy marriage, Hughes heard that Frieda was getting divorced and intended to start a business in Truro but – as he wrote to Peter Redgrove, to whom he still felt close[22] – he was satisfied that she was fully alive.

Ted's continuing fantasies about escaping to Scotland are confirmed in several undated letters to Emma Tennant, although he made few attempts to contact her. He and Jill Barber had not yet broken off all contact. Once Hughes had formed a close relationship with a woman, he expected the relationship to continue, even if the intensity diminished or the sexual bond disappeared altogether. He kept one part of his life separate from another, often giving out secret telephone numbers where he could be reached in London by intimate friends only. He still enjoyed meeting his old Cambridge friends. When Daniel Weissbort arrived at Court Green – 'near cracking point', as he described himself[23] – Ted found him really no more than 'lonely like the rest of us'.[24] Ted and Carol received him warmly. Once, quite off the cuff after such a visit, Weissbort gave me a vivid picture of Carol's independent spirit. A man – evidently the Lord Lieutenant of the County – had arrived at the back door with a brace of geese, which Hughes received gratefully. Carol, however, sighed with amusement and said, 'If you're going to eat these, you've got to pluck them – I can't.' Carol was clearly no subjugated wife. Weissbort also remembered that when Ted had brought back a huge salmon, freshly caught, Carol showed little enthusiasm, pointing out that the freezer was already stuffed with fish.

By now Ted and Carol were well knit into the life of Devon county society. This absorption into the life of the local gentry had been facilitated by the fact that Hughes, at the time of the *Observer*/Arvon Poetry Competition, took part in a consortium in an attempt to win the franchise for a local ITV station, which hopefully would make a television programme about the event. The group included bank managers, successful businessmen and large landowners. Because he was known to be enthusiastic about so many of their country pursuits, these people were happy to offer him access to their privileged trout streams.[25] Carol made a perfect companion for the social life that resulted.

Long before his appointment to the post of Laureate, Ted had been invited to meet the Queen. Many of his most passionate concerns at this time – ecology, for example, and the preservation of salmon in British rivers – overlapped with those of other members of the royal family. He was invited to spend a week with the Queen Mother on her Balmoral estate, where he evidently enjoyed himself hugely, catching a fish or two and seeing 'a million deer'. He also saw how the Queen Mother's interest in everything and everybody caused general high spirits in those around her. He admired her physical health: 'There's something about her that's kept very young – like a young woman ... But everybody is so fond of her that she escapes the psychological isolation – for most old people inescapable.'[26]

With so any new sources of amusement, Hughes' interest in reading his own poetry aloud had dwindled and, although he accepted an invitation to read at the Cheltenham Festival, he wrote to Keith Sagar, 'I've told myself I shall never read in public again.'[27]

In spring 1982, Nicholas arranged a research expedition to Kenya to search for fish that only existed at the source of the Nile. Ted went along at the end of this for a couple of weeks' fishing, and was impressed to see how competent his son had become. Ted took great pleasure in observing the fishermen on the great lakes, especially the way they loaded their catch into canoes, put up rag sails and crossed the lake to the nearest town, which was little more than a hundred mud huts on the mainland. For all his lifelong interest in anthropology, this was Hughes' first opportunity to make contact with so primitive and ancient a society. He relished it, writing proudly in a letter to Peter Redgrove that it was as if Nicholas was now living out Hughes' own dreams. He liked what he saw of Kenya, though he was only there for two weeks. Having expected to find menace and unease, he instead discovered 'release and freedom'.[28]

Hughes spent the first three months of 1983 writing 'The Hanged Man and the Dragonfly', an introduction to the prints of Leonard Baskin, who had been so influential on his own perception of the world. He found it tormentingly difficult. Like most of the prose criticism now collected in *Winter Pollen*, this is both a brilliant and revealing essay. 'The Hanged Man' was Baskin's first mature, large-scale work, dating back to 1954, before he knew Hughes. The two men assuredly influenced one another, but Baskin, who was older, had long since formed his own style. Hughes lucidly identifies Baskin's debts – to the calligraphy of Hebrew script, his rabbinic training and the darker influence of the 'knotted sigils and clavicles used for conjuring spirits', for instance – but he also exposes what he himself learned from Baskin. Hughes had made himself familiar enough with that Hebrew tradition to understand that '[it] is a tradition in which the human body is the sole register, the only whole and adequate symbol' of spiritual experience. And that experience must include 'the horror' of evil cruelty. He cites Baskin's love of quoting Kurtz's line from Conrad's *Heart of Darkness*; suddenly it is possible to see a continuity of vision from Eliot's *The Waste Land* to Hughes, and to recognize Hughes' true debt to Baskin. Their personalities were complementary: Hughes was never verbally savage, and in this essay he acknowledged Baskin's powers of 'destructive derision', which he customarily used against anyone he found disguising from himself the harsh reality of the world around him.[29]

After working for a time on *Flowers and Insects* in April and May, he escaped to Africa with Nicholas again, and found there a huge 'self-contained bliss'.[30] These were pleasures he took seriously, and he was determined never to resign himself to a routine and boring life, which he felt had held his old teacher John Fisher in its Yorkshire grip and contributed to his death. He was still most excited by spiritual exploration, and it was Peter Redgrove's continuing passion for Yeats, the occult and Cabbala that made meeting him for an evening at Totleigh Barton such a pleasure. Hughes' own major spiritual insight at this time was in connection with Ted Cornish, a spiritual healer in Okehampton; a market town near Winkleigh about six miles from Court Green. Cornish had been suffering for many years from an illness for which medicine offered no alleviation. It was his discovery that he had the power to dispel his own pain that led him to offer a similar cure to others. Ted's faith in Cornish's powers was so great that he wrote to the Duke of Edinburgh about him, so that he might pass on news of Cornish's successes to a visiting member of an Arab royal family.[31]

The poet Frances Horowitz, whose cancer had advanced to the point where orthodox medicine could do little, was also seeking the help of Ted Cornish at the time, and Hughes – although his letters show him repeatedly refusing prestigious readings – nevertheless gave a benefit reading to help her perilous finances in October 1984. In November, Hughes agreed to a tour of northern schools in the hope of encouraging a love of poetry. In this way he reached and roused more than 6000 school children.[32]

By now, Ted was most deeply excited by the developing lives of his children. On 29 September 1984, he wrote to Myers that Nicholas, then twenty-three had begun a Ph.D. on fish in the Yukan river system. Ted was equally pleased with Frieda, observing the uncanny resemblance to her mother, not only in appearance but in her animation and flow of speech. At twenty-four, Frieda was divorced from her first husband and living with a young man who sold insurance. What Ted noted with quiet pride, however, was that she had begun to paint seriously: 'Beautiful, intense paintings'.[33]

In June 1984, *What is Truth?* was published. This book of poems, written with children in mind, offers an answer to that question through the perceptions of animals and their way of interpreting the world. It has a liveliness and freedom that Hughes had by now altogether regained, and a new humour as he enters the lives of quite ordinary creatures. As the hen sees it, the fox is a 'country superstition' and she has successfully turned Man into her slave in return for eggs. For all the humour, there is an easy lyricism:

> The Hen
> Worships the dust. She finds God everywhere.[34]

The hen imagines 'the odour of tarragon' just as she falls asleep. Animals seem aware of their own creation, or so the delicate poem 'The Hare' suggests. Hughes, who knew most of the superstitions that attach them-selves to that strange creature, chose instead to stress its physiological fragility: 'The life in the hare is a glassy goblet'.[35]

What he continued to value most – apart from his close family – was the freedom to read as he pleased, without pressure, returning to many books for the second time, such as *The Iliad*, works by Dostoevsky and *Moby Dick*. However much he might value this reclusive withdrawal, he was soon to choose against it. When John Betjeman died in 1984, the position of Poet Laureate had to be filled. Larkin was evidently the first choice for the post, but he was already terminally ill with cancer, and indeed might have found the position an uneasy one. When it was offered to Ted in December 1984, he accepted all the more readily because he already believed that there was a close connection between the role of poet and the symbolic place of royalty in society.

SIXTEEN

The Laureate

Once Hughes' appointment as Poet Laureate had been announced, in December 1984, Ted was inundated by congratulations from admirers: poets, old friends, even school friends from primary school, such as Donald Crossley.[1] He heard from fans to whom he had once shown kindness; professors of English Literature such as John Bayley and John Carey; and journalists such as Lynn Barber and Bel Mooney. His old Director of Studies, Matthew Hodgart, wrote suggesting that Pembroke mark the honour in some suitable way. Even the manager of his local National & Westminster Bank wrote a warm letter of congratulation. Several correspondents, including Lord Gowrie, spoke of the honour and *gravitas* that Hughes would bring to the post, and Al Alvarez wrote to claim it was the first time since Tennyson that a major poet had held the position.

From Mexborough came a touching letter from a colleague of John Fisher, reporting the pride that Fisher had always taken in his former pupil's success. Norman Nicholson, too, who seemed to have known Ted's old school teacher, imagined Fisher's sardonic comment as, 'The Queen *will* be pleased.' A letter from a school teacher who had once been an old friend of Olwyn's expressed doubts as to whether she could ever exert Fisher's influence on unruly boys like Ted in her own class. Hughes replied to all these letters personally. He may have been surprised to find how much affection had been generated in a world that he sometimes thought perceived him primarily as Plath's widower. Hughes wrote back humorously to Alvarez in January 1985, saying that, since his appointment as Poet Laureate, he now had several million people a week telling him how to write, instead of the usual thirty or forty.

On 14 February 1985, after publishing *Rain-Charm for the Duchy*,[2] he was delighted to receive a letter communicating the pleasure that the poem had given to Prince Charles and Princess Diana. More surprisingly, perhaps, he received a letter of congratulations on the poem from Professor Donald Davie, saying: 'It is impossible to think that Philip Larkin could have risen to the occasion so adroitly.' Like all laureate poems, 'Rain-Charm for the Duchy' drew snide comment at the time, but 'the Blessed Devout Drench' for the christening of Prince Harry is most ingeniously invoked. Its force lies in the sound and physical reality of a cloudburst of rain in a country town, hammering the top of the car while a girl in high heels crosses the square with a handbag protecting her hair. It is only after setting up the local and particular that Hughes involves the great rivers of the South-West and imagines their dried up riverbeds once again in glorious flow.

It must have seemed as though, after so much grief, the music of Hughes' life had become that traditionally accompanying a homecoming into happy uplands, and that the vengeful ghost of Plath had changed into one of the Eumenides or gone away. Only a few months later, however, in August 1985, Olwyn was sending him the draft manuscript of Linda Wagner-Martin's biography and wondering dubiously whether Wagner-Martin ought to become Plath's official biographer. In the event, the choice fell on Anne Stevenson. She had been originally commissioned to write a short book about Plath in Emma Tennant's *Lives of Modern Women* series for Penguin; now Olwyn persuaded her to write a full biography with the co-operation of the Plath estate.

Stevenson was American, an accomplished poet and the author of a pioneering critical biography of Elizabeth Bishop. Quietly spoken, even mousy in appearance, she had a tough, scholarly mind and at first Olwyn thought her an ideal choice. She negotiated an advance for Stevenson that was five times the size she would have received for writing a book in Tennant's series, and Stevenson took on the task eagerly. Hughes, too, was satisfied with the choice. There is a very impressive letter from Anne Stevenson to Ted dated 26 August 1985,[3] setting out her initial approach to Plath, which he thought struck the right note. Stevenson stresses her understanding of Plath's ambition to be liked and admired by a society that she grew to despise, and promised to address the whole question of trying to 'be' something in a world that pretends there is such a thing as success that can be possessed, like a valuable antique or a title.

Hughes, even more than Stevenson, had come to feel a disdain for any such ambition of this kind, although in his earlier days he had not been indifferent to the lure of fame. He had no wish to offer Stevenson any more than help in checking facts, but felt that he had at last found in her a spirit capable of dealing with the delicate issues of his marriage. As a sign of his relaxation, his poems began once more to flow freely. In 1986, writing *Flowers and Insects*, Hughes continued to explore the working of the natural world with obsessive curiosity. In 'Eclipse', for instance, writing about the mating of spiders, Hughes must surely have remembered Lawrence's detailed observation of clumsy, mating tortoises, although there is perhaps an extra frisson in Hughes' poem, as he expects to see the female spider devour the male at any moment. Instead, we only see the eager female releasing her eggs. His grasshopper, seen as 'A wicker contraption',[4] is particularly successful, and his 'Sunstruck Foxglove', which he gives the physical qualities of a gypsy girl – 'Swollen lips parted, her eyes closing'[5] – is as tender as Lawrence.

In the year following the publication of *Flowers and Insects*, however, and long before any trouble set in over the Plath biography, another storm broke: a lawsuit was brought against Hughes as a result of a 1979 film based on *The Bell Jar*.

Hughes, as representative of the Plath estate, had over the years turned down far more remunerative film deals than the one that led to this film. He always made a point of refusing to condone any use of the mother/daughter relationship as the mainspring of the plot. At this point all earlier negotiations had foundered. When a small film company headed by Jerrold Brandt Jnr. and Michael Todd Jnr. at last met his condition, Hughes allowed the film to go ahead. Marjorie Kellogg was chosen as a scriptwriter, and Larry Peerce, who in 1969 had directed *Goodbye Columbus*, an adaptation of Philip Roth's satirical novel of suburban Jewish life, was appointed as director.

Unfortunately, in order to introduce an alternative tension in the story, the scriptwriter invented new features in a character called Joan Gilling, loosely resembling Jane Andersen, Plath's Smith acquaintance, who had also been a Bradford High School graduate. To Gilling they ascribed a lesbian passion for the central character and the suggestion that she had proposed a suicide pact. This fiction, which is found nowhere in the novel, resulted in a $6 million lawsuit against fourteen defendants – including Hughes, who had had no hand in the script – claiming that the film wrongly portrayed Andersen, who was by then a Harvard psychiatrist.

Hughes changed the lawyer chosen by his publishers to represent his interests and began to prepare his defence, although the formidable expense of American litigation was worrying. Indeed, he could see that if the case went against him he would be facing bankruptcy. All through the spring and summer of 1986 he showed remarkable fortitude in contemplating the prospect of financial ruin, while divesting himself of assets that might secure his family.

Nor was the libel suit his only anxiety. Even as the lawyers began to arrange their case against him, Hughes was writing to Anne Stevenson in September/October 1986, voicing his concern about the effect that her biography of Sylvia would have on Carol. He understood what it must be like for his wife to live at Court Green as if Sylvia were the true owner, even though Carol had been there for sixteen years and Sylvia for only fourteen months. He was also troubled by signs of growing tension between Olwyn and Anne. As the writing of the book that became *Bitter Fame* proceeded, Olwyn began to think that Anne Stevenson was going to be far less easy to work with than she had hoped. Stevenson had flown to Indiana, where she spent ten hours a day for five days reading Sylvia's unexpurgated letters in *Letters Home*, as well as correspondence from Richard Sassoon, Ted, Aurelia, Mrs Prouty, etc. She 'emerged with the impression that, however perverse, self-justifying and ambitious Sylvia was, for most of her life she was not mad'.[6]

For Olwyn, Sylvia's earlier suicide attempt and her obsession with her dead father Otto were the most important factors in Sylvia's inner world. She could not believe that anyone would have been happy with Sylvia, and frequently said as much. Her own love for Ted was fiercely protective, and she loathed the way he had been presented to the world by those who saw his marriage to Plath as part of a war between the genders. She was altogether impatient with Sylvia's American bewilderment at English ways. Anne Stevenson could not see why Olwyn, who had done no archival research and had never been a close friend of Sylvia, should feel that she was the only one with a right to an opinion. Unwilling to present Plath as Olwyn saw her, Anne traced the roots of Sylvia's pain to features of her American upbringing, whilst well understanding why she would see Cambridge as 'quaint, damp, cold and backwards'.

Olwyn's letters – brilliant, abrasive, detailed – are collected in Anne Stevenson's archive in Cambridge University Library, and will be kept under seal until after Stevenson's death.[7] Those of us who knew Olwyn well at this time found that she could barely speak of anything else but Anne's refusal to see the situation as she did, and her obstinacy in wishing to keep the hostile memoirs of Richard Murphy and Dido Merwin separate from her own narrative.

Olwyn wanted the biography to make use of material that showed how Sylvia fell far short of the saintliness that the feminists had attributed to her. Sylvia's uncut journals themselves make the same point. Her lusty promiscuity was as eager as Ted's before their marriage. And, indeed, after their separation she was uninhibited in her sexual approach to both Richard Murphy in Ireland and Al Alvarez on Christmas Eve 1962. However, Stevenson felt that the real issue lay in Olwyn's reluctance to allow her to explore the pain of abandonment that Plath endured.

As disagreement grew between Anne and Olwyn over the question of Sylvia's sanity – with Anne protesting that if Sylvia were schizophrenic, then so were most of the poets she knew[8] – it became clear that Ted and Olwyn did not necessarily see eye to eye. Olwyn had always found Ted too easygoing in his treatment of Sylvia while she was alive. It is hardly surprising that, in her wish to set the record straight, she put more emphasis on Sylvia as psychotic than Ted wanted. Indeed, Hughes was specific in his initial letter to Stevenson that he was unwilling to have Sylvia's poems seen as the product of psychosis, stressing that the writing in them was coherent and lucid. His protectiveness of Sylvia, which had shown itself all through the six years of their marriage until their separation, was again activated when he sensed she was under attack.

Many marriages disintegrate without wives killing themselves and, moreover, not all adulteries lead to marital break-ups. Plath's rudeness and spoiled sulks were equally only one factor among many in a complex story. Hughes made clear in a letter to Anne Stevenson, once he had seen the final manuscript, that his own viewpoint was different from Olwyn's. He did not feel, as did Dido Merwin and Olwyn, that it was unforgivable for Sylvia to burn his papers: 'The only thing I found hard to understand was her sudden discovery of our bad moments as subjects for poems.'[9]. Nor, indeed, did he hold anything against her that she had done. He refused, however, to intervene.

By 27 April 1987, Ted, writing to Lucas Myers, admitted that he had to some extent been drawn into discussions between Anne, Olwyn and her American editor, Peter Davison at Houghton Mifflin; these had become 'rather fraught'.[10] When Stevenson appealed to Hughes for help, Hughes backed off. As he saw it, once Anne had agreed to work with Olwyn, there was no way in which he could allow himself to be involved further in the situation; there were already too many rumours that he had organized an attack on his first wife, to be ghost-written on his instructions. In a note, written 'in a rush', as he puts it, to Anne from Court Green in January 1988, he acknowledges her dilemma. He recommends that her job be that of the judge rather than one of the barristers, and, above all, she must present the 'dangerous, extreme mix' that produced the poems.[11] Although excellent advice, it did not help Stevenson, nor did it change Olwyn's view of how the book ought to be written. Peter Davison, who had known Sylvia well in earlier days, wrote a clear letter to Olwyn, objecting to her 'gradual movement toward taking over authorship of this book, or parts of it, yourself',[12] but by now Olwyn only saw *Bitter Fame* in one light: as her chance to set the record straight and release Ted from the many rumours that had surrounded him. In the ensuing battle, Stevenson was led to claim that *Bitter Fame* had become something like a work of joint authorship. From that point on, the book, although in many ways an excellent account of Plath's life, was certain to be discredited. Olwyn, who writes exceptionally well herself, should probably have written her own memoir.

In the process of dealing with the problems of Stevenson's manuscript, Hughes had begun to reflect on his own mistake in trying to suppress what he knew of Sylvia's personal problems. This he had done for the sake of their children primarily but also to refrain from wounding Aurelia. He had always known that this would lead to his being seen as the villain of the story, but he had not guessed the extent of the damage it would do to his reputation in the United States. By this time his poetry was barely taught in American universities and he wondered ruefully if the situation was not indeed likely to deteriorate further.

The libel case took some months to come to court; it was finally heard in January 1987, in fact, by which time the legal expenses were already huge. Hughes attended the trial. He was by then approaching sixty, but was still ruggedly handsome. The hearing lasted a week. In the event, the plaintiff agreed to an out of court settlement of $150,000, along with a prominent disclaimer in the credits to the film, stating that the characters and events depicted were fictitious. To reach the settlement, Hughes and three other defendants were dropped from the lawsuit, on the grounds that there was no wrongdoing, since, it was declared, 'To the extent the plaintiff was defamed it was by the motion picture alone, not the novel.'[13]

By 30 June 1988, Olwyn was writing cheerfully to Carol Hughes that she felt free for the first time in years, since the trial and her battles with Anne Stevenson were now more or less at an end.[14] She had not calculated on the critical response that Anne Stevenson's book would meet in 1989. After an inconclusive start, Alvarez opened the attack on the grounds that it was rare to read a biography about a subject so plainly disliked by the author. He set the tone for those that followed. The biography did not lay the ghost of Plath, as Olwyn had hoped. On the contrary, the old stories rose again and Hughes' friends watched with horror.

Stephen Spender had written to Hughes the year before, on 14 March 1988, commiserating with him for the way he was being continuously dragged through the most painful events in his past, and marvelling at his courage in continuing to live so rich and creative a life.[15]

It was in the context of the upheaval around *Bitter Fame* that some of Hughes' finest writing in his post as Laureate was published. It is as if he had now totally recovered his early lyricism. His vision of Nature, however terrible the accidents described, always contained a passion for the elemental final beauty of the created world.[16] 'Ravens' from *Moortown Diary* (1989), which describes the death of a lamb, is quintessentially Hughes in its visionary account of the lamb's brief experience of this world as fortunate, since the day was 'blue and warm',

> The magpies gone quiet with domestic happiness
> And skylarks not worrying about anything
> And the blackthorn budding confidently
> And the skyline of hills, after millions of hard years,
> Sitting soft.[17]

Wolfwatching, which was published in the same year, was a Poetry Book Society choice. On 26 September 1989, Olwyn wrote to Ted saying, 'Do you know one of the reasons *Wolfwatching* is so strong? It's your first collection in ages that is not primarily on a theme. Better so.'[18] There are several poems that hark back to his memories of the First World War and his father's silent heroism. But there is also a new figure. Hughes recalled a memory of his Uncle Albert, with his big laugh and impressive muscles, who had carved wooden ducks in his attic. He had been refused a chance of a partnership in the family firm because his brothers' wives disapproved of him. For all his good humour and strength, he took his own life,

> And his daughter
> Who'd climbed up to singsong: 'Supper, Daddy'
> Fell back down the stairs to the bottom.[19]

SEVENTEEN

The Goddess

By July 1989, Hughes was at work on *Shakespeare and the Goddess of Complete Being*[1] – a magnificent, if idiosyncratic, work of scholarship, which extended and enriched his thoughts on Shakespeare's peculiarly vivifying historical situation. He had originally set this out in his introduction to his selection of Shakespeare's poetry for Faber & Faber in 1971. There he proposed a vision of Elizabeth as the ruler of a police state, enforcing Protestant stability, and he endowed Shakespeare with a certain clairvoyance in prefiguring the horrors of the fundamentalist Puritan regime that lay in the future under Cromwell. He also drew attention to Shakespeare's inner landscape of occult neoplatonism with its wish for a transcendence that could include ancient mysticism and magical beliefs, unbounded by medieval Christian theology. It was fundamental to Hughes' own beliefs that such meditation allowed the visionary in him to reach depths in his own mind that he normally found inaccessible; in his attempts to understand the greatest poetry of the English language, it was very natural for him to source that imaginative freedom in the world of Elizabethan thought, which was beyond the reach of pragmatic rationalism of the sciences as exemplified by Francis Bacon.

Hughes was fascinated by *The Chemical Wedding* of Christian Rosenkreutz, published in 1616 when Rosenkreutz was under the spell of Shakespeare's last plays. As Hughes knew, Frances Yates had, in the twentieth century, suggested that an interest in occult neoplatonism was widespread among many Elizabethan actors' societies; certainly the character of Prospero seems to exemplify this passion. Both Catholicism and Protestantism saw such ways of thought as dangerously heretical, and combined to annihilate them.

225

Shakespeare and the Goddess of Complete Being, however, took Hughes' argument much further. That Shakespeare's Catholicism, often guessed at, was dangerous in Elizabethan England is well understood; it is Hughes' belief that the worship of Mary gained additional power from an ancient British worship of a great goddess that is controversial. The 'tragic equation'[2] that Hughes found in a close reading of *Venus and Adonis* and *The Rape of Lucrece* could then be used to explore the secret world of Shakespeare's inner passions. That Venus denied becomes the destroyer is readily enough understood in terms of Hughes' own hatred of sexual puritanism. The other side of the coin is a recognition that Tarquin, who abandons himself to lust, loses his soul in the process. Hughes wrote marvellously about Shakespeare's poetry; the book took an enormous amount of his energy and five years to bring to conclusion. Future scholars will no doubt give more respect to Hughes' insights than his contemporaries, if only in recognition of a life spent reading Shakespeare with the intensity of a fellow poet. Disappointingly, it was not taken seriously by academics; some reviews – for example, one from Professor John Carey – voiced a measured derision; but even if his book had been applauded, Hughes might well have wondered if the huge effort had not in some important way cost him his health. Indeed, he came to believe that his immune system had suffered as a result.

All his life he had determined to devote himself to poetry rather than prose; and although his critical prose – as *Winter Pollen* readily illustrates – is among the finest of the twentieth century, prose was a diversion. What he wanted to be working on instead was a kind of spiritual stocktaking. The 'tragic equation' of *The Goddess* had some pertinence to that, but it was only a hint of what he knew he must do. As the 1990s began, he finished *Capriccio*[3] in collaboration with Leonard Baskin – a beautiful boxed volume, two feet tall, with two wide green stripes and orange-brown leather covers. At $4000 it was far too expensive for most people to buy. Fifty copies of *Capriccio* were issued in the spring of 1990. It was hardly the public baring of his soul that *Birthday Letters* became, but it was a beginning.

There are many richly coloured engravings by Baskin. Among these are huge bedraggled birds, with small heads; these images always haunted Baskin but in this volume are markedly different in tone from the tender poems they illustrate. The poems in *Capriccio* recall Hughes' love affair with Assia Wevill.

At first reading, the memories of Assia that predominate are those that

226

connect her to the European death camps she had so narrowly escaped. It is an intuition about her own inner world, rather than an attempt at self-exculpation. In a key poem she keeps her own death within a locket between her breasts, almost like a pet, and uses it to flirt with him:

> It lent you uncanny power. A secret, bluish
> Demonic flash
> When you smiled and gently bit the locket.[4]

The imagined gesture is erotic here, yet Hughes endows Assia throughout with a tragic sense of living on borrowed time, as if she had only cheated death for a moment, almost as if her beauty were already within death's grasp. In his poem, a faulty clasp allows the locket to keep coming open and Hughes, for all his efforts, cannot secure it safely shut.

Is Hughes writing only with hindsight? Or did Assia's fascination with death lend a peculiar poignancy to her beauty even at the time? Her friend Mira Hamermesh had understood as much. Certainly Hughes came to see Assia's whole personality as layers of protective clothing, and in 'Descent' describes her life as a gradual shedding of such disguises: a gradual stripping off of Germany, Russia, British Columbia and England, down to her skin until her whole being, and that of her daughter, is fully exposed and sacrificed.

Put in this way, her story, like her beauty, is something from a fairy tale, and the end is inevitable. In some of the poems she even prophesies it carelessly herself – not as a matter of anguish, but as a way of escaping the ugliness of middle age.

Hughes does not portray Assia as a 'beautiful middle-aged woman', as Ruth Fainlight described her, with greying hair and a thickening body. In his memory her beauty has not diminished, nor has she lost the power to arouse his desire, but he presents her as a woman as vulnerable as Sylvia. Her unhappiness lies within her own being, as if she had lived on the run all her life. Ted knew that he had handled their relationship badly towards the end, but Assia had changed her mind about their love many times, and he could not believe that she had found it impossible to live without him. He expresses genuine bewilderment at the thought in 'The Error', when he wonders why, if their relationship was bringing so much pain, she didn't simply make good her escape:

I watched you feeding the flames.
Why didn't you wrap yourself in a carpet
Get to a hospital
Drop the whole mistake–[5]

Among the new material at Emory, there is an excellent line drawing of Tolstoy by Ted – presumably copied from the frontispiece to a novel – and inscribed to Assia. That dedication evokes the vision of a woman in an Anna Karenina hat – which Assia often wore – and confirms the impression of her as a heroine in a Russian novel. This is echoed in 'Snow', one of Hughes' loveliest poems in *Capriccio*, where he remembers Assia somewhere in the Pennines, with snow on her black fox fur and sharing warm words that seemed to melt in their mouths. It is his most affectionate poem.

In 'Flame', Hughes recalls a trip they made looking for houses somewhere north of the Tyne, where rents are cheap. Perhaps it was their last trip together that he had in mind, since he himself appears to be on his way to Manchester. By then it seems as if he knew the die was already cast. Some mysteries remain, however, since we can only guess at the letter Assia found in her flat, which the poem mentions, and which led to her last, desperate phone call.

The final poem in the book recalls Assia's response to his appearance at her advertising agency in 1962: the blade of grass without any letter, which was at once the beginning of their love affair and the turning point, after which his life was never to be the same again. Beneath what he instantly recognized as a sexual invitation lay Sylvia's death, and that of Assia and their daughter Shura. From that moment, although he told the story in many ways, he was taking the harsh road of a survivor. Looking back across thirty years, he may have thought of his own years of silence as resembling those of his father, brooding over those who died at Gallipoli.

In February 1993, in the midst of writing *The Goddess*, Hughes sent a letter to Keith Sagar in which he wrote about blundering into the pit of sorting out what might be going on in Coleridge's three poems 'Kubla Khan', 'The Ancient Mariner' and 'Christabel'. This in turn gave rise to a penetrating analysis of those poems in *Winter Pollen*. Ordinarily it is impossible not to think of Hughes as closer to Wordsworth than Coleridge's 'doomed mercurial spirit'[6] but there was one significant resemblance: Hughes recognized Coleridge's deepest psychological make-up in the myth of what made him a poet and of what destroyed him. From this point onwards, Hughes is looking for his own self-portrait in the myths that he tells himself. We should not expect the stories to be consistent.

In 1994, Hughes went to the Macedonian Poetry Festival at Struga, where he received the prestigious golden Crown for Poetry. As it happened, I saw him soon after that trip, since I had been teaching a course at Totleigh Barton. He came over for an evening to enjoy a small party with the students, his Faber editor – the poet Christopher Reid – and James Fenton, a brilliant essayist and enormously popular poet who was the guest reader. Hughes spoke of the trials of his enormous correspondence and of the likelihood that the horrors of what was happening in the rest of Yugoslavia would spill over into Macedonia.

He looked as handsome as ever. When at the end of the evening he came over to give me a polite peck on the cheek and say goodbye, a pretty young Lancashire student called out, 'Aren't you lucky to be kissed by Ted Hughes?' As much taken by her extroversion and animation as her good looks, Hughes bent over to give her a similar peck. An entirely innocent exchange of letters followed, in which, however, Hughes charmingly registered his admiration of her person.

In September of the same year, Hughes gave a reading with Simon Armitage at the South Bank. In the packed audience there was a little rustle of surprise after he read 'The Earthenware Head', because, although the poem had been published before in *New Selected Poems*, to hear him read aloud about a moment in his life with Sylvia was oddly disturbing. The audience applauded wildly, and perhaps their response confirmed what he had already discovered: that it was in poetry that he must confront his ghosts.

'Goethe called his work one big confession, didn't he?'[7] Hughes told Drue Heinz when interviewed in 1995 for *Paris Review*. That he should agree to give such an interview was itself startling. He had been asked this almost every year for more than a decade and had always refused. Now the invitation accorded with his willingness to let memories of the past enter his poetry. He puzzled over that in the interview itself: 'The real mystery is this strange need. Why do we have to blab? Why do human beings need to confess? Maybe, if you don't have that secret confession, you don't have a poem – don't even have a story. Don't have a writer.'[8]

All his work in the last decade of his life contains elements of personal autobiography, although the poems about his relationship with Sylvia – there are eight included in Faber's *New Selected Poems 1957–1994* –

attracted little attention at the time. That the critics did not seize upon them may have encouraged him, but he remained wary of their likely reception. At first he put his personal thoughts into the public domain in the form of asides and interpolations, which could be seen as referring to his own past, or as part of the original poem. When he completed his magnificent *Tales from Ovid* in September 1996, he described it as 'a holiday in a rest home'[9] to Ann Skea.

Rather than imitate the metres of the Latin classic, familiar yet half forgotten, Hughes uses the language and rhythms of a contemporary voice from the opening account of Creation onwards:

> God, or some such artist as resourceful,
> Began to sort it out.
> Land here, sky there.[10]

He makes us marvel freshly at the mystery of life appearing from chaos and the interconnected ecology involved in its survival. First vegetable life, then animals, then men find their place, as if Ovid had read Genesis – or Darwin. In the golden age, mankind is content simply to gather the earth's abundance:

> Blackberry or strawberry, mushroom or truffle,
> Every kind of nut, figs, apples, cherries,
> Apricots and pears.[11]

But soon the ground, which was once owned by everyone, has been 'portioned by surveyors into patches',[12] and Man begins to plunder the ores from the earth and go to war over them. Jove, on a fact-finding trip, soon discovers the greed and cruelty of mankind, and determines to destroy the creatures, first by fire and then by flood.

As Hughes explains in the introduction, Ovid lived in the Rome of Augustus, and wrote his *Metamorphoses* around the time of the birth of Christ. Although the metre is epic, Ovid's theme was change and transformation, as bodies are magically transformed by the power of the gods.

As he worked, Hughes trawled through the teeming underworld of Roman myth, selecting those he needed. Ovid has long been a rich source of stories for the Western world. For Hughes, what was important in Ovid was his understanding that human passion, taken to an extreme, engages with an experience of the supernatural. Memorably, in setting Ovid in the context of our own day, Hughes concludes his introduction by suggesting that Ovid's tales 'establish a rough register of what it feels like to live in the psychological gulf that opens at the end of an era. Among everything else that we see in them, we certainly recognise this.'[13]

The last great flowering of Hughes' poetry was an attempt to tell his own story for the first time. In the summer of 1997, he handed over the manuscript of *Birthday Letters* to Matthew Evans at his Gloucestershire home without much in the way of a preliminary announcement. Evans' reaction was a mixture of excitement and apprehension,[14] and he realized that the situation would have to be handled very delicately. The existence of the manuscript was kept absolutely secret, and the book was offered to *The Times* for serialization in November 1997. As a result, twelve of the poems, with a commentary by Erica Wagner, appeared in *The Times* between 17 and 22 January 1998. The dates were chosen by Hughes as particularly propitious astrologically.

'There were certain poems,' Wagner explained, 'Hughes did not wish taken out of the context of the book; on a photocopy of the book's table of contents "Dreamers", "The Inscription" (taking the place of another poem "The Laburnum" which appeared in the first proof I saw), "The Cast", "The Ventriloquist", and "Life After Death" are marked NO in Hughes' strong, sloping hand.'[15] 'Dreamers' is Hughes' account of falling in love with Assia on their visit to Court Green; 'The Cast' has Otto Plath at the stake like Saint Sebastian, pierced with arrows. In 'Life after Death', Hughes recalls feeding his young son tenderly in the weeks after Plath's death. Perhaps most significantly, 'The Inscription' records a rare visit to Hughes' flat by Plath after their separation, and turns on the discovery of Assia's handwriting in one of his copies of Shakespeare, which replaced that earlier destroyed by Sylvia.

None of the poems in *Birthday Letters* is dated, and it has been suggested that they were written in a manic burst of activity in the year up to Hughes' death. There is a good deal of evidence that this is not so. Aside from those published in 1994 as uncollected poems in *New Selected Poems*, as early as 1989 he had confided to a young translator in Bangladesh that he was already engaged in writing poems about his intimate life.[16]

Ted Hughes had been invited as chief guest of honour at the Second Asian Poetry Festival held in Dhaka in November 1989. Carolyne Wright was in the second month of a two-year Fulbright Fellowship, which allowed her to translate the work of Bangladeshi women poets. Hughes took some interest in her as the only other person of European stock – she was American – and was intrigued by her fluent Bengali. She in turn registered the generosity of his attention and 'a profound and genuine kindness'.[17] Hughes asked her whether she had read *Bitter Fame*, and emphasized that he had only corrected a few facts, while noting that the book had at least conveyed some idea of Plath's complexity: 'But she wasn't so difficult, not at all ... Actually she was quite cheerful, bright, even a bit – how to say this – diffident? She always went along with what others wanted. Only when she was jealous was she difficult.'[18] Hughes also spoke of his children's bewilderment at being abandoned by their mother and how he had told them: 'Don't ever speak ill of your mother ... if not for her you would never have been able to attend such good schools ... Ironic, isn't it ... because during her lifetime she struggled to find a publisher.'[19]

Carolyne was profoundly moved by his talking to her so frankly. She speaks of him describing Plath and himself as 'such kids' and going on to say, 'I've been writing out my own versions of events ... but it will be published posthumously. If people knew the full story ... When they learn what really happened between us, they'll be surprised that it's so mundane.'[20] It seems most likely that he was talking about *Birthday Letters* as early as 1989. It was also clear to Carolyne Wright that Hughes would go on 'living with Plath in the only way now possible – in words – in memory – perhaps to the end of his days.'[21]

By 1995, Hughes had begun to realize that the time had come to put his huge archive of letters in order. Originally he asked for help from Keith Sagar and Ann Skea, scholars who had written critically on his work for many years, but he soon saw that it was a task only he could complete. As he began, he mentioned to Ann Skea that he was 'writing about 100 poems about things I should have resolved thirty years ago. Should have written then, but couldn't.'[22] There are many drafts of unfinished poems about Sylvia as well as to her in the archive at Emory university, and not all appear in either *Birthday Letters* or *Howls and Whispers*.

Some of the early poems in *Birthday Letters* are so detailed as to suggest that Hughes might be supplementing his memory by a journal he kept himself;[23] it may possibly exist in a box of material that is restricted for another twenty years at Emory. There are eleven other poems about Sylvia, published as *Howls and Whispers*,[24] with eleven copperplate etchings by Leonard Baskin. At a cost of $4000, as with the *Capriccio* edition, they could never reach more than a small audience.

When the Forward Prize for Poetry of £10,000 was awarded to Ted Hughes in October 1998 for *Birthday Letters*, illness prevented him from collecting the prize in person. He issued a statement revealing that the work had been a way of making a 'direct, private inner contact'[25] with his first wife.

These poems should be read not as self-exculpation but as a form of self-discovery. 'It is vital to acknowledge Hughes' silence *to himself* through the intervening years,'[26] as Wagner points out. Many holocaust survivors adopt this strategy, although psychiatrists divide on whether it is a wise one. With hindsight, Hughes regretted it. He had always eschewed confessional poetry in the narrow sense. This whole book resonates with loss and love. Hughes himself thought the poems 'unpublishably raw and unguarded' and only released them because he could not 'bear to be blocked any longer'.[27] Even if Ann Skea's numerological account of how the book came to be set out is accurate, what most readers will take from the book remains intensely personal.

Hughes told the Israeli journalist Eilat Negev in 1996 that all of Sylvia's life was powered by a single Oedipal story, and that the power of her poems came from her ability to cling to the feelings of an eight-year-old girl, emotions that simmered for twenty years: 'And this naked little girl is at the bottom of all this.'[28] He seemed in that year to believe that Sylvia's suicide was inevitable[29] and that the whole thing depended on her childhood history, as if he were merely a spectator, or at worst a catalyst, in this Greek tragedy.[30] Yet the tone and the temperature of the poems are very different as the book progresses.

Erica Wagner points out that the last third of *Birthday Letters*, which is preoccupied 'with the aftermath of Sylvia Plath's death and the spiritual fate of Plath, and the poet himself, may date from the time of his illness'.[31] In 'Suttee', the most bitter poem in the book, Ted analyses the strange, patient dedication that they both gave to bringing Sylvia's new self, and true poetic voice, to birth, until the burning child sucked the oxygen out of both of them. At no point does Hughes pretend to understand Sylvia's moods. 'The Rabbit Catcher' was originally the title of a Plath poem, and her anger there, directed against the snares of poachers, is intertwined with the thought of her husband's fingers round her throat. The sexual conjectures raised by Jacqueline Rose, in her analysis of this poem in *The Haunting of Sylvia Plath*, brought a furious letter from Hughes at the intrusion. His own poem with the same title in *Birthday Letters* does not address Rose's hypothesis. Instead Ted goes back to his memory of what had triggered Sylvia's fury that morning:

> What had I done? I had
> Somehow misunderstood. Inaccessible
> In your dybbuk fury, babies
> Hurled into the car, you drove.[32]

The matter-of-fact explanation behind this poem, namely that Ted was more sympathetic to a rural poverty that traditionally supplemented the stewpot with a little poaching, lacks the terrifying clutch of the Plath original, but Ted was not writing to stun or to startle, but to understand.

Even Al Alvarez, who might have been expected to look for signs of Ted attempting to whitewash his own guilt, seems to have heard the note of genuine grief in the poetry, and understand its value: 'Hughes takes the bare bones on which biographies have been hung – Cambridge, Spain, America, Devon – and does what no biographer, however diligent and impartial, could ever do: say what it felt like to be there with her.'[33] Noting the fatalism that runs through the poems, John Carey saw how it fitted with the rest of Hughes' work, as part of his vision of a universe in which 'responsibility became a figment valid only in a world of lawyers as moralists'.[34]

The last poems in *Birthday Letters* are the most controversial, dancing as each does with the most memorable poems in *Ariel*. Their own plangent comments run in counterpoint to her music. Several critics thought they were the weakest in the book and certainly they are the least carefully honed. Several blame the writing of poetry, and his own part in conjuring it from Plath's inner world, for her death. In 'The Table', inspired by the elm table Ted made for Sylvia's writing desk, Otto is resurrected as she writes and Hughes transfers the desire Sylvia felt to get back to her dead father on to Otto himself: 'He had got what he wanted' and now all the 'peanut-crunchers' in the world can enjoy his dead daughter's glory.[35] In writing about Plath's terrors, which her writing at once activates and transmutes, he seems to believe that what she was doing was bound to rob her of her husband, children, body and life. Overtly, in 'Dream Life',[36] poetry is given 'blood-sticky feet'. In 'Suttee', too, Hughes accuses the *poems*, which he had struggled to release in her, of being responsible for her death. Both of them had no idea what the poems might be, but

I had delivered an explosion
Of screams that were flames.[37]

That this reiteration is not part of a craven attempt to acquit himself is established in 'Fairy Tale', where he acknowledges the part played by his adultery with Assia Wevill in unlocking the door to the ogre that seized her. He unlocks that dangerous forty-ninth door, after all,

With a blade of grass. You never knew
What a skeleton key I had found
In a single blade of grass.[38]

No one who knows Hughes' story could mistake the echo of Assia's artful beckoning him to her with the pressed grass, unaccompanied by any letter.

Ann Skea argues, in an academic paper entitled 'Poetry and Magic',[39] for a cabbalistic frame of reference for *Birthday Letters*. Since she is a formidable Hughes scholar, and was someone Ted knew well enough to consider as a possible helper in the huge task of ordering the archive of his manuscripts, the suggestion must be taken seriously. Moreover, she argues the case with remarkable cogency.

Cabbala is both an occult number theory – which offers a magical way of reading the Hebrew Bible, where all letters have a numerical value – and also a mystical and magical discipline by which neophytes can understand the world. Hughes' own knowledge of Renaissance alchemy and of adepts like Giordano Bruno and Pico Della Mirandola can be found not only throughout *Shakespeare and The Goddess of Complete Being* but also in *Cave Birds* and *Remains of Elmet*.

However, Hughes himself described the poems in *Birthday Letters* as '*raw*',[40] so I was initially sceptical of any such schematic process in their making. Ann Skea makes the point that Cabbala, 'if nothing else, provided him with a protective structure within which to negotiate with the energies and conjure into being the people and events of his past'.[43] It may well be that Hughes used both Renaissance meditations and the cards of the tarot pack to initiate such a process. Skea, however, goes further, and reads the order of the poems – which is not strictly chronological – in terms of a cabbalistic map. Along these routes, she suggests, Ted and Sylvia set out on a spiritual journey. On the way, Ted has already taken a wrong turning in denying the challenge of the fox cub before meeting

Assia Wevill, as Lilith. The ingenuity with which Skea organizes her considerable knowledge of the arcana is remarkable, and it is essential to recognize that this is the way Ted thought about his life, even though more questions arise than are answered. Why, for instance, were eight poems released separately in *New Selected Poems* in 1995?

Hughes still had to confront the hatred that had dogged him ever since Sylvia's death. Indeed, what purported to be a group of self-styled militant feminists took to putting twigs and berries on the doorsteps of Harold Pinter and John Osborne as well as Hughes. All three men had wives who had died, supposedly as a result of being abandoned by their husbands. Pinter had two conversations about the matter with Ted, whom he described as alarmed by the form of the threat. These hints of witchcraft would have affected Ted more than Pinter, who had never dabbled in such matters, but Ted had also been much more persecuted. In fact, it was Pinter who, through a friend, was able to track down not the *pack* of feminists that they had imagined but instead a lone woman. She, it appeared, was susceptible to persuasion that she was committing a form of terrorism herself for which she could be in some peril, and the manifestations ceased.

EIGHTEEN

The Last Flowering

In the summer of 1996 Hughes suffered from shingles, a painful virus of the herpes variety, which attacks the neural fibres of the body. Andrew Motion recalled its effects on the poet's temple, and reports him saying that he attributed the crash in his immune system to years spent writing too much prose. When he was writing about the blinding of Gloucester in *King Lear*, the rash blinded him in one eye, as he confided to Marina Warner, one of the few people to react with a scholarly sympathy to *Shakespeare and the Goddess of Complete Being*. Yet a far more serious disease had begun to take hold. In 1997 he was diagnosed as having cancer of the colon. Christopher Reid, his editor at Faber, knew that he was seriously ill, but neither asked for nor was told any particular details.

Hughes believed that the illness had begun as early as 1990. Even if that were so, it is one of the most operable of cancers and should not have been a death sentence. His speculation as to the date of its onset suggests that it was not caught early. Hughes had always taken the claims of Ted Cornish, the Okehampton healer, very seriously and had for a time in the 1980s tried to encourage research into his remarkable success rate when conventional medicine failed. Indeed, on 21 November 1985, he had mentioned Cornish's healing powers to Philip Larkin, who was then dying. If Hughes called on Cornish in his own last illness, however, no miraculous cure was forthcoming. Hughes is said to have undergone chemotherapy in 1998, which caused his hair to fall out.[1] This may have been the case, although his hair was fully restored by the time he received his Order of Merit from the Queen in October 1998, as a photograph of that occasion[2] makes plain.

Susan Sonntag has written well about the common error of seeing illness as a form of self-betrayal and Hughes said on several occasions that he had been stricken in his body for neglecting the muse of poetry in favour of critical prose. The poems of the last decade do not bear out this sense of neglect. In sickness Hughes may have felt that his rich imagination was failing him, yet he was producing a large body of remarkable work nonetheless. The last great flowering of Hughes' translated poetry continued. In February 1995, he finished his translation of Wedekind's *Spring Awakening*, perhaps attracted by its rebellion against sexual repression. Unlike the *Oresteia*, which was commissioned and which has a magnificence of a kind very close to the poetry of Hughes' earlier period, the translation of Euripides' *Alcestis* was entirely Hughes' own idea. In any writer's hands, the myth is a strange tale, of a king who allows his wife to die in his place, since no one else can be found who loves him enough to do so. If Hughes had his own first wife's death in mind, the myth is hardly congruent with what we know of Sylvia's motivation, but, in one respect at least there is an echo. It took this biographer back to pondering Hughes' strange remark, 'It was her or me,' made to Suzette Macedo.[3]

In *Alcestis*, the main focus is on King Admetos. It is Admetos whom Death regards as his prize. Ten thousand necessary projects wait on his word. He is as much a healer and shaman as he is a ruler, a magic figure whose continued existence ensures the survival of his kingdom; this is a claim made without irony. As for his pain, since 'nothing has ever hurt him', he does not yet know what the loss of his wife will mean.

Alcestis, in contrast, understands exactly what will give her most pain: she sits on the marital bed and imagines Admetos being happy there in the future with his successor. The promise that she exacts from Admetos is demanded in the name of their children, as if a stepmother would be bound to displace them with her own children. Admetos duly promises not to marry again, but to mourn her for the rest of his life. His father is much less sympathetic to his grief when he tackles Admetos after Alcestis' death; it is precisely his son's self-importance that he mocks:

> You think your life is so priceless
> Others must die to preserve it.
> You think the entire country
> Gets its oxygen only when you breathe in . . .[4]

The singularly literal, plain language makes the point brutally against Hughes himself as someone who has enjoyed a few decades of good fortune and flattery. It is impossible to think that in the last years of his life he was not aware of the parallel. Perhaps he even has in mind the moment when he decided not to die himself[5] and found that his heart fibrillations had ceased as a result – which was, as Myers guesses, in 1962 when he decided to have an affair with Assia Wevill.

The dialogue between Prometheus and God – which is entirely Hughes' interpolation – is a reflection of the godless age in which Hughes had to confront his own death, as men freed from belief must:

> To grope his own way into the mine shaft, into the bank-vault
> Of his own ego.[6]

Man in our time has had to live without his soul, and is unsupported by any sense of other worlds; the Chorus urges Admetus to submit to the rule of necessity. Hughes may have felt that he had at least managed to do that, even if his own first wife could not be miraculously restored to him by a demigod. In one poem in *Howls and Whispers*[7] Hughes mocks himself cruelly as the husband of Electra who cannot understand what is troubling his wife. In another, he is haunted by elusive glimpses of Sylvia and admits a wish to join her, although he fears he has lost the chance of doing so. In a poem of hallucinatory loveliness, he imagines Sylvia's poems themselves as a dark city, which he can sometimes drive through at night.

Although Hughes continued to reply to correspondents who wrote mainly to ask for help or his autograph, his attendance at literary receptions had always been sporadic, and by now his response was usually to refuse. It is often Carol Hughes' clear hand that now replies on his behalf. Nor was it only the huge secretarial burden of his correspondence that she had begun to take on. From October 1990, she was ready to assume some of the responsibilities previously shouldered by Olwyn.

All Olwyn's friends had been urging her for some time to release herself from the self-imposed task of defending her younger brother. Friends found that it was almost impossible to talk to her about anything else. And she herself was quite eager to hand over to Faber & Faber the task of granting permission. She had not, however, expected to find that all powers of decision would be taken out of her hands.

There is a letter from Olwyn in the archive in Emory,[8] in which she comments on a conversation with Ted and Carol that led her to think she was expected to sever all connections with what was, after all, her live-lihood. The suggestion shocked her. Had this happened fifteen years earlier she might well have decided on a different route for her life, but she felt a little old to change direction in her sixties. Fortunately, when she set this out crisply in a letter, it soon became clear that Ted had no intention of reducing her income or denying her a generous commission on the royalties of his own and Sylvia's work. But certainly her power over the estate was henceforward reduced.

Hughes' own calendar remained overwhelmed by appointments, although he took on few readings – an exception being at the University of East Anglia, at the invitation of Andrew Motion. For this reading at UEA he received £1000 plus VAT, and Ted may well have had provision for his family in mind. Andrew wrote on 15 January 1996 to ask if Ted would be coming with Carol, and whether he wanted to be booked into the guest suite, since university economies put a hotel out of the question. Hughes has marked the letter 'alone'.[9]

He was beginning to wonder whether, or at what point, to publish the poems that became *Birthday Letters*. A sizeable proportion of the book was ready for publication as early as 1995[10] but he remained undecided about when to release it. In September 1997, the Moortown farm was sold, along with Hughes' favourite bull. In conversation with Ann Skea he spoke of choosing two possible dates for publication of *Birthday Letters*, using horoscopes, although even as late as October he was still wondering about whether to publish at all. By November his decision was firm, but he asked Keith Sagar not to speak of it, in case a whole 'entrenched weaponry be mounted against it. Totally vulnerable as it is'.[11] Perhaps Hughes was encouraged to publish what he had written of *Birthday Letters* by letters from friends, notably Thom Gunn.[12] Gunn thought it essential that he should publish any pieces he had already written, and add anything else that would make the story complete. He not only thought that such a book would be good for the record, he felt it would promote Hughes' own well-being, too. A very different man, with a completely different set of beliefs, Gunn shared Hughes' sense of the power of poetry. It is worth noting, however, that he also advises Hughes not to be too obviously on the defensive.

In January 1998, Hughes' *Tales of Ovid* won the Whitbread Book of the Year Award. Hughes was known to be ill, but none of his friends guessed how ill. Even Daniel Weissbort, who had himself suffered from cancer and had frequently seen Hughes in his last summer as they worked together on the translations of Amichai, seemed fairly confident that he was recovering. Most people knew nothing of his illness. Fay Godwin, the photographer who had collaborated with Hughes on

Remains of Elmet, for instance, heard of his death as a complete shock: 'He was my contemporary, a strong reference point in my life, a source of generosity and inspiration; and I still cannot believe that he has been felled.'[13]

Hughes and I exchanged letters some time in January 1998, after he had been working with Daniel Weissbort on the translation of *The Prophet* for an edition of translations of Pushkin by leading contemporary poets, which I had been editing for the Folio Society and Carcanet. His main concern was that Weissbort should be given sufficient credit for the work that he had put in while furnishing a literal version. At the same time he asked if anyone had tackled Pushkin's huge poem *The Bronze Horseman.* In fact there was a piece already commissioned, but I was so delighted to hear of his interest that I wrote back eagerly to encourage him. It so happened that the Baskins were saying at Court Green. My husband had never quite forgiven me for the breach in our relations with Leonard, which came about as a result of my robust defence of Olwyn in 1976,[14] and I sent an invitation to Leonard too, hoping for a reconciliation over dinner in London.

In January 1997, *Birthday Letters* was already topping the bestseller lists. In March it went on to win the W.H. Smith Award. Hughes continued to work with a will, putting together, with Daniel Weissbort, the 250 best translations of poems by his old friend Yehuda Amichai, Israel's leading poet.

Shortly after having won the Forward Prize for Poetry for *Birthday Letters* Hughes was appointed a member of the Queen's Order of Merit, a distinction bestowed on only twenty-four people at any one time. The photograph of him receiving the honour shows him to be singularly calm, considering what he must have known of the state of his health.

He wrote many letters in the remaining weeks of his life, including a letter to John Carey, with whom he had quarrelled so violently when *Shakespeare and the Goddess of Complete Being* was published. Hughes included the traditional image of a duck that can also be read as a rabbit, suggesting that both their versions of Shakespeare were possible truths.

He died of a heart attack on 28 October 1998 in London Bridge Hospital, a private clinic close to Guy's Hospital where he had been receiving treatment for metastatic cancer of the colon. His daughter Frieda was with him. When in January 1999 he was posthumously awarded the T.S. Eliot Prize for *Birthday Letters,* it was Frieda who received it for him, looking – as many whispered – exactly like her dead mother, and reading from the letter in which he explains the strange release that writing about his life with Sylvia had brought him.[15]

Epilogue

October was dark and wet, with floods in London as well as the countryside. It was Olwyn who rang me early on 29 October 1998 to tell me that Ted had died, and to give me the date of the funeral in North Tawton. My husband and I made our way down to Devon by train through gusting winds and fields of mud. At The George in Hatherleigh were several of Ted's old friends. There was Nathaniel Minton from Ted's Cambridge days, whom we met for the first time, and Michael Baldwin, whom I remembered from the 1970s in London.

The next day, Court Green was filled with a lifetime of Ted's friends from university onwards, some of whom had crossed the Atlantic to be there. The funeral was held in the church next to Court Green, a bleak, bare building with dark beams and whitewashed walls. Reverend Terence McCaughey, now Senior Lecturer Emeritus at Trinity College, Dublin – Ted's singing companion from days at The Anchor in Cambridge – took the service, and the Nobel Laureate Seamus Heaney read one of Ted's poems. The pews were packed, with local villagers as well as Londoners. We all gazed in silence at his huge coffin. After the ceremony, his close family – Carol, Frieda and Nicholas, and his sister Olwyn – left for Exeter, where his body was to be cremated. Court Green itself was locked, and several of us milled around North Tawton, feeling bewildered.

On 13 May 1999, a service of thanksgiving for the life of Ted Hughes was held at Westminster Abbey, attended by the Queen Mother and the Prince of Wales. As that date is the anniversary of the death of Ted's mother, Seamus Heaney read Ted's moving poem about her. The singer Shusha Guppy sang from a lyric Ted had adapted, and poems from *Wodwo*, *Season Songs* and *River* were read by, among others, Gray Gowrie. Then the programme announced the 'Song' from Shakespeare's *Cymbeline*.

There was a little shuffle of conjecture among the listeners, since no reader was named. Then Ted's rich, quiet voice spoke the first lines:

> Fear no more the heat of the sun,
> Nor the furious winter's rages;
> Thou thy worldly task hast done,
> Home art gone, and ta'en thy wages;
> Golden lads and girls all must,
> As chimney-sweepers, come to dust.

Some poets struggle for a lifetime to find a voice that is truly theirs. Hughes discovered his own early, and it was closely connected to the Yorkshire cadences that now gave shape to Shakespeare's miraculous lyric. His poetry grew from the man he was 'as naturally as leaves from a tree'[1] and, for all the impatience he often expressed at how little he was producing, the body of his work is formidable. As the date of his death recedes, his stature seems only to increase.

Notes

The following abbreviations have been used: EF for Elaine Feinstein; TH for Ted Hughes; SCD for Special Collections Department, Robert W. Woodruff Library, Emory University, Atlanta, Georgia.

Introduction, pp. 1–3
[1] MSS 644, SCD, box 18, ff. 10, business correspondence.

Chapter 1: Childhood, pp. 5–20
[1] In 1625 Nicholas Ferrar founded a small monastic community at Little Gidding, which brought together elements of Protestant and Catholic spirituality. It fascinated T.S. Eliot among others.
[2] TH, 'Mount Zion', *New Selected Poems 1957–1994* (Faber & Faber, 1995), p. 168.
[3] TH, 'The Rock', in *Writers on Themselves* (BBC, 1964), collected in Geoffrey Summerfield *Worlds* (Penguin, 1974) p. 126.
[4] EF interview with Donald Crossley, January 2000.
[5] TH, 'Dust As We Are', *New Selected Poems,* p. 269.
[6] EF interview with Donald Crossley, January 2000.
[7] Letter to Anne Stevenson, Sep/Oct. Cambridge University Library, from her papers held in Cambridge University Library, ADD MS9 4451.

[8] The first story in TH, *Difficulties of a Bridegroom, Collected Short Stories* (Faber & Faber, 1995).
[9] TH, 'Poetry in the Making', (1967); reissued in *Winter Pollen* William Scammel (ed.) (Faber & Faber, 1995), p. 10.
[10] EF interview with Donald Crossley, January 2000.
[11] EF telephone conversation with John Wholey, March 2001.
[12] Drue Heinz, 'The Art of Poetry', *Paris Review,* no. 134, 1995, p. 59.
[13] Keith Sagar, *The Laughter of Foxes* (Liverpool University Press, 2000), p. 39.
[14] TH, 'The Rock', *Worlds,* p. 124.
[15] Sagar, *Laughter of Foxes,* p. 104 (quoted in *The Poet Speaks: Ted Hughes speaks to Peter Orr,* (British Council, 1987).
[16] Margaret Drabble, *The Peppered Moth,* (Viking, 2001) p. 8 and *passim.*
[17] MSS 854, SCD, *passim.*
[18] MSS 854, SCD, box 1, ff. 6, letters to Gerald Hughes.
[19] Lucas Myers, *Crow Steered, Bergs Appeared* (Proctor Press, 2001), p. 68.

[20] Heinz, 'Art of Poetry', p. 68.

[21] EF telephone conversation with John Wholey, March 2001.

[22] Tom Pero, 'An Interview with Ted Hughes', *Wild Steelhead & Salmon*, Winter 1999 (partially reprinted in the *Guardian*, 9 January 1999).

[23] Heinz, 'Art of Poetry', p. 59.

[24] MSS 854, SCD, a fragment among letters to Gerald Hughes.

[25] Before English coinage was decimalized, there were twenty shillings in a pound, and twelve pence in a shilling. One shilling and ten pence – less than the current ten-pence coin – would have bought a fairly substantial quantity of a cheaper cut of meat.

[26] Norman Longmate, *How We Lived Then* (Hutchinson, 1971).

[27] EF telephone conversation with John Wholey, March 2001.

[28] MSS 644, SCD, box 28, ff. 2.

[29] From TH boyhood poem, quoted by Sagar, *Laughter of Foxes*, p. 42.

[30] TH, 'Fantastic Happenings and Gory Adventures', *Winter Pollen*, pp. 4–5.

[31] Sagar, *Laughter of Foxes*, p. 43.

[32] MSS 854, SCD, box 1, ff. 20, letters to Gerald Hughes.

[33] Sagar, *Laughter of Foxes*, p. 43.

[34] Letter from Dr Gwen Black, received by EF in October 1999.

[35] MSS 644, SCD, box 28, ff. 1, general correspondence.

[36] TH, 'Fantastic Happenings and Gory Adventures', *Winter Pollen*, p. 6.

[37] EF interview with Donald Crossley, January 2000.

[38] Letter from Dr Gwen Black to EF, October 1999.

[39] EF telephone conversation with Alice Wholey, March 2001.

[40] Email to EF from Michael Boddy, 14 February 2001. These pranks included an amazingly foolish wiring-up of a steel urinal to an electricity supply, which caused great pain to the next man who used it.

[41] Heinz, 'Art of Poetry', p. 85.

Chapter 2: Pembroke College, pp. 21–35

[1] Founded in 1347.

[2] Karl Miller, *Rebecca's Vest* (Hamish Hamilton, 1993), p. 128.

[3] EF interview with Michael Podro, October 2000.

[4] Notably Fred Grubb, in conversation with EF September, 2000.

[5] TH, 'Soliloquy' from *The Hawk in the Rain*, in *New Selected Poems*, p. 7.

[6] As a result of its being bought from him by Glen Fallows, as related in 'Ted Hughes: Reminiscences', written for *Martlet*, 1999, a Pembroke College magazine. Fallows is the former Head of English at Slough Grammar School.

[7] Fallows, 'Reminiscences', p. 8.

[8] When Hughes came to read Anthropology in his third year.

[9] EF interview with David Ross, 1999.

[10] Miller, *Rebecca's Vest*, p. 129.

[11] Brian Cox, 'Ted Hughes (1930–1998): A Personal Retrospect', *Hudson Review*, vol. LII, no. 1 (Spring 1999), p. 32.

[12] Letter from John Honey MA, D.Phil., FR Hist. Soc., Professor of History, Botswana University, to EF, posted 8 December 1999.

[13] An undergraduate reading English at Selwyn, 1949–52, two years ahead of TH.

[14] Letter from John Coggrave to EF, 16 October 1999.

[15] Ibid.

[16] Fallows, 'Reminiscences', p. 8.

[17] Cox, 'Ted Hughes', p. 32.

[18] D.D. Bradley, 'Ted Hughes 1930–98', *Pembroke College Cambridge Annual Gazette*, no. 73 (September 1999), p. 23.

19 Fallows, 'Reminiscences', p. 8.

20 Ibid.

21 EF interview with Brian Cox, 1999.

22 Cox, 'Ted Hughes', pp. 30.

23 EF interview with Cox.

24 Fallows, 'Reminiscences', p. 23.

25 Both were handsome young men; in addition, Mander came from a rich and aristocratic family.

26 Thom Gunn, *The Occasions of Poetry* (Faber & Faber, 1982), p. 154.

27 Ibid.

28 MSS 854, SCD, , box 1, ff. 1, letters to Gerald Hughes.

29 Ibid.

30 MSS 854, SCD, , box 1, ff. 2, letters to Gerald Hughes.

31 Letter from Professor John Honey to EF, posted 8 December 1999.

32 Daiches is an eminent lecturer in English.

33 Letter from Professor John Honey to EF, posted 8 December 1999.

34 Quoted by Sagar, in *Laughter of Foxes*, p. 46.

35 Email from Michael Boddy to EF, 14 February 2001.

36 Email from Daniel Weissbort to EF, 2000.

37 EF interview with David Ross, 1999.

38 EF interview with Peter Redgrove, September 1999.

39 Ibid.

40 Bradley, 'Ted Hughes', p. 23.

41 Letter from John Coggrave to EF, 16 October 1999.

42 EF with Peter Redgrove, September 1999.

43 Ibid.

44 Philip Hobsbaum, 'Ted Hughes at Cambridge', *Dark Horse*, no. 8 (Autumn 1999), p. 6.

45 Hobsbaum, 'Ted Hughes', p. 6.

46 Hobsbaum, 'Ted Hughes', p. 8.

47 EF interview with Karl Miller, November 1999.

48 Heinz, 'The Art of Poetry', p. 68.

49 'Off the Page' (1988), Thames Television.

50 MSS 854, SCD, box 1, ff. 4, letters to Gerald Hughes.

51 Ibid.

52 MSS 854, SCD, box 1, ff. 4, letters to Gerald Hughes.

53 Ibid.

Chapter 3: St Botolph's, pp. 36–49

1 Lucas Myers memoir, Appendix I in Anne Stevenson, *Bitter Fame* (Viking, 1989), p. 308.

2 Email from Michael Boddy to EF, March 2001.

3 Myers, *Crow Steered, Bergs Appeared*, p. 34.

4 Email from Michael Boddy to EF, February 2001.

5 Email from Michael Boddy to EF, March 2001.

6 Ibid.

7 Ibid.

8 Heinz, 'The Art of Poetry', p. 76.

9 See Donald Davie, *Remembering the Movement*, ed. Elaine Feinstein, (*Prospect*, 1959).

10 Heinz, 'The Art of Poetry', p. 77.

11 Letter from Professor John Honey to EF, posted 8 December 1999.

12 Email from Michael Boddy.

13 Email from Michael Boddy to EF, February 2001.

14 MSS 865, SCD, box 1, ff. 1, letter to Lucas Myers from Helen Hitchcock, 12 October 1955.

15 Robert Graves, *The White Goddess* (Faber & Faber, 1948), p. 24.

16 EF interview with David Ross, 1999.

17 Myers, *Crow Steered, Bergs Appeared*, p. 9.

18 Myers, *Crow Steered, Bergs Appeared*, p. 8.

19 Al Alvarez, *The Savage God* (Weidenfeld & Nicolson, 1971), p. 44.

20 Heinz, 'The Art of Poetry', p. 87.

21 David Ross in an interview with EF; his presence is confirmed by Lucas Myers, *Crow Steered, Bergs Appeared*, and by Michael Boddy.

22 EF interview with David Ross, 1999.

23 Daniel Weissbort in conversation with EF.

24 Hobsbaum, 'Ted Hughes', p. 9.

25 Ibid.

26 Myers, Appendix I, in Stevenson, *Bitter Fame*, p. 310.

27 Myers, Appendix I, in Stevenson, *Bitter Fame*, p. 311.

28 TH, 'The Thought Fox', from *Hawk in the Rain*, in *New Selected Poems*, p. 3.

29 MSS 644, SCD, box 18, ff. 10, letter to Aurelia Plath, January 1975.

30 MSS 854, SCD, box 1, ff. 4, letters to Gerald Hughes.

31 Hobsbaum, 'Ted Hughes', p. 10.

32 Hobsbaum, 'Ted Hughes'.

33 Heinz, 'The Art of Poetry', p. 68.

34 Antonia Byatt in conversation with EF, March 1998.

35 TH, 'Paris, 1954', *Howls and Whispers* (Gehenna Press, Northampton, 1998).

36 Myers, Appendix I, in Stevenson, *Bitter Fame*, p. 310.

37 Michael Boddy is a dissenting voice here. Unlike Daniel Weissbort and David Ross, he is convinced that Joe Lyde was in the States at the time, and attributes Ted's mention of Lyde in *Birthday Letters* to a generous wish to perpetuate Lyde's memory.

38 EF interview with David Ross, 1999.

39 Myers, Appendix I, in Stevenson, *Bitter Fame*, p. 312.

40 Lucas Myers in conversation with EF.

41 Myers, *Crow Steered, Bergs Appeared*, p. 33.

42 A house for foreign students at Newnham across the gardens of the college.

43 Myers, *Crow Steered, Bergs Appeared*, p. 30.

44 TH, 'Fallgrief's Girlfriends' from *Hawk in the Rain*, in *New Selected Poems*, p. 9.

45 EF interview with David Ross, 1999.

46 Later on Professor J. Plumb, Professor of History, Master of Christ's College.

47 Karen Kukil (ed.), *The Journals of Sylvia Plath 1950–1962* (Faber & Faber, 2000), p. 210.

48 TH, 'St Botolph's', *Birthday Letters* (Faber & Faber, 1998), p. 15.

49 Ibid.

50 Myers, *Crow Steered, Bergs Appeared*, p. 32.

51 Kukil (ed.), *Journals of Sylvia Plath*, p. 211.

52 Ibid.

53 Ibid.

54 TH, 'St Botolph's', *Birthday Letters*, p. 15.

55 MSS 865, SCD, box 1, ff. 2, correspondence with Lucas Myers, 18 March 1956.

56 Ibid.

Chapter 4: Plath, pp. 50–61

1 Myers, Appendix I, in Stevenson, *Bitter Fame*, p. 313.

2 Ibid.

3 Ibid.

4 Clark University Press, Worcester, Massachusetts, 1935.

5 Aurelia Plath (ed.), *Sylvia Plath's Letters Home: Correspondence 1950–1963* (Faber & Faber, 1975), p. 123.

6 Stevenson, *Bitter Fame*, p. 44.

7 Quoted in Stevenson, *Bitter Fame*, p. 45.

8 Lewis Wolpert, *The Malignant Sadness* (Faber & Faber, 1999).

9 Stevenson, *Bitter Fame*, p. 47.

[10] She gives her recollections in Edward Butscher, *Sylvia Plath: the Woman and the Work* (Peter Owen, 1979).

[11] Gordon Lameyer also gives an account of his relationship to Plath in Butscher, *Sylvia Plath*.

[12] Another contributor to Butscher's collection of essays, *Sylvia Plath*.

[13] Kukil (ed.), *Journals of Sylvia Plath*, p. 233.

[14] Email from Michael Boddy to EF, March 2001.

[15] TH, '18 Rugby Street', *Birthday Letters*, p. 20.

[16] Ibid.

[17] TH, '18 Rugby Street', *Birthday Letters*, p. 24.

[18] Email from Michael Boddy to EF, February 2001.

[19] Email from Michael Boddy to EF, March 2001.

[20] Erica Wagner, *Ariel's Gift* (Faber & Faber, 2000), p. 41.

[21] Anne Stevenson in *Bitter Fame* points out none of these survives, and she questions their existence.

[22] *Letters Home*, p. 233.

[23] Myers, *Crow Steered, Bergs Appeared*, p. 52.

[24] Myers, *Crow Steered, Bergs Appeared*, p. 34.

[25] Heinz, 'The Art of Poetry', p. 77.

[26] Butscher, *Sylvia Plath*, p. 61.

[27] Heinz, 'The Art of Poetry', p. 77.

[28] See TH, 'Fidelity', *Birthday Letters*, p. 29.

[29] As she was indeed to me, when I was her pupil.

[30] MSS 644, SCD, box 18, ff. 10, business correspondence.

[31] TH, 'Your Paris', *Birthday Letters*, p. 38.

Chapter 5: Marriage, pp. 62–75
[1] TH, 'Fate Playing', *Birthday Letters*, p. 32.

[2] Stevenson, *Bitter Fame*, p. 92.

[3] TH, 'Drawing', *Birthday Letters*, p. 44.

[4] Kukil (ed) *Journals of Sylvia Plath*, Appendix 9, p. 570.

[5] Kukil (ed.), *Journals of Sylvia Plath*, p. 251.

[6] TH, *Birthday Letters*, 'You hated Spain', p. 39.

[7] TH, *Birthday Letters*, 'Fever', p. 47.

[8] EF interview with Keith Sagar, February 1999.

[9] Sylvia Plath, 'Pursuit', *Collected Poems* (Faber & Faber, 1981), p. 22.

[10] Ibid.

[11] Introduction to Butscher, *Sylvia Plath*, p. 24.

[12] A Fellow of the college appointed to be responsible for the students' moral welfare.

[13] Anne Stevenson comments in *Bitter Fame* that £20 of this, together with the key to Olwyn's flat, had been left for Ted the summer before in Paris.

[14] Stevenson, *Bitter Fame*, p 99.

[15] Ibid.

[16] Ibid.

[17] Stevenson, *Bitter Fame*, p. 100.

[18] EF interview with John Press, June 2000.

[19] TH, 'The Hawk in the Rain', from *The Hawk in the Rain* (Faber & Faber, 1957).

[20] Ibid.

[21] From 'Horses', from *New Selected Poems*, p. 8. If there is one word that sings through several poems in this collection it is the word 'horizon'.

[22] Ekbert Fass, *Ted Hughes: The Unaccommodated Universe* (Black Sparrow Press, 1980), p. 203.

[23] Plath (ed.), *Letters Home*, pp. 268–9.

[24] TH, 'Wuthering Heights', *Birthday Letters*, p. 61.

[25] MSS 854, SCD, box 1, ff. 6, letters to Gerald Hughes.
[26] TH, 'Thrushes', from *Lupercal*, in *New Selected Poems*, p. 39.
[27] TH, '55 Eltisley', *Birthday Letters*, p. 49.
[28] EF in conversation with Daniel Weissbort.
[29] Sagar, *The Laughter of Foxes*, p. 47.
[30] Plath (ed.), *Letters Home*, p. 294.
[31] TH, 'Ouija', *Birthday Letters*, p. 53.
[32] EF interview with Karl Miller, November 1999.
[33] See Butscher, *Sylvia Plath*, p. 55.
[34] At 1957 values, £1 = $2.80, so this would be the equivalent of £1700, considerably more than a Cambridge lecturer's salary at the time.
[35] Plath (ed.), *Letters Home*, p. 290.
[36] Very few 1st Class degrees – rarely more than five or six – were awarded in the English Tripos. A 2:1 degree would have allowed Sylvia to continue to do research.
[37] Stevenson, *Bitter Fame*, p. 110.
[38] Ibid.

Chapter 6: America, pp. 76–93
[1] Heinz, 'The Art of Poetry', p. 77.
[2] MSS 865, SCD, box 1, ff. 3, letter to Lucas Myers, 22 July.
[3] TH, 'Flounders', *Birthday Letters*, p. 65.
[4] Kindly shown to EF in MS.
[5] See Stevenson, *Bitter Fame*.
[6] MSS 865, SCD, box 1, ff. 3, letter to Lucas Myers, 22 July.
[7] Ibid.
[8] Dan Huws and David Ross, who were both married by this time.
[9] MSS 865, SCD, box 1, ff. 3, letter to Lucas Myers, 22 July.
[10] TH, 'The Blue Flannel Suit', *Birthday Letters*, p. 67.
[11] MSS 865, SCD, box 1, ff. 4.
[12] Ibid.

[13] MSS 854, SCD, box 1, letters to Gerald Hughes.
[14] EF interview with Clarissa Roche, 1999.
[15] Ibid.
[16] Stevenson, *Bitter Fame*, p. 193.
[17] Dido Merwin, Appendix II, in Stevenson, *Bitter Fame*, p. 117.
[18] MSS 856, SCD, box 1, ff. 4, letters to W.S. Merwin.
[19] Kukil, (ed.), *The Journals of Sylvia Plath*, p. 347.
[20] MSS 865, SCD, box 1, ff. 4, Winter 1958.
[21] Ibid.
[22] EF interview with Clarissa Roche, 1999.
[23] Kukil, (ed.), *The Journals of Sylvia Plath*, p. 354.
[24] Kukil, (ed.), *The Journals of Sylvia Plath*, p. 352.
[25] Kukil, (ed.), *The Journals of Sylvia Plath*, p. 368.
[26] MSS 865, SCD, box 1, ff. 4, May 1958.
[27] Stevenson, *Bitter Fame*, p. 123.
[28] Kukil, (ed.), *Journals of Sylvia Plath*, p. 485.
[29] MSS 865, SCD, box 1, ff. 4, May 1958.
[30] Lupercal, according to legend, was the cave in Rome where the she-wolf suckled the city's founders, Romulus and Remus.
[31] TH, 'Snowdrop', from *Lupercal*, in *New Selected Poems*, p. 40.
[32] TH, 'Hawk Roosting', from *Lupercal*, in *New Selected Poems*, p. 29.
[33] TH interview with Erbert Faas.
[34] TH, 'Crow Hill', from *Lupercal*, in *New Selected Poems*, p. 25.
[35] Played by TH.
[36] EF interview with Clarissa Roche, 1999.
[37] Email from Michael Boddy.
[38] Kukil, (ed.), *Journals of Sylvia Plath*, p. 388.

39 Kukil, (ed.), *Journals of Sylvia Plath*, p. 390.

40 SCD, series 1.5, box 63, ff. 6. A box of miscellaneous photocopies.

41 Kukil, (ed.), *Journals of Sylvia Plath*, p. 392.

42 Kukil, (ed.), *Journals of Sylvia Plath*, p. 401.

43 Kukil, (ed.), *Journals of Sylvia Plath*, p. 451.

44 MSS 644, SCD, box 18, ff. 10, letter to Aurelia Plath, January 1975.

45 Kukil, (ed.), *Journals of Sylvia Plath*, p. 445.

46 Kukil, (ed.), *Journals of Sylvia Plath*, p. 430. This was a point she made to Suzette Macedo later (see EF interview with Suzette Macedo, 1999). To Beuscher she speaks of her mother as a murderess of maleness.

47 Kukil, (ed.), *Journals of Sylvia Plath*, p. 476.

48 Tim Kendall, *Sylvia Plath*, seen in MS.

49 SCD, series 1.5, box 63, ff. 6.

50 Kukil, (ed.), *Journals of Sylvia Plath*, p. 473.

51 Plath, 'Electra on Azalea Path', *Collected Poems*, p. 116.

52 MSS 865, SCD, box 1, ff. 4, letter to Lucas Myers, spring 1958.

53 Diane Wood Middlebrook, *Anne Sexton, a biography* (Vintage, 1992), p. 111.

54 Wood Middlebrook, *Anne Sexton*, p. 107.

55 Kukil, (ed.), *Journals of Sylvia Plath*, p. 475. It was an opinion that Hughes was to voice years later.

56 Stevenson, *Bitter Fame*, p. 155.

57 It is an attitude naturally easier for the victorious.

58 MSS 865, SCD, box 1, ff. 5, letter to Lucas Myers, 9 June 1959.

59 Ibid.

60 MSS 644, SCD, box 18, ff. 10, letter to Aurelia Plath, January 1975.

61 Kukil, (ed.), *Journals of Sylvia Plath*, p. 500.

62 Kukil, (ed.), *Journals of Sylvia Plath*, p. 501.

63 Myers, *Crow Steered, Bergs Appeared*, p. 69.

64 Kukil, (ed.), *Journals of Sylvia Plath*, p. 517.

Chapter 7: A Family Man, pp. 94–110

1 See Stevenson, *Bitter Fame*, p. 178.

2 MSS 854, SCD.

3 Myers, *Crow Steered, Bergs Appeared*, p. 65.

4 Stevenson, *Bitter Fame*, p. 177.

5 TH, 'Stubbing Wharfe', *Birthday Letters*, p. 106.

6 Letter quoted in Stevenson, *Bitter Fame*, p. 182.

7 Quoted in Stevenson, *Bitter Fame*, p. 189.

8 EF interview with David Ross, October 1999.

9 EF interview with Peter Redgrove, September 1999.

10 Ibid.

11 Myers, *Crow Steered, Bergs Appeared*, p. 77.

12 Myers' memoir, Appendix I, in Stevenson, *Bitter Fame*, p. 318.

13 Alvarez, *The Savage God*, p. 21.

14 Quoted in Stevenson, *Bitter Fame*, p. 186.

15 Myers, Appendix I, in Stevenson, *Bitter Fame*, p. 319.

16 Stevenson, *Bitter Fame*, p. 187.

17 MSS 854, SCD, box 1, ff. 9, letter from Edith Hughes among the letters to Gerald Hughes.

18 Letter from Myers quoted in Stevenson, *Bitter Fame*, p. 189.

19 Al Alvarez, *Where Did It All Go Right?* (Richard Cohen Books, 2000), p. 98.

20 Ted usually wore grey trousers.

21 Al Alvarez, *Where Did It All Go Right?* p. 284.

22 MSS 866, SCD, *passim*.

23 MSS 865, SCD, box 1, ff. 6.

24 Ibid.

25 Paul Alexander, *Rough Magic* (Da Capo Press, 1999), p. 252. He cites letters, both published and unpublished, to Aurelia Plath.

26 Edith's letter to Gerald, which mentions both the radio programme and Sylvia's appendectomy, must refer to the 1960 Christmas visit to Yorkshire.

27 Plath, 'Tulips', *Collected Poems*, p. 161.

28 Ibid.

29 TH, 'Epiphany', *Birthday Letters*, p. 115.

30 Cambridge University Library ADD MSS 9445.

31 Alvarez, *The Savage God*, p. 22.

32 EF interview with Ruth Fainlight, February 2000.

33 EF interview with Suzette Macedo, October 1999.

34 Ibid.

35 Ibid.

36 MSS 644, SCD, box 18, ff. 10, letter to Aurelia Plath, January 1975.

37 Ibid.

38 Ibid.

39 Dido Merwin, Appendix II, in Stevenson, *Bitter Fame*, p. 341.

Chapter 8: Devon, 111–124

1 11 September 1961; the letter is in the private possession of Ruth Fainlight.

2 EF interview with Peter Redgrove September 1999.

3 TH, 'The Table', *Birthday Letters*, p. 138.

4 Plath, 'Mirror', *Collected Poems*, p. 173.

5 MSS 865, SCD, TH letter to Myers late 1961.

6 TH, 'The Lodger', *Birthday Letters*, p. 124.

7 Myers, *Crow Steered, Bergs Appeared*, p. 79.

8 Myers, *Crow Steered, Bergs Appeared*, p. 78.

9 TH, letter to Anne Stevenson, Cambridge University Library, ADD MS 94451, September/October 1986.

10 TH, 'The Rag Rug', *Birthday Letters*, p. 135.

11 TH, 'Error', *Birthday Letters*, p. 122.

12 Plath, 'Blackberrying', *Collected Poems*, p. 168.

13 TH, 'Publishing Sylvia Plath', *Winter Pollen*, p. 165.

14 Plath, letter 4 March 1962 to Ruth Fainlight.

15 MSS 866, SCD, box 1, ff. 20, letter to Bill Merwin, 14 March 1962.

16 TH, 'Setebos', *Birthday Letters*, p. 133.

17 EF interview with Elizabeth Compton Sigmund, September 1999.

18 Janet Malcolm, *The Silent Woman*, p. 168.

19 EF interview with Elizabeth Compton Sigmund, September 1999.

20 Ibid.

21 Ibid.

22 EF telephone conversation with Alice Wholey, March 2001.

23 EF interview with Elizabeth Compton Sigmund, September 1999.

24 Letter dated 16 April 1962, in the private possession of Ruth Fainlight.

25 Ibid.

26 At this point in the interview, unexpectedly, Ruth began to cry, and remarked, 'I'm getting quite overwrought.'

27 Letter to Ruth Fainlight, 12 May 1962.

28 EF interview with Suzette Macedo, October 1999.

29 Aurelia Plath, *Letters Home*, p. 454.

30 EF interview with Mira Hamermesh, April 2000.

31 Ibid.

32 EF interview with Suzette Macedo, October 1999.

33 Jean Hart was a singer, and Malcolm worked in advertising.

34 EF interview with Suzette Macedo, October 1999.

35 Ibid.

36 Ibid.

37 Ibid.

38 Interview with Al Alvarez, May 2000.

39 A slovenly and untidy person.

40 EF interview with Suzette Macedo, October 1999.

41 Ibid.

42 TH, 'Dreamers', *Birthday Letters*, p. 157.

43 Ibid.

44 ADD MSS 94451, Cambridge University Library, letter from Olwyn Hughes to Anne Stevenson, February 1989.

45 ADD MSS 94451 Cambridge University library, letter from David Wevill to Anne Stevenson.

46 From 'Chlorophyl', the last poem in *Capriccio*, Gehenna Press, 1990.

Chapter 9: The Single Life, 125–143

1 Stevenson, *Bitter Fame*, p. 244.

2 EF interview with Suzette Macedo, October 1999.

3 Ibid.

4 Ibid.

5 Ibid.

6 Interview with Elizabeth Compton Sigmund, September 1999.

7 Ibid.

8 EF interview with Brian Cox, 1999.

9 Cox, 'Ted Hughes 1930–98', p. 36.

10 Quoted by Elizabeth Compton Sigmund in her interview with EF, September 1999.

11 Letter from Aurelia Plath to Elizabeth Compton Sigmund, quoted from memory.

12 Butscher, (ed.) p. 84.

13 EF interview with Elizabeth Compton Sigmund, September 1999.

14 This letter, written in September 1962, is in Ruth Fainlight's possession.

15 Ibid.

16 Stevenson, *Bitter Fame*, Murphy, Appendix III, p. 254.

17 See Murphy memoir, Appendix III, in Stevenson, *Bitter Fame*, p. 352.

18 MSS 644, SCD, box 18, ff. 10, letter to Aurelia Plath, January 1975.

19 MSS 854, SCD, box 1, ff. 11, letters to Gerald Hughes.

20 MSS 644, SCD, box 18, ff. 10, letter to Aurelia Plath, 1975.

21 Ibid.

22 Plath, 'Stings', *Collected Poems*, p. 214.

23 The film *Stepford Wives*, released in the mid-1970s and based on a novel by Ira Levin, made use of a similar idea as a science-fiction horror story.

24 EF interview with Suzette Macedo, October 1999.

25 Plath, 'Daddy', *Collected Poems*, p. 222.

26 Plath, 'Daddy', *Collected Poems*, p. 183.

27 Plath, 'Lady Lazarus', *Collected Poems*, p. 244.

28 Letter to Ruth Fainlight, 22 October 1962.

29 MSS 644, SCD, box 18, ff. 10, letter to Aurelia Plath, 1975.

30 Letter to Ruth Fainlight, 22 October 1962.

31 TH, *Howls and Whispers*, p. 296.

32 EF interview with Elizabeth Compton Sigmund, September 1999.

33 EF with Suzette Macedo, October 1999.

34 Ibid.

35 Ibid.

36 Ibid.

37 Alvarez, *The Savage God*, p. 41.

38 Ibid.

[39] Plath, (ed.), *Letters Home*, p. 493.

[40] Janet Malcolm, *The Silent Woman*, p. 193.

[41] Stevenson, *Bitter Fame*, p. 286.

[42] Ted mentions this in a letter to Aurelia Plath dated January 1975, at a time when Aurelia was putting together *Letters Home* for publication.

[43] Stevenson, *Bitter Fame*, p. 285.

[44] Clarissa Roche, memoir in Butscher, *Sylvia Plath*.

[45] MSS 866, SCD, box 1, ff. 23, letters to W.S. Merwin.

[46] EF interview with David Ross, 1999.

[47] EF interview with Joel Finler, February 2001.

[48] TH, 'The Inscription', *Birthday Letters*, p. 172.

[49] Ibid.

[50] EF interview with Suzette Macedo, October 1999.

Chapter 10: The Inheritance, pp. 144–161

[1] Plath, 'Edge', *Collected Poems*, p. 272.

[2] *Observer*, Al Alvarez, 'A Poet's Epitaph', 17 February 1963.

[3] EF interview with Suzette Macedo, October 1999.

[4] See Alexander, *Rough Magic*, 2nd edition (1999).

[5] Part of Trevor Thomas, 'Last Encounters', a 27-page typewritten and photocopied manuscript (1989) was published in the *Independent*. The Press Council asked them to apologize.

[6] EF interview with David Ross, October 1999.

[7] Heinz, 'The Art of Poetry', p. 77.

[8] EF interview with David Ross, October 1999.

[9] Quoted in TH, 'Publishing Sylvia Plath', in *Winter Pollen*, p. 165.

[10] TH, 'The Minotaur', *Birthday Letters*, p. 120.

[11] EF interview with Al Alvarez.

[12] Ibid.

[13] EF interview with Al Alvarez.

[14] Anne Alvarez works as a psychotherapist.

[15] EF interview with Anne Alvarez.

[16] Ibid.

[17] Elizabeth Sigmund, 'I realised Sylvia knew about Assia's pregnancy', *Guardian*, 23 April 1999.

[18] Abortions were illegal in those days, so an unwanted pregnancy was always something of a crisis.

[19] EF interview with Suzette Macedo, October 1999.

[20] EF interview with Elizabeth Compton Sigmund, September 1999.

[21] Janet Malcolm, *The Silent Woman*, (Alfred A Knopf, 1993), p. 133.

[22] MSS 854, SCD, box 1, 2nd air-letter, 22 July 1963.

[23] Ibid.

[24] EF interview with Elizabeth Compton Sigmund, September 1999.

[25] Letter dated 27 January 2001; copy sent to EF by Lucas Myers, February 2001.

[26] MSS 854, SCD, box 1, ff. 12, letters to Gerald Hughes, 19 June 1963.

[27] Ibid.

[28] EF interview with Al Alvarez and wife Anne.

[29] EF interview with Elizabeth Compton Sigmund, September 1999.

[30] According to Suzette Macedo: EF interview with Suzette Macedo, October 1999.

[31] Ibid.

[32] MSS 854 ff 13 SCD, letter to Gerald Hughes, 1964.

[33] Not all of them were contemporary poets. Some of the author's earliest translations of Marina Tsvetaeva appeared in *Modern Poetry in Translation*.

[34] MSS 854, SCD, box 1, ff. 12, letters to Gerald Hughes, 19 June 1963.

[35] Ibid.

[36] Letter from David Wevill, 20 June 1989, ADD MSS 94451, papers of Anne Stevenson, Cambridge University Library.

[37] Myers, *Crow Steered, Bergs Appeared*, p. 129.

[38] Myers, *Crow Steered, Bergs Appeared*, p. 128.

[39] According to Suzette Macedo: EF interview with Suzette Macedo, October 1999.

[40] A letter found among MSS 865, SCD, box 1, ff. 11, note to Lucas Myers dated 13 March 1965.

[41] Ibid.

[42] Ibid.

[43] Ibid.

[44] Ibid.

[45] EF interview with Suzette Macedo, October 1999.

[46] MSS 865, SCD, box 1, ff. 13, letters to Lucas Myers, Winter/Spring 1967.

[47] MSS 865, SCD, box 1, ff. 13, letter to Lucas Myers, 23 February 1967.

[48] TH, 'Her Husband', from *Wodwo* (Faber & Faber, 1967) published in *New Selected Poems*, p. 56.

[49] Ibid.

[50] TH, 'Full Moon and Little Frieda', from *Wodwo*, in *New Selected Poems*, p. 87.

[51] TH, 'Wodwo', from *Wodwo*, in *New Selected Poems*, p. 87.

[52] MSS 854, SCD, box 1, ff. 16, letters to Gerald Hughes, April 1967.

[53] EF interview with Peter Redgrove, September 1999.

[54] SCD, series 1.5, box 63.

[55] EF interview with Ruth Fainlight.

[56] EF interview with Elizabeth Compton Sigmund, September 1999.

[57] MSS 854, SCD, box 1, ff. 13, letters to Gerald Hughes.

[58] TH, 'Crow on the Beach', in *Winter Pollen*, p. 241.

[59] Ibid.

Chapter 11: Assia, pp. 162–173

[1] EF interview with Karl Miller, November 1999. He agrees that he took none of the poems for publication in the *Listener*. He found in them alarming evidence of Plath's instability, and he would have welcomed some personal help being given to her.

[2] MSS 854, SCD, box 1, ff. 16, 27 April 1967.

[3] MSS 867, SCD, box 1, ff. 2, letter to Peter Redgrove.

[4] Letters in Brenda Hedden's possession, shown to EF 3 May 2001.

[5] Letters from TH in Brenda Hedden's possession, quoted to EF in a fax dated 24 May 2001.

[6] Eilat Negev, 'Haunted by the ghosts of love' *Guardian*, 10 April 1999.

[7] Fax from Brenda Hedden to EF dated 24 May 2001.

[8] Ibid.

[9] MSS 867 box 1, ff. 3, letter to Peter Redgrove, 1970.

[10] Brenda Hedden in a telephone conversation with EF, March 2001.

[11] Brenda Hedden in a telephone conversation with EF, March 2001.

[12] EF interview with Fay Weldon, November 1999.

[13] EF interview with Ruth Fainlight, February 2000.

[14] Giles Gordon was Fay Weldon's literary agent.

[15] EF interview with Fay Weldon.

[16] Ibid.

[17] TH, 'Dreamers', *Birthday Letters*, p. 157.

[18] EF interview with Fay Weldon.

[19] Ibid.

[20] Eda Zoritte-Megged's memoir, typescript in EF's hands.

[21] Ibid.

[22] Ibid.

[23] Ibid.

24 The Hebrew word for 'commandment'.
25 Eda Zoritte-Megged's memoirs, typescript in EF's hands.
26 Ibid.
27 Ibid.
28 Al Alvarez, read to EF from an entry dated May 2 in a diary he had been keeping at the time, which quotes Olwyn as saying, 'She could hardly leave Ted with yet another motherless child.'
29 EF interview with Ruth Fainlight, February 2000.
30 TH, 'Fanaticism', *Capriccio* (Gehenna Press, 1990).
31 TH, 'The Tin Roof' *Capriccio* (Gehenna Press, 1990).
32 Eilat Negev, *Guardian*, 10 April 1999.
33 Letter from Jill Neville, dated 16 October 1969.
34 Yehuda Amichai, *Selected Poems*, ed. Ted Hughes and Daniel Weissbort (Faber & Faber, 2001).

Chapter 12: Surviving, pp. 174–186
1 MSS 854, SCD, box 1, ff. 18, letters to Gerald Hughes, 27 October 1969.
2 Fax from Brenda Hedden to EF, dated 27 May 2001.
3 MSS 854, SCD, box 1, ff. 18, letters to Gerald Hughes, 27 October 1969.
4 Ibid.
5 TH, introduction to Vasko Popa, *Collected Poems* (Penguin, 1969), in *Winter Pollen*, p. 222.
6 MSS 867, SCD, box 1, ff. 3, letter to Peter Redgrove.
7 Fax from Brenda Hedden to EF, dated 27 May 2001.
8 EF interview with Peter Redgrove, September 1999.
9 Fax from Brenda Hedden to EF, 2 June 2001, as modified over the telephone.
10 Sagar, *Laughter of Foxes*, p. 125.

11 TH, 'A Childish Prank', from *Crow*, in *New Selected Poems*, p. 91.
12 TH, 'Examination at the Womb Door', from *Crow*, in *New Selected Poems*, p. 90.
13 Ibid.
14 EF interview with Dannie Abse, 1999.
15 Al Alvarez, *The Savage God*, (Weidenfeld & Nicolson, 1971).
16 Letter to Al Alvarez from TH, held by British Library.
17 Ibid.
18 Ibid.
19 Ibid.
20 Al Alvarez's letter to Ted Hughes, held by the British Museum.
21 TH letter to Alvarez held by British Library.
22 Ibid.
23 MSS 854, SCD, box 1, ff. 20, letters to Gerald Hughes.
24 Ibid.
25 SCD, box of photocopies, series 1.5, box 63, ff. 6, letter to Janet Malcolm.
26 Ibid.
27 MSS 865, SCD, letter to Lucas Myers, February 1972.
28 MSS 644, SCD, box 20, ff. 16, general correspondence.
29 Ibid.

Chapter 13: The Accused, pp. 187–196
1 Marjorie Perloff, 'On the road to Ariel: the transitional poetry of Sylvia Plath', *Iowa Review*, Spring 1973.
2 In Iowa.
3 The poem was included in Robin Morgan, *Monster* (1972).
4 Robin Morgan, 'The Arraignment'.
5 In the 1990s, Hughes and Harold Pinter for a time received insane threats of an equally terrifying nature from what purported to be an active feminist cell, but the police discovered that a single unstable woman was behind them.

[6] MSS 865, SCD, box 15, letters to Lucas Myers.

[7] EF was a member of this committee.

[8] Quoted in letter from David Pease to EF, 8 December 1999.

[9] Ibid.

[10] My own meeting with her came about through her relationship to my then editor, Michael Dempsey, with whom Emma had a child.

[11] In my case, he thought my translations and biography might accelerate Tsvetaeva's recognition as a genius in the West. It was an act of generosity to a dead and then still-neglected poet whom he venerated.

[12] SCD, MSS 644, box 1, ff. 12, Harper & Row correspondence.

[13] MSS 644, SCD box 1.5, ff. 10, business correspondence.

[14] His financial papers were always in good order, as his accountant Michael Henshaw has confirmed to me.

[15] A few chapters of this novel, 'Falcon's Yard', exist in draft in the SCD.

[16] MSS 644, SCD, box 18, ff. 10, letter to Aurelia Plath, 28 January 1975.

[17] MSS 644, SCD, box 18, ff. 1, letter to Aurelia Plath, 28 January 1975.

[18] TH, 'Sheep', reprinted in *New Selected Poems*, p. 136.

[19] TH, 'The Day He Died', *New Selected Poems*, p. 190.

Chapter 14: Australia, pp. 197–206

[1] Letter to Keith Sagar, quoted in Nick Gammage (ed.), *The Epic Poise: A Celebration of Ted Hughes* (Faber & Faber, 1999), p. 239.

[2] Emma Tennant, *Burnt Diaries* (Canongate, 1999), p. 131.

[3] Email from Jill Barber to EF, and EF conversation with Jill Barber in Weng Wat restaurant, Haverstock Hill, NW3, in 1999.

[4] Letter to Jill Barber's mother in Australia from Zoom Syndication, 220

Queenstown Road, London, SW8.

[5] MSS 865, SCD, box 1, ff. 18, letters to Lucas Myers.

[6] I remember having breakfast with them somewhere in Notting Hill.

[7] Letter from Jill Barber, supplied to EF by email.

[8] Tennant, *Burnt Diaries*, p. 165.

[9] Telephone conversation EF and Jill Barber, July 2001.

[10] A copy is in EF's hands.

[11] Letter from Jill Barber, supplied to EF by email.

[12] Ibid.

[13] Jill Barber in conversation with EF at a Hampstead restaurant, 1999.

[14] Email from Jill Barber to EF.

[15] Tennant, *Burnt Diaries*, p. 105.

[16] TH, Introduction to János Pilinszky, *Selected Poems* (Carcanet Press, 1976), in *Winter Pollen*, p. 233.

[17] Published by the Seaburg Press, New York, 1976.

[18] MSS 644, SCD, box 6, ff. 15, general correspondence.

[19] Quoted in Sagar, *Laughter of Foxes*, p. 104.

[20] TH, *Gaudete* (Faber & Faber, 1977), p. 45.

[21] TH, *Gaudete*, p. 179.

[22] TH, *Gaudete*, p. 186.

[23] See Sagar, *Laughter of Foxes*, pp. 104 *et seq*.

[24] MSS 644, SCD, box 1, ff. 12, business correspondence, Harper & Row.

[25] MSS 644, SCD, box 1, ff. 15, business correspondence, Harper & Row.

[26] Jill Barber, *Mail on Sunday*, 'Ted Hughes, My Secret Lover', 13 May 2001.

[27] Ibid.

[28] MSS 854, SCD, box 1, ff. 26, letters to Gerald Hughes.

Chapter 15: Responsibility, pp. 207–217

[1] MSS 854, SCD, box 1, ff. 25, letters to Gerald Hughes, 24 August 1976.

[2] MSS 854, SCD, box 1, ff. 27, letters to Gerald Hughes, 1978.

[3] MSS 854, SCD, box 1, ff. 28, letters to Gerald Hughes, 2 May 1977.

[4] Ibid.

[5] TH, 'You Hated Spain' and 'The Earthenware Head', in *New Selected Poems*, pp. 294–5.

[6] MSS 854, SCD, box 1, letters to Gerald Hughes, 17 June 1979.

[7] MSS 854, SCD, box 1, ff. 29, letters to Gerald Hughes.

[8] MSS 854, SCD, box 1, ff. 30, letters to Gerald Hughes.

[9] MSS 854, SCD, box 1, ff. 31, letters to Gerald Hughes.

[10] Ibid.

[11] Ibid.

[12] MSS 854, SCD, box 1, ff. 26, letters to Gerald Hughes, 30 August 1979.

[13] TH, 'The River', *New Selected Poems*, p. 243.

[14] TH, 'October Salmon', *New Selected Poems*, p. 262 MSS 644.

[15] TH, 'The Gulkana', *New Selected Poems*, p. 250.

[16] MSS 854, SCD, box 1, ff. 31, letters to Gerald Hughes, February 1981.

[17] Ibid.

[18] Sagar, *Laughter of Foxes*, p. xxvii.

[19] Ibid.

[20] Special Collections Department, Robert W. Woodruff Library, Emory University, Atlanta, Georgia.

[21] MSS 854, SCD, box 1, ff. 30, letters to Gerald Hughes, 8 May 1980.

[22] MSS 867, SCD.

[23] MSS 865, SCD, box 1, ff. 18, letters to Lucas Myers.

[24] Ibid.

[25] MSS, 854, SCD, box 1, ff. 30, letters to Gerald Hughes.

[26] MSS 854, SCD, box 1, ff. 31, letters to Gerald Hughes.

[27] Sagar, *Laughter of Foxes*, p. xxvii.

[28] MSS 867, SCD, box 1, letters to Peter Redgrove.

[29] TH, 'The Hanged Man and the Dragonfly', *Winter Pollen*, p. 84.

[30] MSS 854, SCD, box 1, letters to Gerald Hughes.

[31] There is a draft of the letter at Emory University, but it is not clear whether it was ever sent, or if he received a reply.

[32] Letter to Keith Sagar, quoted in Sagar, *Laughter of Foxes*, p. xviii.

[33] MSS 865, SCD, box 1, ff. 19, letter to Lucas Myers.

[34] TH, 'The Hen', *New Selected Poems*, p. 236.

[35] TH, 'The Hare', *New Selected Poems*, p. 238.

Chapter 16: The Laureate, pp. 218–224

[1] See Chapter 1.

[2] TH, *Rain-Charm for the Duchy and Other Laureate Poems* (Faber & Faber, 1992). The Duchy of Cornwall, contiguous with Devon.

[3] MSS 644, SCD, box 2, general correspondence.

[4] TH, 'In the Likeness of a Grasshopper', from *Flowers and Insects*, in *New Selected Poems*, p. 232.

[5] TH, 'Sunstruck Foxglove', from *Flowers and Insects*, in *New Selected Poems*, p. 227.

[6] Letter from Anne Stevenson, Cambridge University Library, ADD MSS 94451.

[7] Anne Stevenson Archive, letter 13 February 1988. Anne Stevenson was kind enough to open her archive for me, though it is in principle closed until after her death.

[8] Letter from Anne Stevenson, Cambridge University Library, ADD MSS 94451.

[9] Stevenson papers, Cambridge University Library, ADD MSS 94451.

[10] Ibid.

[11] Ibid.

[12] Ibid.

[13] According to Paul Alexander, *Rough Magic* (Da Capo Press, 1999).

[14] Cambridge University Library, ADD MSS 94451.

[15] MSS 644, SCD, general correspondence.

[16] TH, 'Crow on the Beach', *Winter Pollen*, p. 241.

[17] TH, 'Ravens', from *Moortown Diary*, in *New Selected Poems*, p. 184.

[18] MSS 644, SCD, general correspondence, letter from Olwyn Hughes, 26 September 1989.

[19] TH, 'Sacrifice', *Wolfwatching*, in *New Selected Poems*, p. 273.

Chapter 17: The Goddess, pp. 225–236
[1] TH, *Shakespeare and the Goddess of Complete Being* (Faber & Faber, 1992).

[2] Ibid.

[3] Gehenna Press, 1990.

[4] TH, 'The Locket', also found in *New Selected Poems*, p. 306.

[5] TH, 'Error', also found in *New Selected Poems*, p. 312.

[6] See J. Beer, Ted Hughes and The Daughter of Incomplete Being, p. 252 in MS.

[7] Heinz, 'The Art of Poetry', p. 75.

[8] Heinz, 'The Art of Poetry', p. 75.

[9] Sagar, *Laughter of Foxes*, p. xxxii.

[10] TH, *Tales from Ovid*, (Faber & Faber, 1997), p. 4.

[11] TH, *Tales from Ovid*, p. 9.

[12] TH, *Tales from Ovid*, p. 12.

[13] TH, introduction to *Tales from Ovid*, p. xi.

[14] Wagner, *Ariel's Gift*, p. 24.

[15] Wagner, *Ariel's Gift*, p. 25.

[16] Carolyn Wright, 'What Happens in the Heart', *Poetry Review*, vol. 89, no. 3, Autumn 1999, p. 3.

[17] *Poetry Review*, vol. 89, no. 3, Autumn 1999, p. 5.

[18] Ibid.

[19] Ibid.

[20] Ibid.

[21] Ibid.

[22] Sagar, *Laughter of Foxes*, p. xxxii.

[23] There is a suggestion that such a journal may exist in a letter to Aurelia Plath, MSS 644, SCD, box 18, ff. 10, letter to Aurelia Plath, January 1975.

[24] TH, *Howls and Whispers* (Gehenna Press, 1998).

[25] Eilat Negev, 'Interview with Ted Hughes', Daily Telegraph, 31 October 1996.

[26] Wagner, *Ariel's Gift*, p. 5.

[27] Ibid.

[28] Newman (ed.), *The Art of Sylvia Plath*, p. 187.

[29] EF interview with Al Alvarez, 2000.

[30] Ibid.

[31] Wagner, *Ariel's Gift*, p. 3.

[32] TH, 'The Rabbit Catcher', *Birthday Letters*, p. 144.

[33] Al Alvarez, *New Yorker*, 2 February 1998.

[34] *Sunday Times.*

[35] TH, 'The Table', *Birthday Letters*, p. 138.

[36] TH, 'Dream Life', *Birthday Letters*, p. 141.

[37] TH, 'Suttee', *Birthday Letters*, p. 149.

[38] TH, 'Fairy Tale', *Birthday Letters*, p. 159.

[39] Ann Skea, 'Poetry and Magic', Ted Hughes 2000 International Conference, Université Lumier, Lyon 2, France.

[40] Letter by TH, read out by Frieda Hughes when accepting the Whitbread Book of the Year Award on his behalf, January 1998.

[41] Ann Skea, 'Poetry and Magic', Ted Hughes 2000 International Conference, Université Lumier, Lyon 2, France.

Chapter 18: The Last Flowering, pp. 237–242
[1] John Cornwell, 'Bard of Prey',

Sunday Times, 3 October 1999.
[2] See picture section.
[3] See p. 145.
[4] TH, *The Alcestis of Euripides* (Faber & Faber, 1999), p. 43.
[5] Myers, *Crow Steered, Bergs Appeared,* p. 79.
[6] TH, *Alcestis,* p. 58.
[7] TH, 'The Hidden Orestes', *Howls and Whispers.*
[8] MSS 644, SCD, general correspondence, letter from Olwyn Hughes.
[9] SCD, general correspondence.

[10] I have been told this by a close friend, who does not wish to be named.
[11] Sagar, *Laughter of Foxes,* p. xxxiii.
[12] SCD, box 1, letters from Thom Gunn, 14 April 1991. General correspondence.
[13] Gammage (ed.), *Epic Poise,* p. 107.
[14] I defended her against the charge of colluding with Ted's adulteries.
[15] EF present on the occasion.

Epilogue: pp. 243–244
[1] John Keats, *Letters.*

Select Bibliography

Manuscript Sources
The most important archive of Hughes material is MS 644 at the Department of Special Collections, Robert Woodruff Library, The University of Emory, Atlanta, Georgia. It includes files of correspondence running from 1959 to 1997 and about 97 per cent of this material is open to scholars. There are boxes filed under particular correspondents, boxes filed under business dealings – with, for instance, Hughes' publisher, the British Broadcasting Corporation, or the Arvon Foundation. Access to some letters is restricted, and there is also a sealed box whose contents are unknown, which cannot be opened until twenty years after Hughes' death. These form part of the original sale of MSS of Ted Hughes to Emory. A further sequence of letters from his brother, Gerald Hughes, MS 854, runs from 1952 to 1991 and was acquired by the Robert Woodruff Library in 2000. Unrestricted access is given to these, with the exception of twenty-nine letters which are unavailable until 2028. There are other exchanges of letters for instance, those with Lucas Myers which were separately acquired.

There are also important collections of Hughes' MSS held by the British Museum, King's College London (as part of the archive of Modern Poetry in Translation), and the universities of Aberystwyth, Liverpool and Leeds. Cambridge University Library holds the papers of Anne Stevenson (CUL ADD MS 944512), which is sealed until after her death, but which she has generously allowed me to read. A number of letters remain in private hands and copies have been sent to me. There are also MSS of work completed after March 1997, including *Birthday Letters*, *Oresteia*, *Phèdre* and *Alcestis*, which remain in the care of the Estate.

Books by Ted Hughes
Unless otherwise stated, all titles are published by Faber & Faber, London, and by Harper and Row, New York.

The Hawk in the Rain (1957)
Lupercal (1960)
Meet My Folks! (1961; US edn. Bobbs-Merrill, 1973)
How the Whale Became (1963; US edn. Atheneum, 1964)
The Earth-Owl and Other Moon People (1963)
Nessie the Mannerless Monster (1964; US edn. Bobbs-Merrill, 1974)
Recklings (Turret Press, 1966)

Wodwo (1967)
Poetry in the Making (1967; US edn. *Poetry Is*, Doubleday, 1970)
The Iron Man (1968; US edn. *The Iron Giant*)
Seneca's Oedipus (1969; US edn. *The Tiger's Bones*, Viking, 1974)
Crow, From the Life and Songs of the Crow (1970; US edn. 1971)
Eat Crow (radio play; 1971; Rainbow Press)
Poems: Ruth Fainlight, Ted Hughes, Alan Sillitoe (Rainbow Press, 1971)
Prometheus on his Crag (Rainbow Press, 1973)
János Pilinszky (Carcanet, 1976)
Season Songs (US edn. Viking, 1975; Faber 1976, 1985)
Gaudete (1977)
Cave Birds (1978; US edn. Viking, 1979)
Moon-Bells (Chatto, 1978)
A Solstice (Sceptre Press, 1978)
Orts (Rainbow Press, 1978)
Adam and the Sacred Nine (Rainbow Press, 1979)
Remains of Elmet (1979)
Moortown (1979)
Under the North Star (1981; US edn. Viking)
River (1983)
What is the Truth? (1984; also as vol. 2 of the *Collected Animal Poems*, 1995)
Flowers and Insects (US edn. Knopf, 1986)
Tales of the Early World (1988; US edn. Farrar Straus & Giroux (FSG), 1991)
Moortown Diary (1989)
Wolfwatching (1989; US edn. FSG, 1991)
Capriccio (Gehenna Press, 1990)
Shakespeare and the Goddess of Complete Being (1992; US edn. FSG, 1992)
Rain-Charm for the Duchy and Other Laureate Poems (1992)
The Iron Woman (1993; US edn. Dial Books, 1995)
Three Books: Remains of Elmet, Cave Birds, River (1993)
Winter Pollen: a collection of Ted Hughes' occasional prose, ed. William Scammell
    (1994; US edn. Picador, 1995)
New Selected Poems 1957–1994 (1995)
The Dreamfighter (1995)
Difficulties of a Bridegroom (1995; US edn. Picador)
Wedekind's Spring Awakening (1995)
*Collected Animal Poems: The Iron Wolf, What is the Truth?, A March Calf, The
    Thought Fox* (1995)
Lorca's Blood Wedding (1996)
Tales from Ovid (1997; US ed. FSG)
Howls and Whispers (Gehenna Press, Northampton, 1998)
Birthday Letters (1998; US edn. FSG)
Racine's Phèdre (1998)
The Oresteia of Aeschylus (1999; US edn. FSG)
The Alcestis of Euripedes (1999; US eds. FSG)

Uncollected Contributions by Hughes
'Context', in *London Magazine*, February 1962
The Poet Speaks (XVI) Ted Hughes Talks to Peter Orr (British Council, 1963)

'The Rock', in *Writers on Themselves* (BBC, 1964); Collected in *Worlds* ed. Geoffrey Summerfield, (Penguin, 1974)
Orghast at Persepolis, A.C.H. Smith (Eyre Methuen, 1972)
Worlds, ed. Geoffrey Summerfield (Penguin, 1974); contains 'The Rock'
'The Hart of the Myster', TH's article on hunting, *Guardian*, 5 July 1997

Criticism and Memoirs

Alexander, Paul, *Rough Magic* (Da Capo Press edn., 1999)
Alvarez, Al, 'Prologue: Sylvia Plath', in *The Savage God: A Study in Suicide* (Weidenfeld & Nicolson, 1971)
—*Where Did It All Go Right?* (Richard Cohen Books, 2000)
Bentley, Paul, *The Poetry of Ted Hughes: Language, Illusion and Beyond* (Longman, 1998)
Bishop, Nicholas, *Remaking Poetry: Ted Hughes and a New Critical Psychology* (Harvester Wheatsheaf, 1991)
Bradley, D.D., 'Ted Hughes 1930–98', *Pembroke College Cambridge Annual Gazette*, no. 73, September 1999, pp. 22–30
Butscher, Edward (ed.), *Sylvia Plath: The Woman and the Work* (1979)
Cox, Brian, 'Ted Hughes (1930–1998): A Personal Retrospect', *Hudson Review*, vol. LII, Spring 1999, pp. 29–43
Davison, Peter, *A Fading Smile: Poets in Boston from Robert Lowell to Sylvia Plath* (W.W. Norton paperback, reprint 1996)
Davie, Donald, *Remembering the Movement*, ed. Elaine Feinstein (Prospect, 1959)
Dyson, S.E. (ed.), *Three Contemporary Poets: Thom Gunn, Ted Hughes and R.S. Thomas* (Macmillan, 1990)
Faas, Ekbert, *Ted Hughes: The Unaccommodated Universe* (Black Sparrow Press, 1980)
Fallows, Glen, 'Ted Hughes: Reminiscences', *Martlet* (an occasional Pembroke College magazine), 1999, pp. 6–9
Gammage, Nick (ed.), *The Epic Poise: A Celebration of Ted Hughes* (Faber & Faber, 1999)
Gifford, Terry, and Roberts, Neil, *Ted Hughes: A Critical Study* (Faber & Faber, 1981)
Graves, Robert, *The White Goddess* (Faber & Faber, 1948)
Gunn, Thom, *The Occasions of Poetry* (Faber & Faber, 1982)
Heinz, Drue, 'The Art of Poetry', *Paris Review*, 134, Spring 1995, pp. 55–94 (interview with TH)
Hirschbert, Stuart, *Myth in the Poetry of Ted Hughes* (Barnes & Noble, 1981)
Hobsbaum, Philip, 'Ted Hughes at Cambridge', *Dark Horse*, no. 8, Autumn 1999, pp. 6–12
Kukil, Karen V. (ed.), *Journals of Sylvia Plath, 1950–1962*, (Faber & Faber, 2000)
Longmate, Norman, *How We Lived Then* (Hutchinson, 1971)
Malcolm, Janet, *The Silent Woman* (Alfred A. Knopf. Inc., 1993)
Miller, Karl, *Rebecca's Vest* (Hamish Hamilton, 1993)
Morgan, Robin, *Monster* (Random House, 1970); reprinted in *Upstairs in the Garden: Poems Selected and New 1968–88* (W. W. Norton, 1990)
Moulin, Joanny, *Ted Hughes: La Langue Remunérée* (L'Harmattan, Paris, 1999)
—(ed.), *Livre Ted Hughes: New Selected Poems* (Editions du Temps, Paris, 1999)
Myers, Lucas, *Crow Steered, Bergs Appeared* (Proctor Press, Tennessee, 2001)

Negev, Eilat, 'Haunted by the Ghosts of Love', *Guardian*, 10 April 1999

Negev, Eilat, 'Ted Hughes Interviewed', *Daily Telegraph*, 31 October 1998

Newman, (ed.), *The Art of Sylvia Plath* (Faber & Faber, 1970)

Pero, Tom, 'An Interview with Ted Hughes', *Wild Steelhead and Salmon* magazine, PO Box 3666, Seattle, Washington, 98124–366, USA, Winter 1999 (extract reprinted in the *Guardian*, 9 January 1999)

Plath, Sylvia, *The Colossus* (Heinemann, 1960)

Plath, Sylvia, *The Bell Jar* (Heinemann, 1963, published under the pseudonym Victoria Lucas)

Plath, Sylvia, *Ariel* (Faber & Faber, 1965)

Plath, Sylvia, *Crossing the Water* (Faber & Faber, 1971)

Plath, Sylvia, *Winter Trees* (Faber & Faber, 1971)

Plath, Sylvia, *Johnny Panic and the Bible of Dreams: Short Stories, Prose and Diary Excerpts* (Faber & Faber, 1977)

Plath, Sylvia, *Collected Poems* (Faber & Faber, 1981)

Plath, Aurelia (ed.), *Sylvia Plath's Letters Home: Correspondence 1950–1963* (Harper & Row, 1975; Faber & Faber, 1975)

Rose, Jacqueline, *The Haunting of Sylvia Plath* (Virago, 1991)

Robinson, Craig, *Ted Hughes as Shepherd of Being* (Macmillan, 1989)

Sagar, Keith, *The Art of Ted Hughes* (Cambridge University Press, 1975; extended edn. 1978)

—*Ted Hughes* (Profile Books, 1981)

—(ed.), *The Achievement of Ted Hughes* (Manchester University Press, 1983)

—(ed.), *The Challenge of Ted Hughes* (Macmillan, 1994)

—*The Laughter of Foxes* (Liverpool University Press, 2000)

Sagar, Keith, and Tabor, S., *Ted Hughes: A Bibliography* (Mansell, 1998)

Scigaj, Leonard M., *The Poetry of Ted Hughes* (University of Iowa Press, 1986)

—*Ted Hughes* (Twayne, 1991)

—(ed.), *Critical Essays on Ted Hughes* (G.K. Hall, 1992)

Skea, Ann, *Ted Hughes: The Poetic Quest* (University of New England Press, Australia, 1994; www.ann.skea.com)

Stella, Maria, *L'Inno e L'Enigma: Saggio su Ted Hughes* (Biblioteca Ianua, Rome, 1988)

Stevenson, Anne, *Bitter Fame*, (Viking, 1989)

Tennant, Emma, *Burnt Diaries* (Canongate, 1999)

Uroff, Margaret, *Sylvia Plath and Ted Hughes* (University of Illinois Press, 1979)

Walder, Dennis, *Ted Hughes* (Open University Press, 1987)

Wagner, Erica, *Ariel's Gift* (Faber & Faber, 2000)

Wagner-Martin, Linda, *Sylvia Plath: A Biography* (Simon & Schuster, New York, 1987; Chatto & Windus, London, 1988)

West, Thomas, *Ted Hughes* (Methuen, 1985)

Wolpert, Lewis, *The Malignant Sadness* (Faber & Faber, 1999)

Wood Middlebrook, Diana, *Anne Sexton: a biography* (Virago, 1992, Houghton Mifflin, 1991)

Wright, Carolyn, 'What happens in the heart', *Poetry Review*, Volga, No. 3, 1999

Zoritte-Megged, Eda, 'Intersections', first printed in Hebrew in *Mosnayim*, no. 9, September/October 1984

Index